Moral Philosophy and Contemporary Problems

EDITED BY

J. D. G. Evans

CAMBRIDGE UNIVERSITY PRESS

CAMBRIDGE NEW YORK
NEW ROCHELLE MELBOURNE SYDNEY

Published by the Press Syndicate of the University of Cambridge
The Pitt Building, Trumpington Street, Cambridge, CB2 1RP
32 East 57th Street, New York, NY 10022, USA
10 Stamford Road, Oakleigh, Melbourne 3166, Australia

Library of Congress catalogue card number: 88-9509

British Library Cataloguing in Publication Data

Moral philosophy and contemporary problems.
—(Royal Institute of Philosophy lecture
series: 22).
1. Social ethics.
I. Evans, J.D.G. (John David Gemmell), 1942–
170

ISBN 0-521-35736-5

Library of Congress Cataloguing in Publication Data

Moral philosophy and contemporary problems/edited by J. D. G.
Evans. p. cm.—(Royal Institute of Philosophy lecture series: 22)
"Supplement to Philosophy 1987."
Bibliography: p.
ISBN 0-521-35736-5
1. Ethics. 2. Social ethics. I. Evans, J. D. G.
(John David Gemmill), 1942– . II. Philosophy. 1987 (Supplement) III. Series: Royal Institute of Philosophy lectures; v. 22.
BJ1012.M6343 1988 88-9509
170—dc19 CIP

ISBN 0 521 35736 5 (pbk.)

Printed and bound by
Adlard & Son Limited,
Leatherhead, Surrey, and Letchworth, Hertfordshire

Contents

Contents

To the memory of
Anna

Introduction

The papers in this volume record the proceedings of the Royal Institute of Philosophy conference held in Queen's University, Belfast, on 12–14 September 1986. It is well to note briefly the antecedents of the conference—especially because it was an unusual honour for Belfast and, I venture to say, a stimulating and enjoyable experience for all the participants.

The Royal Institute had accepted in 1983 an invitation from Queen's to host one of its new series of University-based conferences. The theme proposed at that time was *Moral Philosophy and Contemporary Problems*, which has now become the title of the present volume. When we submitted this proposal, we did so in the hope that in addition to the considerable number of academic philosophers in Ireland who were concerned with issues in moral philosophy, ordinary members of the public would also find it an interesting and accessible topic.

The expectation turned out to be well founded. More than seventy people attended the conference, and lively discussion was joined by the lay people as well as the professional philosophers. The Institute's munificence in sponsoring the conference is gratefully acknowledged on behalf of all who participated. It should also be recorded that Queen's University provided a fine physical setting for the proceedings, and that a bus tour of County Down gave a much appreciated interlude in what was otherwise a continuous and heavily concentrated set of philosophical discussions. Thanks are due above all to Max Wright for ensuring that the conference arrangements worked smoothly.

Moral philosophy is an intellectual activity practised by people who are concerned to apply the most rigorous standards of conceptual exactitude to the problems of real life. Socrates, who founded the subject, would permit no relaxation of intellectual rigour; the human agent is, above all, a thinker. But as Aristotle insisted, such thinking is essentially directed upon doing. The owner of the thoughts is involved in the world of action and change, and it is this involvement that motivates the thinking. This same world also contains other intelligent agents. It is a social and political world; moral thought, by its very nature, has to attend to the actions of other people as well as the one who does the thinking.

The balance between the practical and the intellectual, and the individual and the social, is not easy to maintain. Nor has it always been well observed during the long history of moral philosophy that links the ancient Greeks to contemporary thinkers. In particular, until fairly recent times much moral philosophy countenanced a strong divorce between sophisticated intellectual enquiry and the practical deliberation which ordinarily precedes action. The change in the last two decades has been dramatic. Philosophers are now heavily engaged with problems in medical ethics, the moral decisions of economic life, and yet more general issues of public policy. For the most part philosophers do not themselves question this extension of their involvement; equally significant, it is also accepted by the adjacent disciplines and professions with which they increasingly collaborate. The case for applied ethics seems to be well established and accepted.

But in fact, matters are altogether less secure than this sanguine account suggests. There have been, and still are, philosophers who question the ability of the intellectual to give any useful guidance towards the resolution of real-life problems; and there are non-philosophers who do not accept that philosophers have the right to pronounce on such matters. These are issues that have been debated throughout the history of moral philosophy. It is perhaps a distinctive feature of our time that the debate is now more open, and the audience more receptive, to a variety of viewpoints than previously. I hazard an explanation for this. As the secular age comes to full flower, we are witnessing a burgeoning recognition of the importance of autonomy in human value. The ineluctable fundamental resource for autonomous human agents is their power of reasoning and argument.

These themes are illustrated in the fifteen essays that follow. Certain figures in the history of thought are prominent and recur in many of the essays—above all, Aristotle, Kant, the Utilitarians and Marx. There is considerable interest in the relation between the individual and social dimensions of morality; the question then arises whether groups of people as such can be primary bearers of moral properties. The essays of Keith Graham and David Archard are most directly concerned with this kind of issue. Another large topic in several essays concerns the proper role of the abstract and general in moral thought. There is clearly an ineliminable element of the applied in morality; and, as we have just seen, this is emphasized by many philosophers from Aristotle on. His precursor, Plato, supports a different and less hospitable attitude to the role of the particular; and the tension between these views remains to be appraised in contemporary analysis. Stephen Clark and Onora O'Neill explore this theme.

Plato played a founding role in the development of epistemological sensitivity where matters of moral decision and action are concerned. Moral philosophy has always been concerned with, and sometimes dominated by, the question of the nature of moral expertise and, particularly, of the philosopher's claim to it. Contemporary discussion is less likely to accept the sceptical line that philosophy has nothing to contribute to life; but there remains considerable room for debate about how the philosopher's contribution dovetails into those of other, more self-professedly practical experts.

The essays of Jonathan Gorman, James Brown and Barrie Paskins address this question in broad terms. The remaining papers are more directly concerned with the investigation of actual moral problems. Some of these problems are themselves essentially general—such as those explored in Alan Ryan's discussion of justice and Desmond Clarke's of conscience. Others are slightly more restricted in that they concern a single aspect of life, albeit a pervasive one from which a person could not dissociate himself. The phenomena of leisure and work, treated in the essays of Elizabeth Telfer and Bernard Cullen, fall into this category.

Finally there are the essays which address particular and specialized problems: Bob Brecher on surrogacy, Joseph Mahon on drug-trials, Shyli Karin-Frank on genetic engineering and David Lamb on the criteria of death. It should be noted that for all the particularity of the topic under discussion in each of these essays, more general issues in the theory of moral justification come under survey.

The papers as a whole belie the suggestion that there is any important divide between issues of justification and method in moral theory, on the one hand, and the investigation of actual problems, on the other. Consideration of the latter supplies essential content to moral philosophy, but the demands of rigour and accuracy require us to pay full regard to the former issues as well. The range and depth of topics which are addressed in this volume provide clear illustration and amplification of these themes.

I wish to thank all those who have assisted me in the preparation and production of this volume. This would certainly include all the contributors, who showed great efficiency and co-operation in the way they responded to various editorial instructions and advice. The staff of the Cambridge University Press have performed their task with customary accuracy and dispatch; I should like particularly to thank Trevor Burling for all his help. Finally acknowledgement is due for the extensive and meticulous labours of the secretaries in the Philosophy Department at Queen's—Lindsay Osborne, Mary Emmerson and Alyn Hicks.

J. D. G. Evans
Queen's University
Belfast

Morality, Individuals and Collectives

KEITH GRAHAM

My discussion in this paper is divided into three parts. In section I, I discuss some fairly familiar lines of approach to the question how moral considerations may be shown to have rational appeal. In section II, I suggest how our existence as constituents in collective entities might also influence our practical thinking. In section III, I entertain the idea that identification with collectives might displace moral thinking to some degree, and I offer Marx's class theory as a sample of collective identification for the purposes of practical deliberation.

I

One illuminating way of coming to understand what influences we are rationally susceptible to (and therefore one way of coming to understand, to some extent, what sort of creatures we are) is to consider what influences are seen as problematic. Morality comes very readily to mind here. The problematic nature of moral motivation, encapsulated in the question *Why should I be moral?*, is of impressively ancient lineage. It has been joined in more recent times by a parallel issue: one to do with the problematic rationality of political participation, encapsulated in the question *Why should I bother to vote?* In both, the challenge is laid down to show why a set of external and implicitly irksome considerations should weigh with an individual in the matter of how to act.

The challenge in the question 'Why should I bother to vote?' begins from the empirical truth that in public elections the likelihood of a given individual's vote affecting the outcome is infinitesimally small. But there is always some minimal cost involved in voting (especially if it is raining), so why should a rational agent bother to do so?

Since the result in these circumstances is virtually never determined by one vote, we may try to find some other end which the persistent voter can rationally hope to achieve. We might say that, separately from affecting the result, it is important to you that a good turnout be recorded for your candidate; or that you benefit very considerably from having a democratic system of which the given case of electing someone is a part, so that the cost of voting is offset by the gains from sustaining such a system. But arguments like this are obviously feeble in the extreme, and resurrect just the original problem: they fail to demonstrate that *your* going to vote has any non-negligible instrumental importance for the desired end.

One alternative way of meeting the challenge is then to cease regarding the act of voting as an instrumental act, designed to achieve any obvious end. We might suggest instead, perhaps, that it is an act of self-expression, that in voting one is defining oneself as a (party) voter.[1] But there are still strategies available which would continue to treat voting as an instrumental act. We might say that, although the chances of my affecting the outcome are small, the benefits to others which will follow from a particular result are so massive (because spread over so many people) that a small chance is enough, and it is still rational for me to attempt to affect the outcome.[2] Or we might say that the end to be achieved by voting is something quite different, such as the fulfilment of a commitment or implicit promise or obligation evident from some other part of one's life.

In the case of most of these solutions to the challenge, the question *Why should I bother to vote?* is implicitly being treated as in some ways a less basic question than *Why should I be moral?* We are assuming that the cost, the irksomeness of voting is something which needs to be countered; but that moral considerations, such as obligation or benefit to others, can themselves motivate the agent and so provide the necessary counter. When the motivational force of moral considerations is itself thrown into doubt, we have correspondingly fewer resources to hand in dealing with the voting question. We should note, too, that the question about morality can itself be construed in a more or less basic way, depending on whether it concerns positive or critical morality. That is, in raising the question I may be asking either why I should not remain deaf to the appeals of the particular morality which surrounds me, or why I should not remain deaf to the appeals of morality as such.

How are we to identify morality here? We can do so partly in terms of a distinctive set of concepts, such as justice, freedom and the like. To concentrate on this, however, may be to keep things too local; and we may need to proceed to a more general and abstract level, certainly if we wish to delineate morality as such. As an institution it consists in a set of demands upon individuals which are supposed to temper how they would behave if left to follow their own inclinations or interests, and its role is to afford some protection to other individuals in that way. So there arises a conception of morality which draws an essential contrast between my own good and the good of others and which, as well as appealing to altruism, is universal and unconditional.

[1] Cf. Hollis (1977) 136–8.
[2] Cf. Parfit (1984) 73–4.

There is a deeply ambivalent element in our attitude towards morality, which proceeds from these features, and explains how the question *Why should I be moral?* can come to seem so troublesome. On the one hand we feel that the dictates of morality should have a particularly strong hold over us—they are not to depend on what we happen to want, they must be categorical—and on the other hand we are unsure whether anything could really have such features. Hence the well-known dilemma that any attempt to display the appeal of morality will suffer from either circularity or irrelevance: circularity if we suppose we already have a prior susceptibility to moral considerations, irrelevance if those considerations are linked to desires which an agent just happens to have.[3]

This conception of morality does not come neat. It comes surrounded by other philosophical, psychological and sociological assumptions, which gain expression in pre-philosophical common sense, as well as in philosophical and other academic theorizing. There is, for example, the implicit contrast between self-interest and morality (though morality might on some views just be equated with the interests of others), and the associated idea that the rationality of self-interest is *un*problematic. There is, often, an accompanying story about human nature or the circumstances in which human beings find themselves, which explains why the institution of morality should be necessary at all. We suffer, perhaps, from limited sympathy for others and/or limited resources and knowledge, and in consequence if morality did not exist the result would be something nasty, brutish and short.[4]

A complete disentangling of these background assumptions would pay dividends. To take only the philosophical ones, the dichotomy of morality and self-interest is too crude and far from exhaustive of the types of consideration which can have rational appeal (as I hope to show later). Equally, the idea of the rationality of self-interest is anything but unproblematic. There is a powerful tradition (again both in academic studies and elsewhere) which would identify rational, self-interested action with action that meshes in, in an appropriately efficient way, with an agent's desires or inclinations: in effect the tradition which follows Hume in thinking that reason is and ought only to be the slave of the passions. I confess to being puzzled that this view of the nature of rational motivation should be as widely supported as it is. It seems plain to me that an action's meshing in with an agent's desires is neither a necessary nor a sufficient condition of that action's being rational; and this because desires are themselves susceptible to assessment in terms

[3] Cf. Graham (1986b) 21–2.

[4] Cf. Mackie (1977) 107–14, Lukes (1985) 32, Warnock (1971) 26.

of rationality. If, for example, I do what will serve my desire to eat a housebrick I am not behaving rationally, because in almost all conceivable circumstances that desire is itself insane.

An attempt might be made to shore up the claim that rationality can be measured only relative to desire. It might be argued that the usual insanity of a desire like this one is seen to be so only in the light of the more enduring or long-term desires of the agent in question. But the reply to this is that there is no reason why the more enduring or long-term desires should not be just as insane, and therefore fail to be rational. I should argue that we can be entitled to make this sort of claim about particular desires, even in the absence of any answer to the vastly more difficult question what, in general, the criteria of rationality are which a desire must meet.[5] Moreover, the converse seems equally true. Just as a piece of behaviour may be irrational, despite serving a desire, because the desire itself is defective, so an action may be rational, despite serving no current desire of the agent, because the agent lacks a desire which it would be rational to have. (Suppose that I am needlessly neglectful of myself in some major way. In that case feeding myself may be rational even if it is something I do not want to do.)

I am arguing, therefore, for the possibility of a more radical criticism of desires than anything which is allowed for in the Humean tradition: criticism of them not just where they get mixed up with false beliefs or where they fail to gel with *other* desires, but on their own account, as it were. The area of needs illustrates well the point of disagreement. My suggestion is that if I need something, it is irrational for me not to want it, I have a reason to want it, whether that is recognized by me or not. In contrast, Bernard Williams argues that if an agent needs something but is uninterested in it, and if this lack of interest is not explicable in any of the ways which the Humean tradition allows as grounds for criticizing desires (lack of information, or unperceived connection with pre-existing desires), then the agent has no internal reason (the only kind of reason the Humean tradition allows) to pursue that thing.[6]

Williams is suspicious of the idea that there can be reasons for acting which are unconnected with pre-existing desires, on the grounds that reasons have an explanatory role. An agent would have a reason of the kind I am sponsoring even before they know anything about it, so the mere existence of the reason could never explain why they act. To the suggestion that coming to acquire a belief that the reason holds *constitutes* coming to be motivated by it, Williams objects that no plausible account of this can be given which does not collapse back into

[5] For a more patient discussion of intrinsically irrational desires, see Parfit (1984) 120–6.

[6] Williams (1981a) 105.

something like the Humean account, resting on pre-existing motivations.[7] But why not? Unless we have *already* bought the Humean idea of the inertness of reason, why should the *perception* of the world not itself be constitutive of an *inclination* to act in a certain way? To say that a rational agent has a disposition to do what they believe there is a reason to do is not necessarily to re-import the desire/belief model in a way which allows independent existence to desire.

In one other respect, however, Williams issues a useful caveat. He objects that someone who sponsors desire-independent reasons in the way that I have must set some special store by the criticism of agents for *irrationality*, and therefore incurs a special onus to make that term precise, when in fact it is a virtue to leave indeterminate exactly what is to count as a rational deliberative process.[8] The admonition is useful, but in my view entirely general. It is equally unilluminating to equate, at the outset, self-interest with the pursuit of contingent desire, or rationality with self-interest, either on that construction of self-interest or on some better construction which cuts it free from the close association with contingent desires. For the purposes of this enquiry we should define rational action, uninformatively but also non-question-beggingly, simply as action which there is good reason for. It is compatible with this definition to recognize that there can be more than one kind of good reason, and the challenge in the question *Why be moral?* can be interpreted as the challenge to show that and how moral reasons are themselves one kind of good reason. That at least leaves all the options open.

Broadly speaking, we can distinguish two strategies, not themselves entirely separate, which may be adopted in trying to show that moral considerations are capable of furnishing one kind of good reason. These appeal respectively to an idea of our *essential sameness* and an idea of our *essential oneness*. I address the first strategy in the remainder of this section, and the second strategy in the following section. Each contains insights of some importance but neither, I shall argue, offers quite the kind of justification of morality which is sought.

The appeal to essential sameness can begin from the point we had reached in considering the rationality of self-interest. I had suggested that an action was not necessarily rational by virtue of meshing in with a desire which an agent happens to have. The smallest modification to that position would be to say that the action must at least mesh in with the desires which agents *would* have *if* they knew what was good for them. But there is still a residual problem in displaying how and why doing what is for your own good is rational. Suppose there is a bomb in

[7] Williams (1981a) 106–9.

[8] Williams (1981a) 110.

the doorway and we regard this as a case where I have a good reason to make myself scarce. Then it seems to me to display very poorly the rationality of that action to describe it as meeting my interests, as it were *qua* mine. If you break it to me gently that I am suffering from a bad case of mistaken identity and am in fact not Keith Graham but Tina Turner, I do not conclude that I have suddenly lost the reason I had for moving. In a similar way, if I experience resentment when you stamp on my toes it is a very inadequate representation of the grounds of that resentment to advert to the fact that, after all, the toes are mine. That is not the consideration which I believe gives you a reason for refraining from this action. Rather it is the fact that this is no way to treat a *person*, or (if your or my sympathies are more narrowly drawn) that it is no way to treat your *brother*, or an *officer and a gentleman*. In other words, the attempt is made here to explain self-interest by reference to values impersonally specified: the rationality of my own actions is grounded in general descriptions which involve no use of token-reflexives at all. In this way, it encourages me to regard my own interests as those of a person, impersonally conceived, as it were.

We might thus try to establish the motivational efficacy of moral considerations, the possibility of rational altruism.[9] But even if we allow that my interests arise via the possession of certain general features, which may be possessed by others as well as myself, still it may be objected that this merely gives *each individual* who possesses them a reason for acting in a given way. It would need more argument to show that those reasons carry across from one person to another, so that it would be rational for *me* to show active and practical concern for *another*, to take on that person's interests as if they were my own. To employ the most recent terminology in which these issues are couched, it has to be shown that some reasons are agent-neutral rather than agent-relative.[10]

If no reasons are agent-neutral, then a rational concern for the interests of others has not been established. Moreover, even if my examples demonstrate that there *are* agent-neutral reasons, it may be felt that they do so only because they deal in the currency of basic physical sensations, and that this will not legitimate the much more general concern for others of the kind which morality demands. Yet, on the other hand, it will not do for *all* reasons to be agent-neutral. That would leave us with the absurdity that, when I conceive some particular, contingent and innocuous project (say, cycling a distance of 600 kilometres non-stop), either there is a reason for *anyone* to promote this end or there is no reason for *me, specifically* to do so. And while we

[9] Cf. Nagel (1970).

[10] Cf. Nagel (1986) 152, Parfit (1984) 143.

might wish to build an argument on our basic sameness, we should certainly wish to avoid such thoroughgoing sameness. More seriously, it could be argued, following Bernard Williams, that agent-relative reasons are themselves essential to morality, in the form of dictating that individuals have reason to pay special regard to those to whom they stand in special relations.

I do not profess to know how to disentangle this issue. I share Nagel's feeling that it is self-evident that such things as pain are bad and that there is a reason, for *anyone*, to eliminate them, so that it is not possible to argue to this as a conclusion from something more obvious; and that extension is possible from this case to others.[11] But none of this constitutes an argument. Instead, I call attention to another feature of this attempt to ground the demands of morality in our basic sameness, which may be thought entirely unproblematic. It is clear that this appeal to our essential sameness deals exclusively in the interests of individual human beings. It tries to show why we have reason to make imaginative leaps beyond the physical boundaries separating one human being from another, or at least oneself from others; but it leaves those boundaries themselves intact.

But how could this possibly be otherwise?, it might be said. How can we divest the world of what it manifestly contains, namely separate people? We cannot, of course. But the *significance* of physically separate entities can be very differently conceived in different theoretical standpoints. Certainly for some the fact of our separate existences is of paramount moral importance in explaining the side-constraints on what we may do.[12] But that is not the only possible approach. There are approaches where the individual human being is submerged or immersed in some larger unit, such as a country, a state, a party or a class. Here it is possible to argue, and some do argue, that physically separate existence counts for less than membership of the larger community. We might perhaps surmise that underlying these particular examples there is some more general idea of community which might be of assistance in coming to grips with morality. Is there a defensible sense of *moral* community, of essential oneness, which can give a grounding to a generalized concern for others?

II

I have argued elsewhere[13] for a recognition of collective entities as part of the moral world, as it were, and suggested that such a recognition is

[11] Nagel (1986) 159–60, 171–2.
[12] For example, Nozick (1974) 33.
[13] Graham (1986a) 95–116.

especially pertinent to questions of practical rationality.[14] These facts are most clearly seen in the case of formally constituted collective entities whose powers of action are explicitly defined. A club, for instance, may expel a member, a university senate may close a department, a state may declare war. Generally, entities of this kind may decide on and carry out courses of action which are unavailable to individual human beings (though of course the entities consist of nothing but individual human beings carrying out actions which they *are* capable of). Once collective entities have been identified in this way, it may be appropriate to extend the term to less formally constituted bodies whose powers of action are themselves less clearly defined. Many interesting puzzles can then be raised about collectives, for example what degree of cohesion and conscious awareness is required before a number of people can constitute a collective, what is the smallest collective (a marriage?) and what is the largest (the human race?).

It might be allowed that we should recognize collective entities displaying these features, but why should we allow that this has any particular relevance to the moral world? The answer to that lies in the fact that we confront collectives in two ways—as it were, externally and internally. Collectives make decisions and do things which have an impact on the world. If we wish to adopt any attitude of appraisal to what they do, to express the view that it is regrettable or reprehensible, for example, then we relate to them externally. And we do sometimes wish to express such views. But questions of appraisal become more acute when we realize that we must also relate to collectives internally. At some time or another we are part of collectives, and we may have the option of endorsing or refusing to endorse what the collective of which we are a part does. In that way we may or may not *actively identify* with the collective.

An individual's decision whether to identify with a collective, either in general or in connection with some particular action of the collective, will obviously be complex; and many different considerations will feed into an assessment of whether a decision so to identify would be rational—or, better, to what degree it would be rational. One major consideration concerns the way in which the collective arrives at its decisions, and whether the individual has an opportunity for democratic participation in them.[15] Certainly on a plausible view of the nature of persons as autonomous beings this would be a prerequisite for rationally identifying with the decisions of a collective of which one was a member. Much will also depend on the nature of the particular

[14] Graham (1986b) 29–31.
[15] Graham (1986a) 110–14.

collective and the purposes and functions it has. But, on the other hand, much will depend on the nature of the particular individual. I have needs and interests *qua* individual, by virtue of being a particular type of physical organism, by virtue of being a person of a given description and also by virtue of decisions I may take about what projects I wish to pursue. All of this will affect the circumstances in which it will be rational for me to identify with some collective.[16]

Nevertheless, we should not allow these complications to obscure the *principle* of such identification. It is possible to imagine cases where all the circumstances are propitious: for example, where I voluntarily join together with others in some collective enterprise which serves either a pre-existing interest which I have or one which I have myself created, and where the collective makes its decisions in a suitably democratic fashion to which I am party. Here it is entirely sensible for me to 'think outside myself', focusing on the collective enterprise, and regarding its decisions as I would my own. And in cases which fall away from this favourable one in various ways, there will still be many reasons, if not necessarily conclusive ones, for that form of identification. Rather than calling into question the principle of such identification, what the complications do is indicate the possibility of *mis*identification, of immersing oneself in some collective which one does not have reason to identify with. In one idiom, this might amount to a form of false consciousness.

Two further points about identification with collectives should be mentioned. They arise out of problems about where to draw the boundary around the concept of a collective, as I am using the term. Though this would be a matter of some controversy, I should want to argue for the possibility and existence of *invisible* collectives: that is, collectives which engage in corporate actions of a kind not ascribable separately to their members, but whose members are unaware that this is occurring. This would be a kind of analogue of unconscious action on the part of an individual agent.[17] Clearly the question of active identification with the collective is one which could not arise for the

[16] Even F. H. Bradley, in his enthusiasm for the individual's active identification with the collective, recognized that I might find myself in a collective which was in a 'confused or rotten condition' (Bradley (1962) 203). The grounds for active identification with its actions would in those circumstances be weak to vanishing point.

[17] The analogy is not perfect, and more than one phenomenon might be placed under the heading of invisible collectives. A number of people might be entirely unaware that they constituted a collective; or they might be aware of this, but entirely ignorant of the nature of the acts performed by the collective; or ignorant of *some* of those acts; or ignorant of some possible descriptions of those acts.

individual constituents of the collective while they were in this state of ignorance; but precisely because they would be contributing to actions, and therefore producing results, of which they were unaware, we might think it of paramount importance that such an issue should be raised, that the protagonists' inadequate and incomplete view of their own behaviour should be supplemented. Of course, anyone who has little time for the idea of unconscious individual action, or the idea of redescribing actions in terms unavailable to those whose actions are under review, will disagree with me. I therefore pass to a second case, which is perhaps less controversial (at least theoretically), but I believe in the end more important.

Imagine a number of people who share a common social condition. They stand in a particular kind of position of subordination to others in their society, and in consequence of the relations which grow up around this subordination they suffer or run the risk of suffering from one or more of a number of serious privations. They share not only a common condition but a common interest in ridding themselves of it, in favour of quite different conditions of existence. But suppose these people realize none of this. It is not reflected in their thoughts or their vocabulary; their descriptions of themselves and others emphasize differences rather than similarities (or at least rather than *these* similarities); and they engage in no corporate action together. Then they do not constitute a collective.

Suppose finally, however, that if these people did realize the facts about their common condition and the common interest to which it gives rise, then their combined talents and powers would be sufficient for them corporately to change social relations, in a way in which it would not make sense to think of their doing as individuals, and in fact in such a way that they would cease to be members of the group originally described. They then constitute not an invisible but a *potential* collective. I should want to say that those individuals may have rational grounds for identifying with this potential collective, and derivatively they may have rational grounds for making it an *actual* collective. Not only that, but this might very well be a major source of rational motivation with its origin outside the individual as such. And, of course, none of this would be apparent if we confined our attention to social descriptions and collectives already before people's minds in the circumstances described.

It might be objected that no such rational motivations can be established, for reasons connected with the free-rider problem.[18] As an individual in that situation, I can reason that I have grounds for

[18] This was enunciated by Olson (1965) and discussed more recently by Buchanan (1982) and Elster (1985).

wanting that outcome but not for doing anything towards it: either others will bring about the outcome, in which case my efforts would be wasted and I can still enjoy the benefits; or they will not, in which case my efforts will again be wasted and there are not even any benefits to enjoy. This will apply in any case of 'public goods', that is, goods which are available to all members of a group and cannot be confined to those who actually took part in their production.[19] Hence, 'collective action is beset by the difficulty that it often pays to defect'.[20]

I do not profess to offer a solution, in any orthodox sense, to this problem. I merely observe that, as normally set up, it involves two assumptions which my own discussion is designed to question. First, when it is expressed as a problem about what it is rational to do, it fails to pay heed to the admonition, mentioned in section I, against question-begging conceptions of rationality. It implicitly identifies what is rational with what serves individuals' interests, and indeed takes the latter notion in a fairly crude and straightforward way. But (to employ the neutral definition of rationality recommended earlier) it is far from obvious that considerations of the kind envisaged exhaust what an individual may have reason to do. I may wish *to be associated with* the efforts of a particular group, and there may be good reasons for that wish; I may have a good reason for doing something as an act of self-expression; I may act in a particular way because I regard so acting as appropriate or fitting, given my nature, or what dignity demands, or whatever. The rationality of stances such as these would go unnoticed or misrepresented on the question-begging conception of rationality.

I said that rationality had been identified with individuals' interests. It is not necessarily identified with *self*-interest. That is to say, the free-rider problem does not depend for its substance on a definition of rationality in terms of egoism. Buchanan correctly notes that it arises equally if 'the individual contemplating contribution or non-contribution is not a maximizer of his own utility but a maximizer of overall utility for the group'.[21] As such an individual I can still reason that my own efforts will be 'a subtraction from the group's utility' if the desired outcome can be achieved without them.[22] But, as well as confirming the narrow conception of rationality, this observation also makes clear the second assumption which I wish to challenge: this is the assumption that what individuals have good reason to do turns solely on the expected utilities *for individuals*. (The utility of the group, as Buchanan uses the term, just is the sum of utilities of its individual

[19] Cf. Buchanan (1982) 89.
[20] Elster (1985) 347.
[21] Buchanan (1982) 90.
[22] Ibid.

members.) As Elster puts it, 'The motivation to engage in collective action involves, centrally, the structure of the gains and losses associated with it for the individual'.[23] But precisely what I have tried to suggest is that, in sufficiently propitious circumstances, an individual may have good reason to 'think for' the collective, and to act on a consideration of what is reasonable for the collective, where the collective is not just a collection of individuals but a corporate entity with its own identity and its own decisions and actions. It remains to add that a challenge can be made to the ledger-book conception of rationality, which sees it exhausted in 'gains' and 'losses', as much in the case of collectives as in the case of individuals.[24]

Let me also clarify what I do *not* intend to establish in my discussion of collectives. It is not my intention to join with those theorists who wish (whatever this means) to eliminate the individual, or to argue that the individual is a mere 'construction'. Individuals are there, walking around in the world. Nor is it their existence as mere physical objects that is certain in this way. However much the character and the choices of individuals may be moulded or determined by social circumstances, it is they who give expression to those characters and give effect to those choices. My intention, therefore, is not to replace individuals but to complement them, with other entities which are significant in their own right for our understanding of the social world we live in. And I have tried to indicate how this may affect practical thinking, by tempering

[23] Elster (1985) 351.

[24] Discussions of the free-rider problem tend to be a mixture of theory intended to explain people's behaviour and theory intended to establish how people ought to behave. The two are connected, because we presumably believe that people sometimes behave rationally; but they are distinct. The emphasis in my own remarks is on understanding the conceptual equipment *potentially* available to us on such occasions, rather than on understanding why people currently behave as they do. It is *explanatory* individualism that Elster sponsors (Elster (1985) 5, 359), and he is critical of that methodological collectivism which 'assumes that there are supra-individual entities that are prior to individuals in the explanatory order' (ibid. 6). Though I might disagree with Elster about this, the claims I make here do not commit me to doing so. My claim is that there are prior collective entities, whose significance is not properly understood, in the *explananda* rather than in the *explanans*. Indeed, for reasons mentioned at the beginning of section III, the lack of assimilation of the considerations I am outlining makes an explanation of people's actual behaviour in individualist terms perhaps more plausible. People behave as they do partly because they think in individualist terms. I believe that they think in those terms where they should not, and therefore sometimes behave as they should not. But I do not underestimate the difficulty of changing these habits. See further note 31.

the approach which presupposes a world exhausted by the inventory of atomic individuals, with their atomic, individual concerns.

The answer implicit in my discussion, therefore, to the question what this has to do with morality is that it challenges some of the presuppositions surrounding the institution of morality, mentioned at the outset. When we recognize the existence of collectives, it will no longer do to imagine me as a self-contained individual, on the one hand motivated by unproblematic self-interest, and on the other hand possibly motivated by problematic external demands arising from other individuals like myself. Part of my identity consists in being a constituent in supra-individual corporate entities, and part of my practical thinking should reflect this. Accordingly, I no longer feel only the pressure to take account of the needs and interests of other individual creatures like myself, in addition to my own needs and interests. In cases where active identification is appropriate, the needs of the collective will also weigh with me. And a collective such as a party, or a nation, or a class, may have interests which are quite distinct from the interests either of a given individual or even of all the individuals who go to compose it at a given time.

All the same, it may well be felt that what I have done is to make matters worse, by calling attention to a set of considerations which raise parallel problems to those of morality rather than the same problems. I have, after all, conceded that the interests which other individuals have *qua* individuals will continue to press on us and cause a motivational problem. And dealing with that looks like a different exercise from dealing with the question of where to identify with the decisions and interests of some particular corporate entity to which I belong. Apart from anything else, the latter lacks the generality typical of moral considerations, and therefore seems analogous to the practical thinking of self-interest rather than morality.

Now there is one rejoinder which, if it were sound, would perhaps meet these points. Suppose we could regard all those individuals which fall within the concern of morality as composing one large corporate entity. Then the kind of thinking which I have suggested should characterize practical deliberation *qua* member of a collective might come a lot closer to moral thinking. In those circumstances 'the good of the collective' and 'the requirements of morality' might very well apply to one and the same thing, even if carrying different connotations. And the sense of community concomitant with reasoned identification with the corporate entity might itself carry motivational efficacy which would serve the ends of morality. The problem, however, is that the moral realm does not constitute a collective entity in the required way. Not only is there no collective action of the kind which I have made definitional of a collective, but there is arguably no commonality of condition, or anything similar, either. In this connection MacIntyre has argued convincingly that, whereas we may think of particular contexts, such as schools or hospitals, in which the idea of community in some shared project is appropriate, precisely what is missing in modern life is the sense of any community which is concerned with the whole of life, 'with man's good as such'.[25]

III

At this point we reach a kind of watershed. I have pointed to a form of practical thinking which is not the same as moral thinking, but perhaps exhibits some similarities and may also in some ways be as important. This prompts the subversive thought that this form of practical thinking might at certain points *displace* morality. Whether it could or should do so will depend on many considerations, including, for example, how far we believe that membership of collectives does or ought to constitute a major part of our lives. But it would also depend on the availability of ways of reasoning appropriate to collective identification. The mere recognition of this aspect of our existence will not suffice: we also need the conceptual resources to do justice to it in a coherent and sustained way. We need the equipment to engage in collective practical thinking. Precisely because moral thinking, with its quite different individualist assumptions, has been so central in our tradition this is not likely to be easy to achieve.

What I want to suggest is that Marx's theories, and in particular his theory of class, can help us in this regard. Two caveats need to be entered, however. The first is that in my view Marx's theories have been very poorly understood, as much by would-be supporters as by critics, so that what I refer to here is a body of theory which is available but has gone to a large extent unnoticed or misinterpreted. The second is that I can do little more here than gesture to a source of possible help in the enterprise of providing a backing for thinking in terms of collectives. A full-scale defence is obviously beyond the scope of a few comments in a paper of this length.

Marx's ambivalence towards morality has been well documented in recent times.[26] It is well illustrated in what I should call the *inevitability*

[25] MacIntyre (1981) 146. But don't all people share an interest, say, in the preservation of the earth as a safe habitat, and don't they then constitute a potential collective in the way described earlier? In a sense, yes. But if some of the claims Marx makes about the nature of class-divided society are correct (if, for example, people have irreconcilably different views and interests in the matter of the *form* in which the earth should be preserved), then calls to actualize *this* potential collective are premature.

[26] See, e.g., Lukes (1985), Miller (1984).

problem and the *ideology problem*. On some readings, Marx sees the downfall of capitalism as the unavoidable outcome of ineluctable historical forces. But if that is the case, why does he condemn capitalism for its moral evils, and why does he exhort its victims to band together in the interests of taking action to secure a result which is guaranteed in any case? That question is made all the more urgent by the ideological status which Marx allots to morality. His official view is that as an institution it merely reflects the processes occurring in material life, the realm of production, so that morality, along with law and religion, represents so many bourgeois prejudices, behind which lurk bourgeois interests. Yet that simply makes all the more pressing the question why, in that case, he should engage so much in what looks, at the literal verbal level, to be moral condemnation of the capitalist system.

My own view is that Marx's theory of class, when properly understood, helps to soften some of this paradoxicality. It also connects in an interesting way with the issue of collective identification.

We are familiar from the *Communist Manifesto* with the claim that the history of all hitherto existing society is the history of class struggle, and with the idea that class membership is to be defined by reference to one's position in a network of productive relations, and more specifically to one's relation to the *means* of wealth production.[27] No doubt part of what Marx is doing in constructing a theory around these ideas is calling attention to facts about individual human beings, certain common features which characterize their condition and so on. But that is not all. He also calls attention to the creation of a new kind of collective entity in the work process. Just as the offensive power of a squadron is essentially different from the sum of the offensive powers of individual soldiers, so the mechanical forces operated by isolated workers differ from the social force which arises from co-operation.[28] A new collective power is born, an intrinsically collective one, and this leads Marx to speak of the 'collective worker', an entity which possesses excellences deriving from qualities which represent one-sidedness or imperfections in individuals.[29] It is then this collective worker which becomes responsible for production. 'The product is transformed from the direct product of the individual producer into a social product, the joint product of a collective labourer, i.e. a combination of workers, each of whom stands at a different distance from the actual manipulation of the object of labour'.[30]

[27] Marx and Engels (1967).
[28] Marx (1976) 443.
[29] Marx (1976) 468–9.
[30] Marx (1976) 643.

These claims have important consequences for a proper understanding of Marx's theory of exploitation, based as it is on the idea of extraction of value and surplus value from that entity which produces objects of exchange. They also feed into our discussion of collectives in an interesting way. Effectively, until Marx provides his conceptualization of the nature of social relations in capitalist society, members of the working class constitute what I referred to earlier as an *invisible* collective. They do not have a sense of themselves as combining into a corporate entity, and they do not self-consciously and explicitly engage in corporate action in the way in which a committee or a jury does. Nevertheless, they do so combine, and collectively they achieve what they could not as individuals: at a concrete level, prodigious feats of labour which would be beyond the powers of individuals; at a more theorized level, the creation of surplus value which is appropriated by the capitalist class who own the means of production and buy their labour power. (This should remind us that another important collective entity around in Marx's theory is the capitalist class, to whom the workers stand in important relations. A worker is distinguished from a chattel slave by not being the property of any particular capitalist: but the worker must sell his or her energies to *some* member of the capitalist class, and therefore in effect belongs to that class considered as a whole.)

The point, however, is to change the world, and Marx's conceptualization is also intended to be instrumental in fostering what is already a *potential* collective, in my earlier terminology. Instead of unconsciously forming a collective which sustains a privileged class, the workers can consciously combine to form a different collective which achieves the liberation of human beings from the onerous conditions of class-divided society, a corporate entity which dispossesses the capitalist class of their monopoly of wealth and converts it into the common property of the whole society. That, on Marx's optimistic view, will herald precisely the state of affairs where the free development of each will coincide with the free development of all, and one possible interpretation of that obscure idea is precisely that there will cease to be tensions between the interests of individuals and the interests of the social collective which they compose.

Where, then, does Marx stand on the issue of morality? He sees class identification as a sound and primary motivating force.[31] By contrast, a

[31] Buchanan entertains the possibility that the proletarian might ask not 'What should I do?' but 'What should *we* do?' and thus avoid the free-rider problem. But he objects that this assumes what Marx must establish: that this new way of conceiving decisions could be arrived at in the isolating, egoistic environment of capitalism (Buchanan (1982) 191, n27). That seems to me to

moralistic attitude proceeds from an inadequate understanding of dynamics actually at work in human society, and therefore provides an unsound basis for rational motivation. For Marx, it is as much the bourgeois *conception* of morality as its content which is suspect. I called attention earlier to the universality and unconditionality of moral appeals and to the idea that moral demands incumbent on an agent arose from a consideration of the interests of others. But Marx would object that universality and unconditionality precisely fail to take account of the crucially different class locations of different agents, and the concentration on individuals fails to take acount of the corporate entities which individuals are part of, as a major feature of their lives.

Marx's appeal to workers to transform society is thus not itself a moral appeal, but it occupies ground closely adjacent to morality, because it is concerned with what people have good reason to do. It is also itself not devoid of judgments of value in some looser sense—ideas for example of what constitutes a worthwhile human life and what conditions it is reasonable to expect human beings to tolerate—and that is part of the explanation of why in his practical exhortation Marx often employs some of the same vocabulary as bourgeois moralists.[32] Moreover, given the importance which he assigns to the need for proletarian self-emancipation, his talk of the inevitability of this transformation should be seen as expressing what he expects to see happen as a result of human endeavour, rather than its happening despite human efforts. If Marx is a determinist, his is not the kind of determinism which renders otiose the language of practical exhortation.

The question remains whether we could or should accept a framework of this kind as being to any extent a replacement for the moral point of view. The most I am entitled to suggest, on the basis of the arguments of this paper, is that the collective identification implicit in Marx's class theory is of a type which we have independent grounds for finding a place for and which is relatively neglected in the moral point of view. How far we should accept the particular substance of Marx's theory is a much wider and more complicated question. Our answer to it will turn on many considerations, including the extent to which we

---

put the problem in exactly the right place. Even if there *is* a theoretical resolution available, will it have any practical effect? One part of the answer (and one way of making sense of Marx's own life) is that Marx saw a role for his own theories in helping to shape and change proletarian consciousness. In that respect he was optimistic: he could not be expected to foresee the dire consequences of his posthumous Leninization (cf. Graham (1986a) 204–30).

[32] In a number of respects the position I adopt coincides with that adopted by Miller (1984), though his discussion is mostly couched in terms of individual human beings and their different class locations rather than corporate entities themselves.

accept his claim about the causal influence of class position on other aspects of our existence. But it would certainly provide interesting material for answering a question closely related to the question *Why should I bother to vote?*, which has receded as the discussion progressed. That would be the question not *Why should I be moral?* but *Why should I be political?*[33]

[33] For helpful written comments on an earlier draft I am extremely grateful to David Archard, G. A. Cohen and Martin Hollis.

The Marxist Ethic of Self-realization: Individuality and Community

DAVID ARCHARD

If, for Marx and Marxists, communism would be the most ideal of human societies, this is because it would make possible the maximum use of human and natural resources to the equal benefit of all. This means that, under communism, human beings would 'realize themselves'. In direct and pointed contrast to capitalism wherein all individuals lead alienated, stunted, and fragmented lives, communism for Marx would provide the preconditions for a flowering, a full and final development of all human potentialities.

In his recent work on Marx, Jon Elster has argued that the ideal of self-realization is central to Marx's thought but is nevertheless vitiated by an unresolved tension between the principles of individuality and community.[1] I shall briefly set out some general criticisms of the notion of self-realization before indicating the nature of these more specific criticisms of Elster's (I). I shall state, but not pursue any criticisms of, a number of assumptions made by Elster in his understanding of 'self-realization' (II), before commenting upon the ways in which it is alleged that the values of 'creative self-realization' and 'community' conflict (IV). A brief section (III) exposes a bad argument for such a conflict. In the final, and more substantive, half of the paper I shall argue that there is a sense in which, according to Marx, human beings realize themselves as social individuals, and that, accordingly, the alleged tension of individuality and community is mis-stated. I examine the idea of a 'synthesis' of individuality and community (V), define a notion of *sociality* and distinguish it from harmony (VI), relate both notions to the problem of the individual within society (VII), and sketch the relation of 'sociality' to individual self-realization through creative activity (VIII), before making some brief concluding remarks (IX).

[1] He speaks of a 'conflict' between 'creative self-realization' and 'the value of community' in his (1985) p. 523 and, more bluntly in the shorter (1986) of 'a head-on collision' (p. 48). Similarly Steven Lukes in his (1985) speaks of 'a contradiction, or at least tension, between the individualistic and communitarian impulses in Marx's thought' (p. 96).

I

The idea that it would be good for humans to 'realize themselves' is a powerful and attractive one. It is also a venerable idea going back at least to Aristotle. However, the ethic of self-realization is the subject of familiar criticisms.[2] What are the appropriate ways in which humans realize themselves? If it is said that humans realize themselves by engaging in a wide variety of different activities and projects, it will be replied that depth is thereby sacrificed to breadth. The person who consistently hunts, fishes and disputes all in the one day will probably do none of these activities sufficiently well for her to find any of them, or indeed her life as a whole, fulfilling. If it is said that humans realize themselves by performing only those activities that accord with their nature, that are essentially human, it will be responded that there is no non-evaluative, no non-question begging means of agreeing upon that nature or essence. Why, with Aristotle, should we believe that reason is man's essence, or why indeed, if that is what he believed, should we concur with Marx's conception of human beings as essentially labouring creatures? Moreover, is there any reason to conclude that in doing those things that are argued to accord with his essential nature man would thereby be any happier or better off?

These general criticisms apply to *any* ideal of self-realization but specifically directed at the Marxist ideal is a criticism which may be found expressed in the most recent philosophical writing on Marx. This alleges a tension, conflict or contradiction between individualistic and communitarian principles in Marx's description of self-realization under communism. On the one hand, Marx speaks of individual human beings fulfilling their potentialities; on the other hand, he stresses the value and achievement of the community, human society as a whole. Is it then men or Man, discrete and particular human beings, or the human species whose self-realization communism facilitates? Is it unrealistic of Marx to suggest, as he appears to do, that these principles of individuality and community do not and will never conflict? Is it Utopian to imply that the self-realization of individuals is always and completely compatible with that of the community as a whole? Elster is representative of several critics in believing that the answer to these last two questions must be 'yes'. He himself gives specific reasons for his answer which I will return to in section IV.

II

However, before I proceed further I should state certain assumptions which appear to be made by Elster and others in their descriptions of

[2] See for instance Nielsen (1973) and, of particular relevance to this paper, Plamenatz (1975) Ch. 12.

self-realization. Proper consideration of them lies outside the scope of this particular paper, but it is important, for at least two reasons, to make them explicit. First, it is by no means clear that the assumptions are justified, and there are reasons for believing them false; second, some of the arguments offered for the conclusion that Marx's notion of self-realization involves a conflict between the principles of individuality and community require at least some of these assumptions to be made. These arguments might thus be discounted were the assumptions in question shown to be mistaken. However, since my target is a different one, I shall content myself merely with stating these assumptions.

The first of them is that freedom of choice is a necessary condition of self-realization. That is, an individual can only realize herself in those projects which she herself has chosen. Second, it is assumed that for each individual what is realized is a specific and distinctive essence, such that each individual can only realize herself in one particular way, or at least in a very limited range of ways. This contrasts with, for instance, a view of individuals as each realizing a general human essence, and being able to do so in a range of possible ways. Third, self-realization is not all or nothing, but admits of degrees, and we can sensibly speak both of maximizing self-realization, and of one individual being more self-realized than another.

III

There is a bad reason for thinking that the principles of individuality and community must conflict. This is that, whilst individuality requires that individuals assert themselves in individual, that is different projects, activities and lives, community requires that individuals pursue common, that is the same purposes. In short individuality requires difference, community requires uniformity. But it is of course quite possible for individuals to engage in different activities but nevertheless be in pursuit of a shared end or goal. Several people join together to build an artefact that each could not, individually and separately, succeed in constructing; they agree a division of labour wherein each undertakes a task that is distinct from any other and specific to that individual. Each does something different and yet all pursue the same goal. In so far then as individuality is thought to entail difference, there is no reason to conclude that it thereby automatically conflicts with some principle of community.

Relevant here are remarks by Aristotle in his *Politics*. Aristotle defines the polis as an association (*koinōnia*), but criticizes those who believe that the unity of the ideal polis can best be secured by a uniformity of its membership. On the contrary, Aristotle believed that the self-sufficiency of a polis could only be attained through a differentiation between its members: a better life for all could best be achieved through each providing different, yet complementary, services. They would be complementary insofar as they all served a common, and shared, end or good. What, for Aristotle, ensured that a polis was truly a *koinōnia* was the common purpose, and what made the polis ideal was that the common purpose was the good of all.[3]

IV

Elster does not make use of this bad argument for the incompatibility of the principles of individuality and community. His main claim is that, even in an ideal social arrangement, there will have to be trade-offs—both between individuals within the community, and between individuals and the community as a whole.

If we take this last trade-off first, we may follow Elster and understand the self-realization of the community as the achievements in general of a society, or species—in art, science, and overall culture. Elster argues that such achievements may only be maximized by increasing to the limit the number of individuals attempting to achieve such advances. And with an increase in the number of candidates for success will automatically come an increase in the number of those who fail. 'If only those engage in creative and intellectual work who are certain *ex ante* to succeed, then fewer will do so than are required for the social optimum. If no potential Raphael is to be blocked, then many who wrongly believe themselves to be potential Raphaels will be frustrated'.[4]

Elster intends to speak of a trade-off between two goals—the self-realization of individuals and that of humanity as a whole. This trade-off must clearly be distinguished from any other—for instance, one between satisfactions, or, indeed, between satisfactions on the one hand and self-realization(s) on the other. Yet Elster's examples are not always unambiguous. To simplify matters: let us agree that the potentialities of humanity as a whole are more realized if it produces one rather than no 'Shakespeare'. (The quotation marks indicate that we are less interested in the historically actual Shakespeare than in an individual with literary achievements and talents equivalent to those of the actual Shakespeare.) We can also agree that a 'Shakespeare' is more

[3] Aristotle (1921) B2; see also Mulgan (1977) 13–17 and Newman (1887) 41–4.

[4] Elster (1985) 89.

likely to appear if a large number of individuals attempt and fail to become a 'Shakespeare'. What then is the alleged conflict or trade-off at issue? It is between the gain to humanity as a whole of a 'Shakespeare' and the loss of individuals who are frustrated 'Shakespeares'.

But why should this latter 'loss' be interpreted as one of self-realization? It clearly *may* be a loss in terms of satisfaction: individuals who seek, and fail, to achieve a certain goal may, obviously, end up unhappier than if they had not made the attempt. But there is no reason to believe that they are thereby less realized; indeed there is every reason to conclude that by striving to perfect themselves, measured against the ideal in whatever field of human endeavour they are in, they will make *more* of themselves than had they not made the attempt.

As described by Elster the attempt to self-realize brings unhappiness for most. Yet one might—convincingly—redescribe the example as follows: the aspirant to literary greatness may be initially disappointed to recognize that she is not, and never will be, the equal of Shakespeare. But in her attempt to become such she has pushed herself further than she ever previously has, and now feels happy to work at a level she would not otherwise have attempted to reach. Initially not writing at all, an individual may indeed be unhappy to fail as a 'Shakespeare', but may also be happy at least to achieve *something* as a writer.

The issue of the relationship between self-realization and happiness cannot adequately be dealt with here. I note only that the conflict or trade-off at stake in the 'Shakespeare' example is one between satisfactions and self-realization, which is not that intended by Elster.

There is one way in which there could be a loss in self-realization if individuals were encouraged to strive for success in an inappropriate field of human endeavour; that is the case where they might have succeeded in some other. For example, humanity may be the overall gainer if it produces more 'Shakespeares' than 'Einsteins', yet individuals may fail to realize themselves if, encouraged to become 'Shakespeares', they do not become the 'Einsteins' they could have become. However, this again is not the sort of trade-off or conflict Elster has in mind. His use of human achievement in a particular field, viz. 'Raphael', is only to exemplify a supposedly general conflict—between gains to humanity as a whole and the losses to particular individuals.

Moreover, it is very difficult to see what precise sense could be made of optimizing humanity's self-realization through trade-offs between particular fields of achievement. We *might* be able to specify such an optimum just as we could an optimization of satisfactions (by, for instance, calculating the respective gains to everybody from the works of a 'Shakespeare', an 'Einstein', etc.). However, difficulties in calculation notwithstanding, it seems safe to suggest that a flowering of humanity entails, at a minimum, a fair degree of variety in its achievements. So talk of a trade-off between a 'Shakespeare' and an 'Einstein' would be inappropriate.

Let us turn then to the trade-off between individuals. It is argued that the self-realizing activities of individuals may be incompatible of themselves or as a result of scarce resources. It is the problems that arise from a scarcity of resources which most interest Elster, and it is worth spelling out the argument involved. First, given scarce resources it is impossible for everybody to realize themselves completely. Marx is criticized for sometimes appearing to deny this premise by predicting communist abundance. Second, it must be assumed that insofar as individuals choose different projects of self-realization they will make different demands on these scarce resources. That is, the same degree of self-realization in two individuals may result from a different degree of resource utilization. Third, Marx is generally agreed to have favoured equal maximal self-realization for all, as opposed, say, to a principle of equal resource use.

Given these premises, two problems of trade-off follow. The first is that of the *relatively* expensive project of self-realization. Assume a society composed exclusively and in equal measure of goldsmiths and poets; assume further that the goldsmith requires three times as many units of available resources to achieve the same degree of self-realization as the poet. Then, on a distribution of resources to ensure equal maximal self-realization for all, poets will achieve half as much self-realization as they could have achieved on an equal division of resources. Thus, the poets (and in general those who choose relatively inexpensive projects of self-realization) will be worse off than they would be on some principle other than equal maximal self-realization (such as an equal division of available resources).

The second problem is that of the *excessively* expensive project of self-realization. Assume the same society as before, but this time assume that the goldsmiths require, say, ten times as many units of resources to achieve the same degree of self-realization as the poets. Assuming again a goal of equal maximal self-realization, it must follow not only that the poets are considerably worse off than on an equal distribution of resources but that everyone enjoys a very low level of self- realization. The only reasonable solution would seem to be for the goldsmiths (and in general those with excessively expensive projects of self-realization) to agree to a lesser degree of self-realization than the poets, thus freeing resources which can then be used for the more 'economical' self-realization of these latter.

Both problems can be solved only by a trade-off between individuals: in the first example to the detriment of the poets, and in the latter to that of the goldsmiths. Such a trade-off indicates an incompatibility between the principles of individuality and community. If the goldsmiths, for instance, are prevented from pursuing their projects to their desired end, then they are denied the freedom of choice which is a necessary condition of their self-realization. Besides which the need for coercion means that there cannot be real community, namely an absence of irresolvable conflict between individuals. We may note here the importance of the three assumptions stated earlier. They preclude the goldsmiths from being equally self-realized in some activity other than goldsmithery; and, in general, from being self-realized in any activity other than one of their own choosing. Otherwise, the 'goldsmiths' could choose (or be coerced) to realize themselves to the same extent as in their goldsmithery but in some other activity which involved fewer resources.

Coercion apart, the only solution would be if individuals altruistically sacrificed some at least of their own self-realization for the sake of others. Elster regards such a solution as utopian, and as conflicting with 'Marx's vision of communism as a society in which *full* self-realization will go together with *full* community'.[5] That is, individuals cannot all realize themselves to the same degree as they would choose to do in circumstances where they were not constrained by sharing resources with others. Thus, with respect to self-realization the principles of individuality and community cannot be reconciled.

V

This particular problem of self-realization is, of course, one example of a very general dilemma: how to reconcile desires and interests within a context of scarcity. It is what Rawls terms 'the circumstances of justice'—a situation of moderate scarcity in which self-interested, mutually disinterested individuals recognize the need to agree principles whereby social association (and its benefits) become possible.[6] Further, it would seem that Marx simply abolishes the dilemma by making one or both of the following two Utopian assumptions: communist abundance abolishes scarcity; individual interests and desires will not come into conflict.

It is thus mistaken to argue that there is a tension, or contradiction, within Marx between the principles of individuality and community. Rather the criticism should be that there *ought* to be such a tension in his work. Insofar as a condition of scarcity obtains, and individuals pursue their different interests, these latter must come into conflict, in

[5] Elster (1985) 524.
[6] Rawls (1972) 126–30.

such a way that only agreed and enforced principles will permit stable social association. Thus when Marx speaks of a 'synthesis' of individuality and community, and thereby implies that individual interests can, without such principles, be brought into harmonious co-ordination he is simply guilty of a romantic Utopianism which ill befits a scientific socialist.

To assess this charge, it is important to understand what precisely Marx understands by a 'synthesis' of individuality and community. In an influential article G. A. Cohen defines a 'dialectical' process as that which something undergoes if 'it passes from a stage where it is undivided from some object, through a stage where it divides itself from it in a manner which creates disunity, to a stage where distinction persists but unity is restored'.[7] Cohen labels these successive stages 'undifferentiated unity', 'differentiated disunity', and 'differentiated unity'. He argues that the three successive stages of the dialectic of labour correspond to the three great epochs of Marxist history: pre-capitalism, capitalism and communism. In pre-capitalist feudal society, the individual is undivided from his work and nature; he is, to use Cohen's suggestive term, 'engulfed' by the conditions of his existence. Under capitalism, the worker acquires a detachment from his natural environment and his work, but only at the cost of an alienation. Man is free and independent, but no longer 'at home' in his world. Under communism, man will be reunited with his world, not in the 'engulfing' manner of pre-capitalist society, but rather through a harmonious integration of differentiated elements. This final achieved unity may be thought of as a 'synthesis' of the pre-capitalist unity and the capitalist differentiation between man and the nature he works upon.

There is a clear analogue to this particular dialectic of labour if man is thought of simply in social terms. In pre-capitalist feudal society, each individual is engulfed by his social role. Marx indeed speaks of 'individuals imprisoned within a certain definition, as feudal lord and vassal, landlord and serf, etc.'[8] In capitalism, the individual is free and independent of such engulfing social roles, but his detachment is again achieved only at the cost of an alienation from his fellows. Under communism, man will be reunited with his species, and yet there will be a differentiation of one individual from another. Communism, in short, will offer a differentiated social unity, a 'synthesis' of individuality and community. Of the first epochs, Marx writes as follows: 'The more deeply we go back into history, the more does the

[7] Cohen (1973/4).
[8] Marx (1973) 163.

individual . . . appear as dependent, as belonging to a greater whole.[9] Relations of personal dependence . . . are the first social forms.[10] Only in the eighteenth century, in 'civil society', do the various forms of social connectedness confront the individual as a mere means towards his private purposes, as external necessity.[11] Personal independence founded on *objective* dependence is the second great form'.[12] Of the final stage, the communist synthesis, Marx notoriously says little except to speak generally of 'free social individuals' enjoying 'mutual relationships', the 'free development of each' being 'the condition for the free development of all'.[13]

I do not propose to evaluate this notion of a 'dialectical process', either in itself or as allegedly explanatory of historical development. I am interested in how to understand the notions of 'individuality', 'community' and their synthesis, and the crucial point is that Elster and others seem to understand these notions in terms of *interests*. Individuality means something like self-interestedness, and community means something like a harmony or oneness of interests. So interpreted Marx's talk of a synthesis of individuality and community seems wildly implausible, if not outright nonsense.

Russell Keat has explicitly tried to apply Cohen's understanding of the dialectic process to the problem of individuality and community, and he, like Elster, interprets this problem as one of interests.[14] Thus, he understands unity to mean a harmony of interests, and differentiation to mean the distinguishability of individual interests. He concludes that Marx's ideal of communist unity can only—and implausibly—be that all individuals share a single common interest. But Keat's understanding of the notions of unity/disunity and differentiated/undifferentiated seems mistaken. He speaks of disunity as appropriate to capitalism because there is a conflict of individual interests; there is differentiation in capitalism since each individual has a sense of personal identity and independence from others.[15] However, the converses of disunity and differentiation, if understood in analogous fashion, do not apply to pre-capitalist societies. These are not free of conflict, not least because all societies are characterized by a struggle between classes: 'Freeman and slave, patrician and plebeian, lord and serf, guild master and journeyman, in a word, oppressor and oppressed stood in

[9] Marx (1973) 84.
[10] Marx (1973) 158.
[11] Marx (1973) 84.
[12] Marx (1973) 158.
[13] Marx and Engels (1967) 105.
[14] Keat (1981).
[15] See for example p. 144.

constant opposition to one another, carried on an uninterrupted, now hidden, now open fight . . .'[16] This quotation also makes it clear that individuals in pre-capitalist societies are distinguishable one from another and have quite distinct interests.

VI

I want to suggest that there is an altogether different sense in which Marx understands the notions of individuality, community and their 'synthesis'. Let us start by applying the notions of unity, differentiation and their respective converses to pre-capitalist, capitalist and communist societies. In pre-capitalist society each individual fills a social position or role; he is nothing but this role, he is 'engulfed' by it, 'imprisoned within a certain definition'.[17] He acts, desires, lives as a serf, for example, and not in the first instance as a human being who happens to live in a society where there are serfs of which he happens to be one. There is, in short, no differentiation between the individual and his social role. At the same time there is unity in this sense. The society to which an individual belongs just *is* the set of relations between these roles. Pre-capitalist society is the set of relations which ordains that each individual in his particular role should fulfil certain obligations and undertake certain offices.

Capitalism has, claims Marx, 'torn asunder' these ties,[18] they are 'exploded, ripped up'.[19] Individuals are distinguished from their social roles; they have a freedom (though it is contentious what this really amounts to) to occupy the various social positions which capitalism distributes. Individuals in capitalism are first of all human beings who happen in this particular society to fulfil the roles of proletarian or bourgeois. There is thus a differentiation between the individual and his social role. At the same time, there is disunity in this sense. Society is distinct from the relations entered into by individuals. Under capitalism each individual is indifferent to others; yet independent of each's will and knowledge, behind their backs as it were, are created forms of social interconnection. And this societal interconnectedness is something set over and against each individual: 'various forms of social connnectedness confront the individual . . . as external necessity',[20] they are 'independent of the knowing and willing of individuals

[16] Marx and Engels (1967) 79.
[17] Marx (1973) 163.
[18] Marx and Engels (1967) 82.
[19] Marx (1973) 163.
[20] Marx (1973) 84.

and . . . presuppose their reciprocal independence and indifference';[21] they 'assume the form of objective powers . . . of things independent of the relations among individuals themselves'.[22]

So what then of the 'differentiated unity' which defines socialism? There is differentiation insofar as individuals are distinct from their social roles. This is part of the sense in which individuals under communism will hunt and fish and yet not be hunters or fishermen.[23] At the same time, there is unity since society just is the relations that individuals enter into. Marx speaks of 'universally developed individuals, whose social relations, *as their own communal relations,* are hence also subordinated to their own communal control'.[24]

What we might term the *sociality* of communist society consists of the fact that individuals relate directly one to another as human beings, that these relations are under their collective control, and that these relations are 'universal', unconfined by any 'local' or 'parochial' ties. The notion of *sociality,* whatever else we might want to say about it, is clearly distinct from that of *harmony,* which makes reference to the interests and desires of individuals. A harmonious society is one without conflict, and this may result (broadly) either from individuals not having incompatible interests (as would be the case if all individuals shared a single common interest or if all interests could be satisfied from superabundant resources) or from each individual always being prepared to renounce his or her own interests in favour of those of others (the Utopian vision of universal altruism which Elster derides).

VII

Regrettably, Marx's talk of a 'synthesis' of individuality and community is normally understood only to mean that he envisages communism as being a harmonious society of this kind, and being so for the implausible reasons already given. But my interpretation above favours a different view—namely that Marx supposed such a 'synthesis' to mean *sociality,* not harmony. At the same time, although the notions are clearly distinct, Marx believed them to be importantly related. We can better recognize this by looking at the ways in which individuals relate to one another within different societies. Between capitalist and communist societies there is in fact a double contrast in this respect. Thus,

[21] Marx (1973) 161.
[22] Marx (1973) 652.
[23] Marx and Engels (1965) 45; see also Cohen (1973/4) 258–9 and Ch. V (7) of his (1978).
[24] Marx (1973) 162 (my emphasis).

the individualism that Marx thought characteristic of capitalism comprised two features: mutual indifference and selfishness. Individuals are uninterested in, and indifferent to, their fellows; the particular interests, activities and ends of each are 'private', pursued without reference to those of others. At the same time, they egotistically pursue their own selfish interests, are concerned with others only as the means to their own private gain, and are always prepared to subordinate the interests and ends of others to their own.

Marx believed that, under capitalism, these two features were interrelated. If one is self-interested in the sense of being interested in a self defined outside and without reference to others, then in the capitalist circumstances of human intercourse one's own interests will be seen as superordinate to those of others. Thus, in criticizing Benthamite utilitarianism as a moral philosophy appropriate to capitalism Marx writes that '. . . each looks only to his own advantages. The only force bringing them together, and putting them in relation with each other, is the selfishness, the gain and the private interest of each. Each pays heed to himself only, and no one worries about the others'.[25] G. G. Brenkert similarly argues that when Marx refers to the egoistic individual presupposed by utilitarianism, he means that such an individual is both selfish (acts 'to promote his own good without regard to the well-being of other sentient beings') and 'private' ('the particular kind of individual characteristic of civil society—viz. one who was defined by and concerned with various private ends').[26]

However, the two senses of self-interestedness (or 'egoism')—as indifference to others (being a 'private' individual) and as selfishness—are clearly distinct. To be disinterested in relation to others and interested in oneself alone does not necessarily mean that one will always act so as one's interests are superordinate to those of others: mutual indifference does not entail selfishness.

When we compare communism with capitalism we should remain aware of this double contrast. Individuals under communism are believed by Marx both to think of themselves in social terms and to acquire a new set of motivations. By contrast with capitalism individuals, under communism, will be interested in the interests of others, and will no longer pursue their own projects 'privately' and without reference to others. This mutual interestedness does not *entail* a form of altruism, whereby each individual is always prepared to subordinate his interests to those of others. But Marx certainly seems to have believed that what we have called sociality would be an important precondition of social harmony—along with equality of condition and

[25] Marx (1976) 280.
[26] Brenkert (1981) 198–9.

an end to exploitation—and he also believed that the new communist society with its new forms of 'communal relations' would make possible new kinds of individual motivation.

It is not clear which of these—very vague and ambiguous—ideas may be termed simple romantic Utopianism. Marx did not believe that individual interests would be replaced by a general social or species interest. Nor did he believe either that differences between individual interests would disappear or that each individual would always subordinate his own interests to those of others. But he may have believed that what differences there were could be resolved in a non-antagonistic manner and without resort to coercion. And he may have been right to assume the following: where each individual has a sense of himself as social and sees his society as his 'communal relations' to others under their 'communal control', there is a willingness to settle, or try to settle, differences between individuals in ways that are fundamentally moral, that is fair and just. Understanding the 'synthesis' of individuality and community as *sociality* is thus important for showing that Marx had at least *some* reason for believing that the relations between individuals under communism would be non-antagonistic. If this 'synthesis' is interpreted simply as harmony, then Marx's belief that the relations between individuals under communism would be harmonious lacks any apparent foundation and appears a straightforwardly Utopian assumption or article of faith.

VIII

We can now try briefly to relate this notion of 'sociality' to the ideal of individual self-realization through creative activity. Returning to the simplified example of a society of goldsmiths and poets, we note that its earlier description required a certain mutual indifference on the part of each to the fate of the other. Thus, it is not counted part of a goldsmith's self-realization that a poet realize himself. This assumption clearly reflects the view of individuals as 'privately' pursuing their own projects and ends without reference to, and being disinterested in relation to those of others. Now Marx clearly believed that in truly human activity, that is authentically social activity, individuals would not be indifferent to one another's fate, and indeed that the action of one individual would be an affirmation or objectification of the other. In an oft-quoted passage from his earlier manuscripts Marx spoke of production carried out 'as human beings'. My production of something would be an objectification of my 'individuality and its particularity'; you, as an other human being, might make use of and gain satisfaction from my product, and I would thus 'have had the *direct* and conscious satisfaction that my work satisfied a *human* need, that it objectified *human* nature, and that it created an object appropriate to the need of another *human* being'. 'In my individual activity I would have directly created your life; in my individual activity I would have immediately *confirmed* and *realized* my true *human* and *social* nature. Our productions would be so many mirrors reflecting our nature'.[27]

In a recent article on self-realization Elster himself quotes this passage and says that 'it may be read as suggesting a distinction between two ways in which the appreciation of other people enhances the satisfaction I derive from work'. This appreciation may either take the form of pleasure derived from my product, or of a critical estimation of the product's merits. Elster claims that since this latter appreciation may include negative assessments and demands a 'coolly evaluative attitude', it is incompatible with the 'warmth and spontaneity' of relations to friends and family. This latter group, says Elster, is the 'only' one who can appreciate, in the first sense, my product, that is derive pleasure from it. He adds that 'the idea that one can derive pleasure from knowing that one provides a service to "society" is . . . unrealistic'. Marx is thus wrong to believe that the same group—others in general or 'society' on the one hand, and close personal friends or relations on the other—can appreciate my product in both senses of the word.[28]

Elster's comments do not seem well judged. There are many who do currently claim to take pleasure from the knowledge that their work is of service to 'society'. He may mean that only some, but not all, could take such pleasure, but this is not clearly stated. Anyway, could one not imagine a society each member of which was the exclusive performer of a distinct service valuable to the others? And why would it be 'unrealistic' to say of this example that each individual derived pleasure from knowing that she provided a service to her 'society'? Why too cannot a group of friends be 'coolly evaluative' of one's work? Elster does not clearly show that they cannot. It may be more true to say that friends cannot be both 'coolly evaluative' and 'warmly spontaneous' *at the same time*. But this may only appear obviously true insofar as Elster's descriptions beg the crucial questions by their implicit contraries—'cool' and 'warm', for instance. There are good reasons for saying, *pace* Elster, that friendship may sometimes require cool judgments, just as criticism may occasionally be warmly spontaneous.

The major defect of Elster's gloss on the Marx passage, however, is that it seems to overstate its content. I agree with Elster that Marx's remarks are not entirely clear, but a reasonable gloss might be as

[27] Marx (1967) 281.
[28] Elster (1985/6) 120.

follows: as a self-realizing goldsmith, for instance, I affirm my own creativity as a human being; I also create something which others are able, as humans, to enjoy. Further, others are able to recognize in my work the creativity of a human; and since they are themselves humans, they can thus recognize that the species to which they belong is realized in my work. I am also, to a corresponding degree, realized in the work of my fellow human, the poet. My individual activity as goldsmith and the other's as a poet are both affirmations or expressions of the capacities we have *qua* humans, and are, thus, to that extent expressions of our communally shared human nature.

Marx is not speaking about the satisfactions or pleasures derived from work. He is talking rather about the extent to which production objectively 'confirms', 'expresses', 'affirms' and 'realizes' human nature. It is important that an individual should recognize her product as an objectification of her own particular and individual creative nature. Under capitalist conditions of production this is not possible and human beings are alienated from their own products. It is also important that humans should recognize products in general as the objectifications of human beings. This is not possible under capitalism, wherein the commodities exchanged do not show themselves to be the visible and evident products of human powers. Truly human production will be different. Whether we produce or consume, we will all recognize what is produced to be the outcome of creative human activity, and it is in this recognition that the activity is human that we also, and simultaneously, 'confirm', 'express', 'affirm' and 'realize' our own nature as human beings.

IX

Jon Elster remarks in the concluding chapter of *Making Sense of Marx* that 'self-realization through creative work is the essence of Marx's communism' and that 'this is the most valuable and enduring element of Marx's thought'.[29] The Marxist notion of self-realization is indeed a valuable and enduring ideal, but, for reasons given, it would be wrong to restrict it to the creative activity of individuals. This would follow if Marx had indeed supposed that the essence of man consists only in his labouring. But Marx also said that the human essence (*Wesen*) is the *Gemeinwesen* of man, that is to say community.[30] In other words, man realizes himself not just in creative activity but in creating within and for a community which he consciously recognizes to be that of his fellow

[29] Elster (1985) 521.
[30] Marx (1967) 271.

species members. What we have termed 'sociality' is thus the realization of the communal nature of human beings.

Were Marx to have understood the 'social individuality' of communist man as only signifying a social harmony wherein all individual interests and desires were totally compatible one with another, he could be justly accused of romantic Utopianism. But insofar as he means something else by the 'synthesis' of individuality and community, namely sociality, he both has a richer notion of human self-realization than is normally thought to be the case and makes more sense of his conviction that communism may indeed be a harmonious and conflict-free society.[31]

[31] I am extremely grateful to the following who commented on earlier drafts of this paper: H. Bunting, P. Carruthers, G. A. Cohen, S. Mills.

Abstract Morality, Concrete Cases

STEPHEN R. L. CLARK

I

Practitioners of disciplines whose problems are debated by moral philosophers regularly complain that the philosophers are engaged in abstract speculation, divorced from 'real-life' consequences and responsibilities, that it is the practitioners (doctor, research scientist, politician) who must take the decisions, and that they cannot (and should not) act in accordance with strict abstract logic.

These charges have some force. It is very irritating to be told what to do by people who are not themselves involved in the day-to-day doing of what is said to be one's duty. It is irritating not only because the preacher may be ignorant of what really needs to be done, because she is ignorant of a range of particular circumstances that cannot easily be described to outsiders, but also because she may have given us no reason to suppose that she would successfully follow her own advice if she were suddenly afflicted with the duties she is so eager to prescribe for others. There are few things easier than the giving of unwanted and inappropriate advice, on the basis of a simplistic model of the situation, to people who are, perforce, much better acquainted with the particular realities, and who will be the ones to bear most of the consequences, material and social, of any error. Consider the comment, by a Puerto Rican lady, on Paul VI's *Humanae Vitae:* 'He no playa the game, he no maka the rules'.

There is more to the objection than offended dignity. Any discipline, any duty, has its own problems, that arise within that discipline and duty and which it is part of the discipline and duty to recognize as problems. What outsiders think problematical may not be so for the practitioner; what practitioners think problematical may be entirely opaque to those who have not had the requisite training or experience. It may seem easy enough, 'in the abstract', to build a bridge across a river—what is needed but ropes, planks, secure endpoints? But the actual attempt to build the thing will undoubtedly reveal a thousand unexpected and particular problems (and the more secure and workman-like we wish the bridge to be, the worse will be the problems) very few of which will be solved by an appeal to 'first principles of bridge-building'. Philosophical claims to superior insight may be as inane as

Aristotle thought Plato's idea of Good:[1] we shall only be able to grasp what is a problem for another discipline if we submit to be trained in that other discipline, and to practise it. Till then we can only be opinionated amateurs. Liberal shibboleth aside, I have no right to an opinion as to the truth or otherwise of Fermat's Last Theorem, the periodicity of gravitational waves, the dangers of cannabis, the linguistic capacities of dolphins, the causes of the Lelantine War, the probable effects of economic sanctions against South Africa, or the net advantages of comprehensive education. Other people may have rationally justifiable beliefs on these matters, but 'what in them is science would in [me] be merely opiniatrety',[2] opinions to which I have no epistemological right.

So issues in the administration of law, the allocation of scarce medical and other resources, the reliability of new engineering techniques, the defence of the realm or the education of children can only usefully be debated by those who are practically and immediately involved in them, trained in the disciplines whose practice throws up the problems, acquainted with the manifold and largely unformalized complexity of real-life situations, and accountable for the consequences of their decisions. The only way of determining what is rightly to be done in these situations is to submit ourselves to a laborious and lengthy discipline, and to put up with the real-life consequences of what we really and truly do. Parents have a right to their opinion on the rearing of children—though even parents have only their own experience to go by, and should be wary of giving unasked advice to other parents; medical researchers who know the likely costs and profits of some particular experimental practice have a right, and even a duty, to judge that practice.

People learn a craft not merely by being taught a set of axioms which include the rules for their own application. We learn the craft by beginning to practise it, perhaps under the guidance and control of an older craftsman: we imitate our guide without necessarily being able then or ever to give a formal account of the sort of thing she does in given situations. Part of what we learn, indeed, is just to see the situations as she does, and act 'appropriately'. Crafts carry their own moral universes with them. The Socratic game of making craftsmen, of whatever craft, look silly by demanding that they give some formal account of the principles on which they 'must' be acting if their craft is to be more than an unreasoning knack is sophistical.[3] All crafts, including Socrates's own, are governed by tacit and unformalized principles:

[1] Aristotle (1915) I, 1096a11ff.

[2] Locke (1959) 115; see Weinsheimer (1984) 21.

[3] See Geach (1969) 117.

one might as well decree that no one knows how to ride a bicycle unless she can give the (unusable and strictly inaccurate) formula that indicates how to turn the handlebars at the angle needed to compensate for the rider's tilt. We do not need any abstract idea of justice or virtue in order to be just and virtuous.[4]

The study of some few abstract principles, accordingly, can have no necessary bearing on the complex, tacitly known realities of those crafts and pursuits that make up the human universe. Some crafts, we can agree, rely more than others on relatively abstract calculation. The archer learns to shoot her arrows by imitation, practice, unformalized assessments of wind speed, humidity and the target's motion. The technicians at Canaveral will have preferred to calculate their missile's progress, even though they also know that unpredictable anomalies will leave the calculations inexact, correct only within a margin of natural and human error. Similarly (though for rather different reasons), whereas a paterfamilias would be ill-advised to lay down any very clear and exactly proportioned punishments for making so and so much noise or disarray after such and such an hour (rules which would only encourage his children to become sea-lawyers!), we may well insist that the laws of the land be more predictably applied, that judges do more than exercise their 'educated judgments' and class prejudice. But even those crafts that rely upon some exactly defined rules do not require their craftsmen to have deduced these rules from 'self-evident' principles, still less from principles that would be intelligible and obvious to just anyone. When craftsmen begin to derive their explicit rules from other rules at some higher level of abstraction, it is the latter which are usually explained through the former, not vice versa. Pythagoras' Theorem is a lot more difficult to understand and prove than the 'Egyptian Rule' of 3–4–5. Abstraction and formal deduction come late in the game: we may, naively, hope one day to have a fully axiomatized science but we do not now, nor in the foreseeable future, expect to deduce new scientific theory from a simple set of axioms. Nor could any reasonable person even hope to have an axiomatized psycho-history, although good diplomats and statesmen may occasionally exercise a craft knowledge of what has happened before, and may yet again.

> Beyond the fairly narrow world of number and measure—the proper domain of *res extensa*—we encounter a universe that is complex and manifold, with surprising contours and ever shifting forms, showing us causes that are neither unfailingly true nor patently false, but typically merely probable.[5]

[4] Berkeley (1948–57) II, 84.

[5] Mooney (1985) 124, after Vico.

Even the realm of number and measure, if by that is meant the universe considered as a physical system, is not well understood merely in terms of an abstractly conceived axiomatic system. How much less the worlds of animal and human life?

One response to the unaxiomatizable complexity of 'real life', and the primacy of craft-disciplines in the management of that life, is to resort to the fiction of 'ideal cases'. In the 'real world' of our everyday experience there is no saying when something dropped from a precisely calculated height will reach the ground (for we cannot predict the effects of gravitational anomalies, sudden gusts of wind, inquisitive magpies, subsidence, or passing children): the best we can do is estimate when it would reach the ground if there were no interference, and hope that by and large the interference that there is will make little enough difference. In the idealized world of Newtonian mechanics things in motion continue so, in a straight line for ever, unless they are subjected to some interfering force—as, of course, they always are. In the similarly idealized world of supposedly realistic fiction individuals maintain their own serious integrity in the face of circumstance, and everything that happens to them is significant. Novelists are not judged 'realistic' if they allow arbitrary coincidence, sudden shifts of mood and habit, utterly inconsequential thoughts: a 'realistic' novelist shows how things would be if there were no world larger than her chosen realm, and all things in it behaved as things of 'that kind' reasonably would. Richard Whately commented on such fictional examples that we cannot take the results for real: 'appeal [is] made to the picture of a man conquering a lion; a result which might just as easily have been reversed, and which would have been so had lions been painters'.[6] Such fictive worlds dictate their morals: being a Mrs Proudie is, axiomatically, being overbearing and of poor theological judgment. But would someone in 'real life' who was sometimes or in part a Mrs Proudie be no more than that? Would she be that unfailingly? There is always more to say about real, concrete individuals, whereas merely abstract entities can be exhaustively described.[7]

Trollope's worlds, of course, like those of other great writers,[8] are often extraordinarily convincing 'real worlds', giving an illusory conviction that there is much more to his characters than he has ever said, that the acts he describes are morally ambiguous and open-ended in something like the way of actions in 'real life', that his characters really could surprise us without thereby forfeiting their integrity as fictional characters. But this is an illusion: Mrs Proudie could not make friends

[6] Whateley (1832) 85.

[7] See Martin (1975) 128.

[8] See Martin (1981) 85.

with the Dean and these be the same books; anyone who treated a real person as 'only a Mrs Proudie' would (for all the moral insights to be found in Trollope) be in moral error. Stereotypes may be unavoidable (and it is therefore as well to have a large and interesting collection) but the real ungovernable beings must always peak around the edges.

> I suppose most men will recollect in their past years how many mistakes they have made about persons, parties, local occurrences, nations and the like, of which at the time they had no actual knowledge of their own . . . In order to find what individual men of flesh and blood were, they fancied that they had nothing to do but to refer to commonplaces, alphabetically arranged. Thus they were well up with the character of a Whig stateman or a Tory magnate, a Wesleyan, a Congregationalist, a parson, a priest, a philanthropist, a writer of controversy, a sceptic; and found themselves prepared without the trouble of direct inquiry to draw the individual after the peculiarities of the type.[9]

The fictions advanced by philosophers, notoriously, lack even such depth and complexity as may be found in realistic fiction. Our stories are derived from the rhetoricians' 'sophistopolis', the imaginary city which used to provide topics for Roman schoolboys.[10] Such topics were wholly 'unrealistic', designed to give full opportunity for cleverness in the resolution of absurd problems. If illness excuses from military service, and love is a sickness, persuade the draft board to excuse you on the ground that you are sick with love. Most genuinely philosophical fictions are designed to show how the application of particular principles would affect the world—if nothing else interfered—and so to confirm or rebut the principles as ones that we could happily incorporate in our normal reasonings. If we were in such and such a situation and we were guided only by such and such a principle, this is what we would do—but of course we are never only in that situation, and we are never guided only by one principle, nor even by any clearly discriminable set of principles.

This is the point at which complaining practitioners regularly aim: in the philosophical fiction the application of a suggested principle leads us to experiment on babies or the mentally disturbed for the increase of scientific knowledge or the alleged benefit of others. The philosophical story-teller usually intends either that we then reject this principle, as having unacceptable implications, or that we alter our ordinary practice: either such experimentation is all right after all, or else other experiments (which have been defended as increasing scientific

[9] Newman (1979) 45.
[10] See Russell (1983) 21.

knowledge or benefiting others) cannot be thus defended. The practitioner usually responds with irritation that, 'of course' other principles come into play, in all real situations, to prevent the unwelcome result. It may not be possible to spell out exactly what principle it is that forbids destructive experimentation on, say, microcephalic human babies and permits it upon chimpanzees, but the practitioner will simply insist that people properly brought up in the honourable manners and approved techniques of contemporary experimental science will find no difficulty in discriminating cases. Babies, even microcephalic babies, occupy a quite different moral slot from chimpanzees, even Ameslan users, even if no clearly acceptable principle that would, on its own, be adequate to moral crises can be formulated. Constant reiteration of the obvious truth that we would behave abominably if this or that were our only principle of action serves only to irritate. Nothing is our only principle of action, and people of sound judgment, suitably reared, will make socially acceptable choices even without being able to say why.

> All empty souls tend to extreme opinion. It is only in those who have built up a rich world of memories and habits of thought that extreme opinions affront the sense of probability. Propositions, for instance, which set all the truth upon one side can only enter rich minds to dislocate and strain, if they can enter at all, and sooner or later the mind expels them by instinct.[11]

The philosophical fictions do not refute the particular principles they had brought in to illustrate, but the general claim that moral (or any other) decisions can be made by rules: as Vico said, 'To apply the geometric method to the running of one's life is like trying to go mad by rule'.[12] The sort of 'moral demonstration' which is 'making a dictionary of words' is either trifling or absurd.[13] The impossibility of refuting a suggested principle by telling stories of how horribly (?) we would behave if this were our only principle is paralleled in the ordinarily scientific sphere. No scientific theory can be straightforwardly refuted by experiment or observation, simply because we can never treat just one hypothesis at a time. We may try to conduct our experiments in carefully controlled conditions, and so reduce the number of unexamined assumptions, but this process can never be complete. All we can hope is that there will come a time when we have excluded all but the most bizarre alternative explanations of our experimental results, and shown that the kind of tacit craft management which continues, in

[11] Yeats (1955) 169.
[12] Vico (1982) 71 (*De Italorum Sapientia* I.7.5).
[13] Berkeley (1948–57) I, 82 (Locke), III, 324 (Spinoza); see Clark (1985).

practice, to give reasonable results even with a lousy theory embodies just too many *ad hoc* accommodations, or is just too difficult to train a novice in. These seem to be the only hopes in moral practice too: we cannot hope to show that a particular principle is unacceptable merely by showing how we would behave if it were our only principle. What happens when moral practice changes is that some previously acceptable act has come to seem anomalous, to require a degree of self-deception or emotional manipulation that can no longer be provided. Philosophical and other fictions have a part to play in this reversal, but they do not quite establish what some philosophers have hoped. Aristotle was right: it is best to rear our future citizens, by imitation and habituation, to an honourable grasp of what it is to live well, not by dull obedience to some finitely statable and easily applicable rules. As Vico argues: 'Geometrical method, having an illusion of completeness, stifles the process of philosophical contemplation that the universe—its forms enclosed within God's being—naturally evokes.[14]

II

Moral, practical, technical reasoning—all those forms of reason that have to do with the concrete worlds of our everyday existence—involve more than the simple application of clearly defined principles. Right action is not what is required by a finitely statable principle under such and such neutrally defined circumstances. Even to identify the relevant circumstances requires a depth of moral and practical experience that is not well captured by any set of abstract principles of a kind that one could simply be taught. Right action is what a suitably trained person of sound judgment and good moral character, able to say what she was doing, would in fact do.[15] A well-governed state, or a person of good moral character, is not one which knows and can recite a set of exactly applicable rules suitable for all eventualities, such that even the silliest or weakest or unfriendliest of officials could apply the rules and still do well.[16] Conversely, Socrates and his successors have not been entirely fair in denigrating the unformalized pieties of honest citizens. The *phronimos* (to adopt Aristotle's term) will be able to say what she is doing, and give some account of why it is virtuous so to do: but she will not necessarily be able always to say how exactly this case differs from some other where she would act differently, nor yet to explain why just this sort of virtue is called upon just here. How she describes the world

[14] Mooney (1985) 122.
[15] Aristotle (1915) II, 1107a1ff.
[16] Aristotle (1915) V, 1137b12ff.

and her own intended action is a function of those tacit understandings, natural and social meanings that she has grown up to share.

This view of moral and practical judgment is so far unfamiliar to mainstream moral philosophers that they often mistake its expression for a mere lack of principle. There is a seductive charm about the idea that we could solve our moral crises by arguing from first principles, whether they be utilitarian or Kantian. There is a similar charm to the idea that we could formulate an absolutely general theory of mass-energy and deduce the entire history of the universe from its axioms. Unfortunately, the fact is that there are no such available axioms in science or statesmanship or personal morality. The idea that parental obligation, for example, is a minor corollary of some abstract duty, binding on all moral beings, to maximize happiness, or to allow all other moral or potentially moralizing beings an equal liberty, is a quite hopeless fantasy, as hopeless and at least as dangerous as the cognate fantasy that one might be able to demonstrate the existence of other minds, or the past, or the reliability of inductive reason from the Cartesian *cogito*. 'The attempt to think without presupposition is unreasonable and vain':[17] in science and practical action alike we move within traditional frameworks that are not, and cannot be, entirely systematized. Our moral governors, accordingly, are not abstractly conceived ideals, but the concrete and incipient realities of our particular human world.

> Love is not directed to abstractions, but to persons; not to persons we do not know, nor to numbers of people but to our own dear ones, our family and neighbours.[18]

Such concrete values are familiar enough within the rhetorical tradition. Orators may appeal to abstractions, but unless their aim is merely obfuscation they must in the end explain what concrete realities are there to be valued. We do not protect lovely and historically evocative buildings because we are enjoined to do so in obedience to an abstract rule (e.g. that no one has a right to destroy what they did not make and cannot replace): on the contrary, such force as this general rule may have derives from the immediate value, obvious to the well-brought-up and pious eye, of this and that building.

Abstract values like Justice or Happiness do feature in rhetorical debate, and are not always resolved or reduced to particular, concrete values such as England, or a particular child. They have the enormous advantage that we can hope thereby to appeal to people of many different backgrounds and traditions. Few people will share my own

[17] Weinsheimer (1984) 27.
[18] Peirce (1931–5) 6.288.

particular and direct concern with the life and fortune of my son, or the health and beauty of some particular, unimportant place. Many more can be caught by an appeal to relatively abstract values, realizable in other things than my son, or an Ellesmere cottage. In a 'society of strangers', to adopt MacIntyre's phrase,[19] it will not do to appeal to too many shared experiences, or historical traditions: the English landscape will not mean the same to an immigrant, even if she likes it as it is. The Mother of Parliaments may, quite reasonably, be regarded with more jaundiced eyes by people whose personal and cultural experience has been focused by a struggle against the British Raj. If people with such differently structured worlds, embodying different particular evaluations, must live and work together, they must perforce rely upon more abstract values precisely because their concrete values are so different. Let us by all means strive to live and work together under the rule of such laws as will allow us our different ideals and worlds.

The trouble is that it is all too easy, especially for a dominant group, to say that such and such a system of law is, as it were, transvaluational—such as to be respected and obeyed whatever our particular attachments—when in fact it is not. Consider Hume's enormously persuasive rhetoric, and note with MacIntyre that

> his final court of appeal can be no more than the appeal to the passions of men of good sense, to a concurrence of feeling among the worldly . . . The passions of some are to be preferred to the passions of others. Whose preferences reign? The preferences of those who accept the stability of property, of those who understand chastity in women as a virtue only because it is a useful device to ensure that property is passed only to legitimate heirs, of those who believe that the passage of time confers legitimacy upon what was originally acquired by violence and aggression. What Hume identifies as the standpoint of universal human nature turns out in fact to be that of the prejudices of the Hanoverian ruling elite. Hume's moral philosophy presupposes allegiance to a particular kind of social structure as much as Aristotle's does.[20]

If abstract values are given enough content to make any significant difference, their content is—to put it mildly—likely to be determined by the attitudes and *Weltanschauung* of the dominant group. Because we pretend, even to ourselves, that the laws of the land are those that any rational being would prescribe, that they depend not at all on particular evaluations, we may be the more shameless in imposing our ideals on others. If, on the other hand, we seriously acknowledge that

[19] MacIntyre (1981) 233.
[20] MacIntyre (1981) 215.

talk of Justice or Happiness 'in the abstract' is so vague as to be effectively meaningless, such values cannot serve to settle any point between bourgeois liberal, Muslim, Marxist, nationalist, animal liberationist or mainstream Christian. 'For quite non-Marxist reasons Marx was in the right when he argued against the English trade-unionists of the 1860s that appeals to justice were pointless, since there are rival conceptions of justice formed by and informing the life of rival groups'.[21]

A nameless sixteenth-century Welshman lamented the cutting of Glyn Cynon:

Many a birch-tree green of cloak
(I'd like to choke the Saxon!)
is now a flaming heap of fire
where iron-workers blacken.
For cutting the branch and bearing away
the wild birds' habitation
may misfortune quickly reach
Rowenna's treacherous children![22]

The poet's complaint is not that an abstract principle of justice has been violated, that the wild birds have been robbed of what is theirs by abstract right, but that the particular meanings which that wood had for him and for his people have been overwritten, a new *gestalt* formed. He may believe that the Saxon is consciously at fault, but would be vulnerable to the obvious retort that his preferred life-style is also an attack on the wild things.

No more the badger's earth we'll sack
nor start a buck from the glade;
no more deer-stalking in my day,
now they've cut Glyn Cynon's shade.

Glyn Cynon is sanctuary and trysting-place, not an aggregate of things 'with rights' against assault.

If a man in sudden plight
took to flight from foe,
for guest-house to the nightingale
in Cynon Vale he'd go . . .
If ever a stag got into a wood
with huntsmen a stride behind,
never again will he turn in his run
with Cynon Wood in mind.

[21] MacIntyre (1981) 235.
[22] Jones (1977) 71; see Clark (1987b).

If the flour-white girl once came
to walk along the brook,
Glyn Cynon's wood was always there
as a fair trysting nook.

The English had their *gestalts* too, their happy places, the visible record of their personal and national past, their own account of property and proper use. A meeting of minds and manners here is not impossible, but there is little reason to expect that 'abstract justice' will settle the point between them. 'To live honestly'—but what duties and privileges are they that constitute the particular being of each honest liver? 'To injure none'—but what counts as injury, and who as a creature that must not be injured? 'To each his own'—but what is one's own, and who is to count as owner? Those Europeans who imagined that they had 'bought' land or labour or security from an Amerindian 'chief' were, in their terms, justly incensed to find that the land would not stay bought. Amerindians, in their terms, were as justly outraged by the greed and superstition of the Europeans. 'Justice', in historical fact, has been the name given to the interest of the stronger, and the efforts of political philosophers to ground a particular dispensation in abstract or universal right are as empty as the parallel efforts of epistemologists to derive our ordinary, traditionally grounded and socially mediated 'knowledge', from axioms that just any rational being would be bound to accept.

Must this account involve the rejection of impartiality as a value? That may certainly seem to be the implication. Practitioners of an established craft resent the impertinent and ill-informed advice of philosophical outsiders (on the grounds that they do not grasp the concrete situation, and have no responsibility for the actual consequences of their own advice). Spokesmen for a culture and tradition not well represented in the ruling elite may be equally resentful of those who pretend to judge them 'impartially', but who entertain no doubts about the whole *gestalt* within which they work.

> Everyone thinks himself free of prejudice because no one is able impartially to examine himself . . . One can see the place one stands only by moving to another, at which point a different place is concealed.[23]

'Impartiality' is either a cloak for unconscious prejudice, or a condition in which no decisions can any longer be taken: one cannot be impartial, for example, between the claims of Western liberal individualism and Muslim fundamentalism when the duties and privileges of a young girl

[23] Weinsheimer (1984) 24.

are in question—unless by speaking from within some other equally intransigent tradition. Nor is the decision to provide hallal meats to Muslim school-children in state-run schools an 'impartial' one: it is, precisely, a decision to be partial to the claims of one sect as against another.

But can we really abandon all the duties of impartial reasoning? Can we really hesitate to call child sacrifice 'murder' merely because those who perform the sacrifice think differently about the act.[24] Was the Holocaust really 'just the accepted Nazi way of doing things'?

> When, in December 1976, Luis Corvalan and Vladimir Bukovski, who had been imprisoned for their beliefs by the Chilean and Russian regimes respectively, were exchanged for each other by international agreement, the Italian communist newspaper *L'Unità* wrote that Corvalan's case 'highlights the necessity to eliminate the fascist regime' in Chile, but that 'Bukovski is an entirely different episode which signals the difficulties of a great country, which has lived through a great revolution, to extend its own conquests into the field of individual rights and liberties'. There could be no clearer case of the double-think whereby tyrannies contrive to apologize for themselves.[25]

L'Unità counted on general disapproval of regimes that imprison people for their beliefs to condemn Chile, and then offered a specious excuse for Russia which could with as much reason have been offered for Chile. The paper could preserve its consistency by admitting that no general issue of principle was at stake: if the enemy uses a particular weapon against us, that is a reason for fighting back the harder, even if our side has also used the weapon. It is not 'using the weapon' or 'imprisoning dissidents' which is, in the abstract, wrong: the enemy's world and programme constitutes a threat to ours, not because these things are done in it with a clear conscience—only because they are done *to* us and our friends instead of *by* us.

L'Unità, in other words, may not (*pace* Martin) have been practising double-think (though it is likely that it hoped to draw upon an ill-formulated moral disquiet to help condemn Chile which it hoped simultaneously to defuse so as not to condemn Russia). It may simply have been relying upon the rejection of impartial morality seemingly implicit in the case I have so far been developing. 'Modern politics is civil war carried on by other means'.[26] But though this position is a possible one, it is noteworthy that such partisans invariably display

[24] Martin (1981) 150.
[25] Martin (1981) 66.
[26] MacIntyre (1981) 236.

acute symptoms of moralizing fervour—almost as much indeed as do those confused would-be liberals who moralistically denounce all those who express a moral judgment! People committed to the defence of 'their own' class, country or sect, and who understand that other people are as fervent in defence of their own, need not pretend to themselves or others that their present enemies could never be their allies, nor that they are properly to be condemned. Nor is it easy to see why anyone should be repelled by the thought of being a traitor, class-traitor or heretic, unless there is some sense in which they would do wrong to be so. Once the thought has taken root that one might as easily and conscientiously have been fighting on the other side, moral outrage at the opposing army, or the turncoat, seems uncalled for. Moralism, at most, would be a rhetorical device, a way of getting under the skin of our opponent, sapping her 'moral fibre'—rather as terrorists, tyrants and other gangsters are reputed to do to their captives, subjects and helpers. The more we all know that it is only a device, the less effective it will be.

III

It is implicit in the case that I have been developing so far that we live and act and have our beings in established crafts and communities. There is nothing humanly recognizable that human individuals *would* be like if they had not grown up in a community, and we cannot sensibly ask ourselves what wholly deracinated, solitary, uninformed 'intelligences' would agree on if they had to, nor what measures they would take to achieve a natural happiness. What constitutes happiness for any of us is partly determined by our view of life, the universe and everything. What identifies a creature as one with which we must achieve some workable relationship is our traditional stock of stereotypes and working practices. Hunter-gatherers, pastoralists and traditional agriculturalists must reckon themselves members, at some workable level, of a community of gods, the dead, the living and the unborn, animals and crops and the historically patterned land. Rationalizing moralists in the Declining West may reckon such things superstitious, not such as rational intelligences would agree to 'in the abstract'. But there could be no rational intelligences in the abstract, and therefore no supracultural, unhistorical agreements of the kind lauded by Rousseau and his successors, nor any non-moral account of 'happiness' such that moral rules could be seen as merely technical advice on how to get 'it'.

Once rationalizing moralism and its attendant mythology of 'pure intelligence behind a veil of ignorance' or pure Benthamite hedonists have been dismissed, it seems that we are condemned to the life of more or less fervent partisans, that we have no recourse but to the 'good faith' and 'traditionally grounded intelligence' of persons reared in class, sect, craft, party and historic nation. The claims of justice and utility alike have usually been considered in a non-historical context, with the unspoken assumption that historical rights and traditionally assessed utilities are not the province of moral minds, or of philosophers. But as Berkeley pointed out, 'though we should grant that (a prince) has originally no right to the crown, yet when (he) is once in possession of it and you have sworn allegiance to him you are no longer at liberty to inquire by what unrighteous steps he might have obtained it'.[27] Once the anti-historical assumption is displaced, must we accept that civil peace is only a temporary expedient, that there can be no appeal to any wider loyalties or goods than those embedded in partisan tradition?

Thus: Albert, an honest mink-farmer, believes himself entitled under the law to keep and slaughter minks, while Belle, a radical zoophile, believes herself entitled to rescue her imprisoned kin. British law, being what it is, is not impartial in this matter: it is, in effect, Albert's Law. Belle may agree that it is better than it would be if it were Cuthbert's—Cuthbert being an honest organizer of dogfights and badger-baiting expeditions—or Drogo's—Drogo being a stereotypically humourless fanatic who would rather organize ritual murders. All sides *may* agree (but some obviously do not) that they would rather not force each other into open war, knowing what that condition is like, but none but Albert (and not even he on every issue) is likely to view the High Courts of Parliament as spokesmen for their moral community. Those Courts are no longer, if ever they were, the place where the representatives of divergent crafts, classes and traditions came together to develop a new moral consensus for the community they ruled. 'Loyalty to my country, to my community—which remains unalterably a central virtue—becomes detached from obedience to the government which happens to rule me'.[28] Respect for individual liberties under the rule of law is not the product of abstract argument (for no such arguments work), but of a historically grounded sense of mutual respect for fellow inhabitants of these offshore islands. What happens when those inhabitants and temporary sojourners no longer share enough of their attitudes and moral categories to support a willing obedience to the Queen in Parliament, when the Law is (plausibly) dismissed as 'Tory Law' or 'Militant Takeover'? Have we no recourse, as MacIntyre seems to suggest, but to cultivate our parties till one of them informs the world-consciousness of a new civil community?

[27] Berkeley (1948–57) VI, 57 (*Advice to the Tories*).
[28] MacIntyre (1981) 237.

'What matters at this stage is the construction of local forms of community within which civility and the intellectual and moral life can be sustained through the new dark ages which are already upon us . . . We are waiting not for a Godot, but for another—doubtless very different—St Benedict.'[29]

I have considerable sympathy with MacIntyre's position,[30] but he is perhaps himself in error. The rationalist implicitly assumes (i) that we can distinguish between 'natural' and 'conventional' morality, (ii) that this distinction will be Newtonian in character, between what 'we' would decide 'ideally' and what we decide when influenced by historical accident, (iii) that we need the distinction if we are to be able to criticize the conventions of our or any other day, and (iv) that such a natural morality will consist of an axiomatizable set of rules. Once doubt is cast on the second and fourth assumptions, it may seem that the first will also fail. If the third remains unchallenged, it must seem that we can only challenge one party's views and actions by appealing to another's, that all moral reflection is incurably partisan. 'The ascendency of faith may be impractical, but the reign of knowledge is incomprehensible. The problem for statesmen of this age is how to educate the masses, and literature and science cannot give the solution'.[31] On these terms the new St Benedict will only be one more cult leader, and people faced by that prospect may decide that a decaying individualism, with all its faults, is preferable. MacIntyre's promised statement of his 'systematic account of [moral] rationality'[32] may provide a non-partisan justification for his preferred 'Benedictines'. In the absence of that account, I offer the following sketch.

A rationally acceptable moral *gestalt,* incorporating a powerful vision of the world and our place in it, as well as a framework for the multiple roles and practices that must be available to us, and a hierarchy of virtue, certainly need not be an axiomatizable set of moral rules. Nor do we need to think that it is the *gestalt* that some unimaginable collection of unfettered individuals would have agreed upon, or even that all present persons, even if 'free from prejudice and self-esteem', would grudgingly admit its charms. Each craft, each culture, even each species structures its world and its corresponding duties differently. That is relativism's strongest point. But each craft, each culture, and each species must in fact take its being from the One World Only. Nothing can claim to be that world which does not allow and explain those manifold perspectives on itself. Nothing can claim to be a sound

[29] MacIntyre (1981) 245.
[30] Clark (1983), (1986), (1987a).
[31] Newman (1979) 88.
[32] MacIntyre (1981) 242.

gestalt that does not allow that World's existence, and its manifold servitors, beyond and around our own tradition.

> What are the implications of living godlessly? For one thing it implies forgetfulness of the encompassing world to which we are so totally bound, both as individuals and as a species. No longer do we feel answerable to this encompassing which is within us, as memory, imagination and consciousness, or without us as soil and sun and air and water. We are forgetful of the fact that these latter are not simply things of our environment but natural powers and fibres of which we are made and which enable us to be sustained in existence every moment . . . Such godless living means for another thing that our species fancies itself to be the purpose and goal of creation perhaps not merely of our tiny earth but also of the inconceivable range and extent of the cosmos.[33]

Gray's description of the godless life, and hence—by contraries—of the ordinary pieties, identifies something of what we must look for in a sound tradition. Gray's book, incidentally, is a fascinating and illuminating study of the concrete realities faced by men at war, and a reminder of the truth contained in the complaint against abstract theorizing with which I began this paper. If we live godlessly, whether because we have lost touch with the faith of our forefathers or because that 'faith' is itself an unrealistic and irreligious one, our 'morality' must indeed be a bargain between desperate ruffians, to look after each others' interests in a hostile world. 'The same atheistical narrow spirit centering all our cares upon private interest and concentrating all our hopes within the enjoyment of this life equally produceth a neglect of what we owe to God and our country.'[34]

The worship we give to gods who exist around and outside our own particular horizon, the doctrines that we tell each other to 'make proper impressions on the mind, producing therein love, hope, gratitude and obedience, and thereby become a lively operative principle, influencing [our] life and actions, agreeably to that notion of saving faith which is required in a Christian',[35] can be understood and applauded without recourse to metaphysical realism about the things called 'gods'. The worship and the doctrines are ways of expressing to ourselves this first demand upon a sane tradition, that it help us to know that we are mortal, that it engage our emotions and attention upon the world as it really is. It may be true, though I shall not argue the point further here,

33 Gray (1967) xviii.

34 Berkeley (1948–57) VI, 63, 79 (*Essay toward preventing the Ruin of Great Britain*).

35 Berkeley (1948–57) III, 297 (Euphranor speaks).

that Berkeley was indeed correct, as well as traditional, in saying that 'he who makes it his business to lessen or root out from the minds of men a religious awe and fear of God doth in effect endeavour to fill his country with highwaymen, housebreakers, murderers, fraudulent dealers, perjured witnesses and every other pest of society', as 'the 2 great Principles of Morality [are] the Being of God & the Freedom of Man'.[36] Theological realism may be a necessary postulate of practical reason, but it is enough for my present purpose that a proper piety, without any ontological commitment to the 'existence' of 'superlunary divinities', be identified as the first requirement for a sane tradition.

Proper piety, worshipful service of a world, unknown to us in many details, and shared with uncounted millions of other lives, is the necessary opposite of mere irreligion. But it is notorious that 'piety' can come in many forms, and it is those 'wars of religion' that have persuaded many humane hearts to demand that a merely 'secular' state be required to keep 'the peace' between warring sects: '*tantum religio potuit suadere malorum*'. The evils, of course, are no less simply because the oppressor is not always recognizably theistic, and it is perhaps time that honest humanists stopped pretending that it is the openly and traditionally religious who are now our chief dangers.

The common error in tyrannical oppression is not that the oppressors (who are not always those in recognized positions of authority) are 'pious' (acknowledging their own mortality, their derivativeness, and choosing to remind themselves through song and story and hypothesis of the One World Only that outlasts all kings), but that they are led on by abstractions. 'We're fundamentally interested in justice, which means we have a greater tolerance for ideas of liquidating a class and so on'.[37] 'Justice' here names something that the speaker cannot clearly specify ('we don't know what comes after the revolution'), for which he is prepared to evacuate the concrete individuals he confronts of all significance.

> 'I may fail,' said Weston. 'But while I live I will not, with such a key in my hand, consent to close the gates of the future on my race. What lies in that future, beyond our present ken, passes imagination to conceive: it is enough for me that there is a Beyond.' 'He is saying', Ransom translated, 'that he will not stop trying to do all this unless you kill him. And he says that though he doesn't know what will happen to the creatures sprung from us, he wants it to happen very much'.[38]

[36] Berkeley (1948–57) VI, 219; see III, 23, I, 63.

[37] Dotson Rader, a 1968 Columbia University revolutionist, cited by Martin (1981) 64.

[38] Lewis (1952) 162.

I recommend Lewis's fantasy strongly, despite its grave inaccuracies of detail, precisely because it makes more nearly clear what too many writers, in the '30s and since, have muddle-headedly conceived.

What is lacking in the oppressor is any strong sense of the present reality of her victims. Such a sense, indeed, may be consciously resisted: 'The whole ability to function as a revolutionary depends upon the ability to depersonalize your enemy . . . If you personalize your enemy you can't act'.[39] Invasive experimentation on non-human creatures with whom we could be on friendly terms, with whom we could in some measure 'identify', similarly requires that they be reduced to the status of 'animal preparations', organic test-tubes. 'Abstractolatry . . . is a method of blinding oneself to facts one does not wish to see, of withdrawing sympathy from people one wishes to oppress, of distancing oneself from human [and other] suffering'.[40] It is possible, in some cases, to add that depersonalizing our victim is not merely a necessary expedient if we are to be able to oppress her: it is the object of the exercise. We oppress because we fear engagement with a real and living presence. That is the heart of wickedness.

Martin himself, whom I have been quoting with some approval, has his blind spots. 'Human beings', he says, 'are the purpose of values . . . One cannot speak of doing good to an insensate object like a stone'.[41] True enough, but there are other creatures we can do good to than the merely human, and other classes than the human and the insensate. Berkeley himself committed the same error in claiming that human action can affect only human beings for good or ill.[42] With this correction, Berkeley's moral vision of 'that great City whose Author and Founder is God'[43] is a splendid evocation of an honourable tradition.

That City, to which all honourable traditions point even in their decay, was not, for Berkeley, something laid up in heaven, an abstract ideal of what might have been. Nor was Berkeley's City simply equivalent to the whole of natural event. What our perceptions, properly trained through the customs and prejudices of our immediate community[44] reveal to us is a complex of communities drawn together through natural affection,[45] such that the whole is sustained despite the self-interest and corruption of its parts by the operation of general laws. Obedience to God requires of us that we learn what is expected of us

[39] Rader (Martn (1981) 64).
[40] Martin (1981) 73.
[41] Martin (1981) 148.
[42] Berkeley (1948–57) VI, 20.
[43] Berkeley (1948–57) III, 129 (Crito speaks).
[44] Berkeley (1948–57) III, 143 (Euphranor speaks), 176 (Crito speaks).
[45] Berkeley (1948–57) VII, 225; see Leary (1977).

through daily conversation with our fellows, and with the archetypical author of the phenomenal universe.

With these last remarks, of course, I have begun to move into larger, even if well-charted waters. In this context, it will perhaps be as well to return to port. We reason and act, inevitably, within historical communities, familial, civil, craft-based and collegiate. But any such community can be pressed to consider what it has forgotten or obscured, any of us can begin to see things differently and more or less realistically. When statesmen, doctors, research-scientists or parents are annoyed by what they take to be ill-informed and merely abstract commentary, they may at times be right. They will certainly not be convinced by abstract appeals to 'natural right' or 'net total of utility'. But they should, in their turn, at least entertain the possibility that they are being reminded of things they will eventually be glad to have remembered, that there is after all a wider world than that defined by their crafts, their immediate parental concerns, even than the presumed well-being of the state. Perhaps it is they who are guilty of 'abstraction', of seeking to conduct their lives and manners without reference to the wider, concrete realities. Their little enclaves of meaning take their significance from the life and world of redeemed humanity, and if they seek a separate, abstracted life (as though what scientists or statesmen do was no affair of common men) they err: 'these eternal principles or characters of human life . . ., when erected into gods, become destructive of humanity. They ought to be the servants, and not the masters of man, or of society . . . for when separated from man or humanity, who is Jesus the Saviour, the vine of eternity, they are thieves and rebels, they are destroyers'.[46] Philosophers may blink and stumble when they find themselves back in the cave (and should make every effort not to); but they may, after all, be bringing back important news, the memory—so to call it—that we are not merely appetitive or custom-bound animals, but fallen and forgetful souls with the capacity to be informed by truth.

[46] Blake (1966) 671 (*Descriptive Catalogue*).

Abstraction, Idealization and Ideology in Ethics

ONORA O'NEILL

Although Burke, Bentham, Hegel and Marx do not often agree, all criticized certain ethical theories, in particular theories of rights, for being too *abstract*. The complaint is still popular. It was common in Existentialist and in Wittgensteinian writing that stressed the importance of *cases* and examples rather than *principles* for the moral life; it has been prominent in recent Hegelian and Aristotelian flavoured writing, which stresses the importance of the virtues; it is reiterated in discussions that stress the distinctiveness and particularity of moral vicissitudes and query the importance of ethical theory.[1] Recent critics of abstraction are opposed not only to theories of rights, and the Kantian notions with which these are linked, but also to consequentialist ethical theories.[2] The two ethical theories that are most influential in the English-speaking world now both stand accused of being too abstract.

On the surface this is a curious complaint. If we take abstract reasoning quite straightforwardly as reasoning which leaves out a great deal, three quite simple defences of abstract approaches to ethics might be offered. First, abstraction is, taken strictly, unavoidable in all reasoning: no use of language can be fully determinate. Second, abstraction is not always objected to in practical reasoning. Accountancy and law are both very abstract types of practical reasoning, yet widely admired and practised, indeed highly rewarded. Third, only abstract principles are likely to have wide scope: if ethical principles are to be relevant to a wide range of situations or of agents, they surely not merely *may* but *must* be abstract.

If reasoning has to be abstract, is often admired for being abstract and apparently gains advantages by being abstract, why should ethical reasoning be persistently and fervently denounced for abstraction? I shall try to get a clearer view of a range of issues that lie behind the charge of abstraction, and to see whether anything can or should be done to answer the charge.

[1] Including MacIntyre (1981), Williams (1985) and Walzer (1983); also, in rather different idioms, Baier (1985b), Blum (1980) and Seidler (1986).

[2] Benthamite utilitarians, we shall see, can avoid the charge of abstraction, but at the cost of implausible assumptions.

Abstract Reasoning and Ideal Agents

Some complaints that ethical reasoning is too abstract object mainly to reliance on abstract views of agents. These complaints are the core of Hegelian and Marxian criticisms of 'abstract individualism'; they resurface in recent objections to 'deontological liberalism'.[3] Abstract ethical and political theories, it is said, make assumptions about agency which are not satisfied by human agents. The theories fail because they ignore the social and historical features that are constitutive of human agency, and assume capacities for reasoning and choosing which human agents simply lack.

The target of this line of criticism is not, however, just abstraction. The objection is not just that much (too much) that is true of human agents is *omitted* in some accounts of agents, but that much (too much) that is false of human agents is *added*. Descriptions of agents in much post-enlightenment ethical and political theory are often *idealized*; they are satisfied only by hypothetical agents whose cognitive and volitional capacities human beings lack. We none of us have cardinal and interpersonally comparable utilities or complete and transitively ordered preferences or complete information. We lack both infallible powers of calculation and independence from the institutional and ideological context we inhabit. We certainly don't have transparent self-knowledge or archangelic insight into others' preferences.

Many supposed 'models of man' idealize in a second sense. They don't merely posit agents with streamlined, super-normal cognitive and volitional capacities. (Perhaps there are theoretical uses for such idealizations.) They also treat enhanced versions of certain capacities as *ideals* for human action. Rational economic men, ideal moral spectators, utilitarian legislators and the legions of rational choosers are taken as *standards* for human economic or political or ethical action. We are to think of idealized agents and their flawless compliance with rational norms as admirable and super-human rather than as irrelevant to human choosing, let alone sub-human.

Appeals to the choice procedure of hypothetical idealized agents can seem relevant and compelling if we concentrate on domains of life where we might want or admire enhanced cognitive or volitional capacities: shopping, for example. They are less convincing in areas of life where we don't want those capacities overdeveloped or know that they won't and perhaps can't be highly developed. We would not admire medical ethics that posited ideal rational patients, or personal relationships designed for ideal rational friends and lovers.

If all criticisms of abstraction in ethics were criticisms of idealizing conceptions of agency, we would know where to head in order to deal

[3] See Seidler (1986), Sandel (1982).

with them. Plenty of people have headed off in those directions. Rational choice theorists try to show how some of the stronger and less plausible assumptions about cognitive and volitional capacities can be weakened. Utilitarians acknowledge the approximate character of utilitarian calculation and the importance of 'putting out to sea with the almanac already calculated'; plausibility is sought at the cost of softening the sharper and more radical implications of felicific calculation. Decision procedures which acknowledge uncertainty, partial information and the constraints of time are advocated. Maximin is preferred to maximizing. Some human rights theorists even emphasize the imperfection of human cognitive and volitional capacities and argue from these to 'welfare' rights. They point out that liberty rights are worthless without agency, that human agency is vulnerable to material and other deprivation, and conclude that liberty rights are not taken seriously unless there are also rights to have basic needs met.[4]

Abstract Reasoning and Formalism in Ethics

Ethical and political discussion can do without idealizing accounts of agency. This does not show that it could also do without abstraction in the strict sense.[5] However, much criticism of abstraction in philosophical ethics suggests that abstraction itself might be dispensable. It is criticism not just of theories that rely on idealized views of agency but of the supposed formalism and emptiness of all practical reasoning that invokes principles or rules. The charge of empty formalism is most frequently levelled against Kant. Kant, it is said, proposes in the Categorical Imperative a formal test of principles of duty, which simply lacks determinate implications for action. Mill speaks for many when he alleges that Kant 'when he begins to deduce from this precept any of the actual duties of morality . . . fails almost grotesquely . . .'.[6] The supposed failure of Kantian formalism is neatly summarized in Péguy's acid quip 'Le kantisme a les mains pures, *mais il n'a pas de mains*'.[7] What is the point of 'hands' kept clean by grasping nothing?

However, objections to formalism are not directed only at Kant. All ethics of principles, and at present theories of human rights in particular, are often charged with formalism whether or not they make idealiz-

[4] Gewirth (1982), Shue (1980).

[5] Formalism and idealization are, however, linked. Principles that could be relevant both for idealized agents and for varying human agents would have to be particularly schematic and indeterminate.

[6] Mill (1962), *Utilitarianism*, Ch.1.

[7] Péguy (1961), *Victor Marie, Comte Hugo*.

ing assumptions about agency. Formalism is said to be both theoretically and ethically inadequate. A range of interconnected objections is repeatedly raised. I shall consider four of them. Two of these objections are mainly theoretical. It is said, first, that ethics of principle underdetermine decisions and offer no 'algorithm for the difficult case'[8] and, second, that we can never formulate plausible exceptionless or universal moral principles.[9] The other two objections are ethical rather than theoretical. It is said, third, that thinking in terms of principles or rules can blunt moral and human sensibilities, lead to decisions that are taken 'by the book' and fail to consider context, and, fourth, that reliance on abstract, i.e. indeterminate principles, is self-undermining and self-defeating.

The two theoretical objections, which are closely connected, are, I think, true under their standard interpretation. They are also, I shall argue, quite insufficient under that interpretation to show that we either should or can avoid appealing to ethical principles or rules. The two ethical objections to abstraction are, I shall argue, unsustainable generalizations from ways in which principles or rules can be misused. I shall consider these objections in turn.

Principles and Algorithms

It is true that principles underdetermine decisions. This is hardly news for those who have advocated ethical theories that make principles or rules central. Kant, for example, insisted that we can have no algorithm for judgment, since every application of a rule would itself need supplementing with further rules.[10] Yet the reasons often given for rejecting reliance on principles or rules appear to be based on no more than the assumption that they would have to be algorithmic—i.e. that they must determine answers for all cases that fall under them and that particular decisions must be given by, and so be deducible from, rules.

If no principle or rule can determine every detail of its own application, even the most highly specified rule can be implemented in varied ways, so there can strictly be no algorithms of action. However, this move would be too easy a rebuttal of the view that ethical principles should be algorithms for action. There is a quite reasonable sense in which some rules of action can be algorithmic: there are algorithms for multiplying and for reaching a draw when playing noughts and crosses although these algorithms do not determine every move of every

[8] Baier (1985b) 226; the criticism is frequent.
[9] Baier (1985b) 216–17; again the point is standard.
[10] Kant (1929) A133/B172.

muscle. The significant point is not that there are strictly no algorithms of action, but that there is no reason to think that ethical principles either are algorithmic in a less strict sense, or have been thought to be so by their advocates.

The view that principles or rules must be algorithmic in the wider sense is often combined with the stronger and even stranger view that any ethical theory which centres on principles must provide a universal practical algorithm for agents. Not only must each principle or rule provide an algorithm for the cases it covers; the set of principles and rules taken together must cover all cases. On such a view an ethic of principles would enable us to calculate what is ethically required in every situation: it would be an algorithm not just for some situations but for life.

The only ethical theory which purportedly offers a life algorithm is classical utilitarianism. Here a set of abstract (and idealizing) assumptions is used to define a procedure which will identify an 'optimal' act in each situation. All 'available' options are to be listed, their expected consequences reckoned and evaluated, and the option with maximal expected utility identified. Actual decision makers can go through none of these steps. Since they lack complete information about what is possible and cannot individuate options exhaustively they cannot list all available options. Since they lack a comprehensive science of society they cannot foresee all expected consequences. Since they lack cardinal and interpersonally comparable utilities they cannot evaluate and maximize. The 'rules of thumb' that would-be utilitarian agents have to fall back on are not algorithmic; they augment or replace calculation with judgment. Classical utilitarianism did not aspire to be an ethic of principles. It relied on strong idealizing assumptions about agency to ground its claim to provide an ethical algorithm. Without these implausible idealizations utilitarianism's calculating aspirations cannot be fulfilled. Any usable utilitarianism depends on judgment to identify options, to predict and evaluate their likely results and to rank them in terms of some decision procedure. This reduces the appeal of calculating utilitarianism: how valuable is high precision calculation in handling low definition materials?

Many critics of abstraction appear to accept the aspirations even if they reject the content of classical utilitarianism. They apparently think that if there are ethical rules or principles they must be algorithmic. As a corollary they suggest that those who propose an ethics of principles must be eager to shuffle off the burdens of responsibility by finding rules that will 'decide for us'. Advocates of ethics of principle can hardly recognize themselves as the targets of these criticisms. Kant reminds us as forcefully as Sartre later did that the thought of 'delegating' hard decisions to 'authorities' or 'codes' tempts but is a symptom of immaturity or bad faith.[11] Algorithmic rules for conduct, let alone life algorithms, are fabulous: they belong in the fairyland of felicific calculation.

Exceptionless Principles

The second complaint that critics of abstraction commonly level against ethics of principles is closely connected to the first. It is that we can find no plausible exceptionless or universal ethical rules or principles. This is a more sweeping objection than the complaint that there are no algorithmic rules. Algorithmic rules would have to be exceptionless; but not all exceptionless rules are algorithmic, since some may fail to specify what is required or forbidden in each situation even in the broadest terms. 'When in doubt do something' is exceptionless, but not much of an algorithm. However, exceptionless rules can cut quite a lot of ice, even if they are not algorithms, provided they constrain action in significant ways. Kant's Categorical Imperative, for example, requires that we reject action on principles that must have exceptions, although it does not purport to identify a correct act for each situation. It provides what Kant terms 'negative instruction'. Many people think that theories of rights constrain action but provide no algorithms for action, let alone life algorithms. Even if we find the complaint that ethical rules provide no algorithms beside the point, the charge that there are no plausible exceptionless ethical rules or principles would tell against a wide range of theories that do not claim to offer algorithms for action but do propose exceptionless principles of action. Is the charge true? If so, must we or had we better do without ethical theories, principles or rules?

The claim that we can find no plausible exceptionless rules or principles is often put as an objection to setting aside context and circumstance in making decisions. Failure to take context and circumstance into account, it is said, makes a fetish of rules or principles. It leads to rigorism in ethics; in and out of utilitarian circles it amounts to superstitious rule worship. The objection of rigorism is often made plausible by pointing to examples (in life as well as in theory) of over-rigid reliance on certain rules.

Within a classical utilitarian context of debate, where we supposedly have access to algorithmic calculation about particular cases, the charge that adherence to exceptionless rules would be superstitious is well taken—unless the rules build in all the indicated exceptions, which makes the charge vacuous. Outside the classical utilitarian context it is

[11] Kant (1970), Sartre (1948).

not obvious what the critics of abstraction expect an 'exceptionless' rule to be. The objection is presumably not that we cannot state plausible ethical rules or principles that are formally universal. It is rather that these formulations are not complete. There may be exceptions even to principles that we take seriously such as 'don't lie' or 'don't kill'. Why is this a deep criticism? That we understand such principles as qualified by *ceteris paribus* clauses is no reason to think that we do not take them seriously or that they do not constrain action. Principles and rules must be indeterminate, so cannot specify all the boundary conditions or all the details of their own application in varying contexts. We cannot deduce their applications. Why should it be a criticism that we cannot? What image do those who criticize the supposed lack of 'exceptionless' rules have of ethical principles or rules? Do they assume that any exceptionless rule or principle would have to be algorithmic? Do they expect ethical rules to tell them what to do, although they do not expect rules of language to tell them what to say?

The claim that there cannot be exceptionless rules would constitute a general criticism of ethics of principles only if 'exceptionless' rules and principles had to provide algorithms for action. However, we have seen that there is no reason for thinking that ethics of principles must consist of algorithms, and good reason to think that they cannot consist of algorithms, even in the broader sense in which there can be some algorithms of action. The criticism simply does not apply either to Kant's ethics, or to recent theories of rights or of obligations, which stress the incompleteness of principles or rules, and deny that they are sufficient for making decisions. Advocates of ethical principles standardly deny they are or can be complete, and insist that they must be supplemented by procedures of deliberation if we are to apply (necessarily incomplete) principles to cases. The charge that advocates of ethics of principles fail to provide plausible exceptionless rules is implausible unless it is understood as the charge that they have failed to provide plausible exceptionless rules *from which decisions can be deduced*. That charge is true, but has little point, since those who advocate ethics of principle don't claim to provide such principles.

For the charge to seem plausible, ethics of principles have to be interpreted as philosophically backward. The results are often textually grotesque. For example, Kant's cases of dutiful action in *Groundwork* are taken as deductions from rather than as illustrations of the Categorical Imperative. Kant did not see his examples in that way; and anybody who has looked at *The Doctrine of Virtue*, or read *Groundwork* with care, can see that Kant (although he held some rigid views) knows that principles of duty alone don't and can't tell us what to do. He could hardly think otherwise given his well-known insistence on the indeterminacy of judgment. Contemporary human rights theorists also assume that the interpretation and application of rights is an intricate and demanding business. Applied ethics is not a matter of deducing decisions from principles. It requires judgment and additional premises because rules are *not* algorithms, because the subsumption of cases under rules is not a mechanical operation, because we need to work out what it would take to institutionalize certain rights and to allocate corresponding obligations in various circumstances. The need for deliberation and casuistry—for procedures by which principles are applied to cases—is taken for granted by non-algorithmic utilitarians as well. Mill clearly holds that deliberation is needed to apply the principle of utility: although nobody would go to sea without the almanac already calculated, nobody would expect the almanac to make the skipper's judgment redundant. Kant and Mill and their respective successors don't disagree that principles and rules are necessary, that they are incomplete and that their application needs deliberation. Their disagreement is over the weight ethical reasoning should place on desire and preference.

Sheltering Behind Rules

The third and fourth criticisms of abstraction in the strict sense point to ethical rather than theoretical deficiencies in ethics of principles. Abstract ethical reasoning which relies on principles or rules can, it is said, blunt moral and human sensibilities, so lead to decisions that are taken 'by the book' and take too little account of context; it may also be self-undermining and self-defeating in deep ways. I believe that there is some, but only some, truth behind these claims. This limited truth may be misinterpreted as evidence that ethics of principles are committed to algorithmic rules, so are theoretically flawed.

Appeals to rules and principles have often been offered in supposed justification of wrongs. The standard examples of disastrous wrongs done by agents who appeal to rules or principles to justify their decisions are not examples of appeals to ethical principles. A classic twentieth century theme is that of officials who shelter behind roles, official rules and the authority of orders, and try to use these to 'justify' wrongdoing. These wrongs can be petty, or in the much-discussed case of Nazi bureaucrats ghastly. What do such cases tell us about ethics of principles? Only a little, I suggest. In the first place, both the rules to which bureaucratic wrong-doers usually appeal and the assumption that these rules outrank other principles of action may lack ethical weight. Secondly, all but the lowest level rules on which bureaucrats rely are far from algorithmic. Postal workers may not have discretion about how much postage to charge, but even junior Home Office officials have some discretion in the application of immigration law; while powerful officials—Eichmann, for example—are constrained but not determined by the policies they implement, and can reveal their commitment (or partial dissent) from the policy by the judgments they make about implementing it. Except in the smallest matters, following orders does not determine action closely: even in small matters it does not fully determine all aspects of action. Only if all rules were algorithmic could they make judgment redundant. Standard bureaucratic excuses such as 'I was only applying the rules' or 'I was only carrying out orders' are disingenuous; they rest on a pretence that all rules are algorithmic.

It is not only bureaucrats who try to shelter behind rules. Sometimes specifically ethical rules or principles are invoked in defence of ethically questionable action. Winch's discussion of Ibsen's character Mrs Solness[12] dissects a case in which ethical principles are misused to 'justify' bad and offensive action. Such bogus 'justifications' do not convince. To do so they would not only have to invoke ethical rules that have weight, but to offer reasons for relying on that particular rule or principle in this particular situation and for applying it in a specific way. Our experience is not much like that of ideal-typical petty bureaucrats. Situations do not come handily pre-classified for subsumption under one and only one ethical rule or principle, which prescribes quite determinate action. Before we apply rules we have to construe the situation we face; when we have done so we may find more than one pertinent rule, and every relevant rule will underdetermine action. Ethical rules and principles offer remarkably little shelter outside ideal-typical petty bureaucratic roles.

Still, rules and principles offer minimal shelter, and are often thought to offer rather more. The truth behind the claim that appeals to abstract principles are ethically blunting is, I think, that such appeals are mainly made by ethically blunt agents. Such agents assume (falsely) that problems and cases confront us uncontroversially as candidates for subsumption under one and only one rule or principle, which can determine fully what ought to be done.

A similar truth lies behind the claim that (ethical) principles and rules are self-defeating. Those who need to refer explicitly to rules in guiding their action often do so in blunt and insensitive ways, just as those who need to refer explicitly to rules of grammar often speak or write in blunt and insensitive ways. Some cite abstract principles yet distance themselves from actual situations; they pay lip-service to impeccable principles that never incommode them. Others undercut their own performance by excessive scrutiny of principles they take

[12] See Winch (1972) and discussion of his paper in Mendus (1985b).

themselves to follow. There are often strong reasons to sustain ways of life in which we neither parade nor perform explicit reasoning about matters like trust or kindness or spontaneity or the pursuit of happiness. Too much concentration on rules or principles can mar performance. This does not show that principles or rules cannot guide reasoning in these matters, but rather that they do so best when deeply absorbed and internalized, as the rules of a language must be deeply absorbed and internalized for effortless and precise speech. In both cases explicit focus on rules and principles may be self-defeating. Yet there are also cases where it is important to refer explicitly to rules and principles. These may include 'hard' cases, the education of children and cases where important principles are confused or flouted. Here the greater danger may lie in failure to formulate and follow rules and principles explicitly.

The Indispensability of Principles

Both the theoretical and the ethical criticisms of abstraction in ethics are unconvincing. They depend upon misconstruing principles or rules as precluding rather than requiring deliberation. The advocates of various sorts of ethics of principles do not claim that there are principles from which specific decisions or requirements can be deduced. They take ethical principles and rules as non-algorithmic, and assume that their application requires deliberation; yet they have been persistently read as taking a different view.

The important point about rules and principles is not that the morally insensitive try to exploit them for shelter, but that even the sensitive cannot dispense with them. Once we reject the view that rules and principles of action must be algorithmic we can see why any plausible view of reasoning about conduct must give principles and rules an important role. Although some critics of abstraction and theory in ethics suggest that deliberation could dispense with rules, and fall back on sensitive articulation of situations, this is as implausible as the thought that principles or rules by themselves could make decisions.

There are two reasons why articulations of situations alone are ethically inadequate. First, descriptions are neither unique to cases nor uncontentious. Cases no more determine unique descriptions than rules pick out fully determinate actions. Reasons have to be given for preferring one rather than another description of a situation; and these reasons lead straight back to more general principles. Secondly, even if a certain description of a situation can be justified, it is by itself inert. It is only when we see situations *of that sort* as requiring action *of this type* that knowledge of some description becomes action guiding. Principles enable us to navigate among descriptions of situations. Fortunately we do not always have to keep our principles in the forefront of consciousness; we have much of the almanac not only calculated but in our bones. That we make our moves directly, intuitively, spontaneously no more shows that we do not need principles than the rapid inferences we draw without explicit laying out of arguments show that we don't rely on principles of inference. In each case reliance on principles has become ingrained—but not redundant—habit. Without these habits we would be wholly at sea.

'Facts' and Cases

Do these arguments show that the entire critique of abstraction (as opposed to idealization) in ethics has been groundless? It seems to me unlikely that so strong and persistent an intellectual current could be superficial. What then are the deeper sources of perennial concern about abstraction? I suggest that abstraction worries us not because some writers maintain that ethical reasoning requires only principles or rules, but because nearly all writers, whether or not they advocate ethical principles, have offered too meagre and cursory an account of deliberation. Perhaps the illusion that all the work in ethical debate is to be done by the major premise has arisen because we are unsure how the minor premise is to be identified and used.

It is not enough to suggest that the minor premise is just a matter of establishing 'the facts'. Situations have no unique descriptions. What we see under one true description as an urgent crisis or problem, may appear under another as mere and trivial routine. Ways of reasoning that assume that 'the facts' of human situations can be uncontroversially stated are likely to be dominated by established and often by establishment views. Without a critical account of the selection of minor premises, ethical reasoning may avoid formalism only to become hostage to local ideology. This is not an idle worry. Writing in applied ethics has to work with some account of the topics to be handled. Neither the selection of topics nor their description is neutrally given. Could any of us demonstrate that contemporary applied ethics is more than the scholasticism of a liberal tradition? What explains the particular agenda of problems that dominates the literature at a given moment?[13]

Those who dispute the relevance of principles in ethical reasoning have also, it seems to me, failed to offer an adequate account of how we are to describe the situations we find. For example, a lot of Wittgen-

[13] Ruddick (1980), O'Neill (1986).

steinian and related writing on ethics suggests that examples carry the whole burden of ethical deliberation, and that the articulation of examples, although subtle, is possible because we can determine 'what we do want to say'. But what we want to say depends much on who we are, and how we understand the world. Outside closed circles there are real and deep controversies about the articulation of cases and examples; even well-established descriptions may be evasive, self-serving or ideologically contentious.

Of course, we may choose to retreat to closed circles, which we define by the possibility of agreeing on the articulation of cases and an agenda of ethical problems. This strategy is likely to push us not merely into relativism but into circles that are smaller than those we actually inhabit. Even within the confines of the Athenian polis—our best image of a moral community—there was dispute about the articulation of examples, and no guarantee that disputants could agree on cases. Does failing to return a knife to its frenzied owner count as failure to give each his due? *Every* articulation of a situation privileges certain categories and descriptions, and is incomplete and potentially controversial even among those who inhabit the same circles. Those who don't live in the same circles may find that disagreement amounts to mutual incomprehension.

This suggests that we need to think more about the means by which understanding, and perhaps agreement, can be sought, and less about the conditions under which they can be taken for granted. We might ask: what are the minimal assumptions we must make for there to be ways of seeking to come to a mutually comprehensible and perhaps agreed-upon account of the minor premises of ethical reasoning? What does deliberation require?

Relativism and Multilingualism

It is difficult to discuss this point without entering into debates about relativism. For present purposes I want to bracket conceptual relativism of the sort that would trap us in permanent conceptual and social isolation. I offer only gestural reasons for doing so.[14]

First, conceptual relativism suggests that we cannot even discuss matters with those in different traditions since we lack a common conceptual framework. The reality of ethical and political conflict, however, suggests that when we are in dispute we do not entirely

[14] For good reasons: a full consideration of the topic has to give an account of how one may, without begging questions, discuss with those who allege that there are barriers that prevent any discussion.

misunderstand. It is because we understand (pretty well) what the other lot mean and are up to that we are in furious dispute. Those who are separated by ethical and political disagreements are more like those who speak different languages. Multilingualism is possible even if perfect translation is not. If we can be ethically and socially as well as linguistically multilingual, we may find more than one way of articulating a situation so as to make it accessible. Many people, I suggest, are at least partly ethically multilingual.

The second reason for bracketing conceptual relativism is practical. If we do not bracket relativism, we have only two options for dealing with those whose ways of thought and life we do not understand. Either we can cut ourselves off and retreat to the cosiness of 'our' shared outlook; or we can impose our ways on others. If we are to have options other than quietism and imperialisms (violent or merely paternalistic) we must bet against relativism.

Betting Against Relativism

What would it be to bet against relativism? Rather than accepting that there is nothing rational to do in the face of deep misunderstanding and disagreements, we would have to look for ways to reach wider mutual comprehension and perhaps some resolution of disagreement. This search cannot be just a blind groping for minor premises that all will understand and perhaps accept. If it is to count as a bet against relativism it must be more than this: indeed it must be guided by principles.

There is a possibility—welcomed by some—that we can make no bets against relativism. It may be said, for example, that we can do no more than accept that the conversation of mankind will lead us and others to new perceptions and descriptions, which will sometimes permit wider understanding and agreement. If this is our situation we can draw no generally acceptable distinction between consciousness raising and consciousness lowering. While we will not be trapped in timeless conceptual capsules, the sense we come to make of others' ethical reasoning will depend on the way we drift with the tide of history. Since the conversation of mankind sometimes takes a distinctly nasty turn, we have reasons to balk at this moderated relativism.

If we balk, one consolation that may be offered us is the claim that all change will at least enlarge horizons, since the tradition retains a comprehension of its past formations. We can understand the Athenians, even if they would have found us baffling. There is a worrying ethnocentrism—specifically Eurocentrism—in assuming that there is only one tradition. Even when we are talking about pasts that are ancestors to our own present there is an implausible optimism in assuming that transitions always happen without loss—it may merely be that when loss is quite general we no longer experience it as such. The present categories of any tradition are always the categories of the rewriters of its history. Historicized relativism substitutes ethnocentrism and optimism for strategies for bridging non-comprehension.

If we are to take seriously the thought that others may not understand our very articulation of situations or, where they understand, may think them pointless or evil, what can we do? Which principles must we follow if we bet against relativism? How can we work towards rather than assume acceptable minor premises? I shall do no more here than gesture towards lines of inquiry that require accounts of practical reasoning to address questions of ideology.

First, in practical reasoning that is not predicated on relativism we must accept that others may not share our views of situations and problems and that we may have to discuss and mediate disagreements. Our first task may be to enable communication. If so the most fundamental of ethical principles may be those by which we question our own and others' perceptions of situations and seek strategies for securing mutual communication, and where possible some agreement on the appropriate minor premises for ethical reasoning.

The beginning of a bet against relativism may be action on principles of tolerating and mediating discursive differences. Such toleration could not be mere indifference to others' views and voices. It would rather be a matter of straining to follow the terms of others' discourse and to grasp their starting points. Such moves towards multilingualism might fail if others were deeply alien and separated from us by impassable conceptual gulfs. There is no guarantee that all bets succeed. However, there is no reason to be sure that this bet must fail: there is little evidence of impassable conceptual barriers between human beings who have not suffered traumatic breakdown.

The principles required to guide a quest for mutual accessibility can be thought of as requiring strategies of decentring: we seek to enlarge our horizons and understand other standpoints.[15] However, trying to communicate with others whom we initially cannot understand needs more than a shift of our own horizon. A shift of horizons would not constitute a bet against relativism if it were only a conversion, during which our own former starting point dropped below the new horizon. Attaining multilingualism is not a matter of forgetting one's native tongue. The objective of building understanding between those who do

[15] This brief discussion draws mainly on Kant's account of shifting horizons and of the *sensus communis* in the First and Third Critiques and in his *Logic* and on Gadamer's rather different use of the metaphor of the horizon.

not share terms of discourse requires a strategy of seeking to grasp both perspectives, not the loss or suppression of some original bearings.

The strategy of seeking multilingualism could be analysed in Kant's terms[16] as a matter of acting on three principles. Those who seek to enlarge their horizon must preserve their own view or voice; they must seek to share others' views; they must strain to render consistent the constantly revised set of views to which action on the first two principles of the strategy may lead. If such a strategy works—there is no guarantee that it will always do so—those who transform their understanding may become conceptually multilingual, and may find their views of the problems they confront and their possibilities for action changed.

But won't multilinguals suffer schizophrenia? Enlarged horizons, in the sense just explained, don't guarantee an integrated viewpoint or a clear basis for action. It is a myth that horizons fuse. Perhaps multilingualism can lead to a sort of breakdown and moral paralysis, or to extreme fragmentation of moral life.[17] However, multilingualism need not disable. It might be continuous with the experience of 'monolinguals', who also find that their one language allows multiple and dissonant possibilities for describing situations. Even within the horizons we grow up with we experience conceptual and ethical hiatuses. Enlarged horizons do not offer our first glimpse of ethical conflict. However, if we are looking only for *strategies* for seeking, and not for *algorithms* for scrutinizing, the minor premises to which we are initially drawn, we do not need a guarantee that every use of a principle of seeking to bridge disagreement about particular situations will bear fruit. We need only to bet that it is not ruled out that a strategy of acting on such principles can work for at least some cases. The strategies to which I have gestured are slender weapons for confronting entrenched ideologies and dominant articulations of the problems to be addressed. Betting on these strategies may be the best we can do if we refuse to be relativists or to rely uncritically upon some locally entrenched account of 'the facts'.

[16] Kant (1978) 293–4.

[17] For recent discussion of the significance of such fragmentation of ethical discourse see above all MacIntyre (1981).

Philosophical Confidence

J. L. GORMAN

Analytical philosophers, if they are true to their training, never forget the first lesson of analytical philosophy: philosophers have no moral authority.

In so far as analytical philosophers believe this, they find it easy to live with. For them even to assert, let alone successfully lay claim to, moral authority would require, first, hard work of some non-analytical and probably mistaken kind and, secondly, personality traits of leadership or confidence or even charisma, which philosophers may accidentally have but which they are certainly not trained to have and had better not rely upon, while they live by analytical standards. Yet a further reason why analytical philosophers find the denial of their moral authority easy to accept is that they never forget the second lesson of analytical philosophy, either: nobody else has any moral authority.

Even though such philosophers may examine at length the possibility of the objectivity of morality, and perhaps offer standards for moral certainty, their analytical work is essentially second order. That their conclusions are neutral by the standards of first order morality is a necessary condition for their acceptability. It is not, of course, a sufficient condition for the acceptability of such analytical conclusions. On the contrary, there is probably no sufficient condition. Analytical philosophers are constitutionally opposed to finality. Revisability of philosophical conclusions is always a possibility, and is taken to entail fence-sitting. Suspension of moral judgment may be seen as the only fully rational procedure. If analytical philosophers do have strong moral convictions—and of course many do—they do not have them as the proper conclusion of a philosophical argument, but only by some accident of personality or education. Like everyone else philosophers may reason from ethical assumptions to ethical conclusions, and with luck be better at avoiding contradictions than some other people, but they do not have, by virtue of their professed subject, a special ability in the determination of moral issues.

This view that philosophers have no moral authority is not simply a parochial belief within linguistic philosophy. If it were just that, it would be already outmoded as philosophers have moved to interest themselves in more substantive issues, in public affairs and in that wide range of matters covered by applied philosophy. The move to applied philosophy over the last ten years or so has been indeed a powerful force, but—to give an influential example—the editors of the *Journal of Applied Philosophy* did not forget their first lesson. In their note on editorial policy in the first issue of this journal in March 1984, they refused to allow that philosophy 'has nothing to say about the pressing dilemmas of life in the later twentieth century',[1] and admitted that the very notion of applied philosophy implies some bridge-building across the gulf between theory and practice, between value and fact. But they were clear that a mere willingness to engage as philosophers with these pressing dilemmas does not mean that philosophers are moral experts. There is no appeal to authority or claim to expertise. The philosophical outsider can participate just as well; indeed, I say *pretend* just as well. Dispassionate philosophical study cannot resolve or dissolve a moral problem, they said. We are thus to understand the contribution of philosophy to the debates over moral dilemmas as simply the benefits of concentration and careful expression, the benefits of a reasonable intelligence. The tools of philosophical analysis and argument can be helpfully used by those with a particular moral commitment, but the commitment itself is not philosophically founded. On the contrary, 'the identification, justification and discussion of values capable of commanding widespread acceptance and endorsement in the contemporary world',[2] which is involved in a wider notion of applied philosophy, was allowed by them to be a political rather than a purely philosophical task.

What is moral authority? The concept of authority is usually studied in its mask of political authority; so let us begin there. Political authority is not just power; rather, it is opposed to power, in that the exercise of power is only required when authority lapses. Thomas Hobbes told us what authority is: 'by authority, is always understood a right of doing any act; and *done by authority*, done by commission, or licence from him whose right it is'.[3] This understanding of authority is not limited to political authority (if such a limitation is possible) and we may use it for the notion of moral authority. Moral authority is not just any kind of authority. Any authority is in itself legitimate in that it embodies a right to act, but even if this right to act is a moral right, that does not make any exercise of authority an exercise of moral authority. Moral authority is the particular right to determine what is right or wrong, what ought to be done, what is good and what is bad, and what our obligations, rights and duties are. The actions which are essential to the exercise of this right are declarative utterances in a context of free and effective communication to others.

[1] Cohen and O'Hear (1984) 3.
[2] Cohen and O'Hear (1984) 4.
[3] Hobbes (1962) 169.

Every one of us may have the freedom or capacity to determine what is right or wrong. It is of the nature of moral judgment that it is universalizable in some way, so that our determination of what is right or wrong will be a determination of what is right or wrong both for ourselves and for everyone else. The utterance of some moral judgment which implies the taking of a moral decision and the requiring of others to follow that decision is an exercise of free speech, but it is not thereby an exercise of moral authority. Moral authority exists only when the utterance of a universalizable moral judgment is by right.

And yet it is a strange kind of right. For, as Hobbes also told us, right and obligation 'in one and the same matter are inconsistent'.[4] Given this widely accepted view, then our rights may always be exercised or not, as we please, without our being obliged so to do. If the exercise of moral authority is a right in this way then it is one which those of us who have it cannot be obliged to exercise. But I think there is no doubt that a person who correctly knows himself or herself to have moral authority will also correctly hold that he or she has a moral duty to speak out. Moral authority is a moral right which we have a moral duty to exercise. Moreover, the rightful exercise of free speech is to an extent limited by the exercise of moral authority. For the right to authoritative moral utterance has as a corollary the duty of others to subordinate their moral judgments to that of the moral authority. Freedom of speech and action are *prima facie* rights of all persons which constrain privilege, and thus require that we guard against those who merely believe, rather than know, that they have moral authority. Thus a moral authority only exists when there is a person or body of persons who has, and not just claims to have, a right and duty to utter universalizable moral judgments, such that others are morally obliged to accept their judgments, subordinate their own judgments to them, and act in accordance with them. To have moral authority is thus to be deferred to. This means that the burden of proof lies on those who oppose an authority. The notion of a right, which includes that of rightful authority, generally embodies this feature: rights exist for some when the appropriate burdens of proof lie upon others.

A corollary of this is that we are to understand moral judgments, where a moral authority exists, as forming a hierarchy of superior to inferior. The moral beliefs held by the members of a community form, as a matter of empirical fact, an inconsistent set. Those moral judgments which are inconsistent with, or otherwise different from, those of the moral authority are morally inferior in virtue of that authority, and are thus not binding. If there is more than one moral authority, therefore, they must speak alike, otherwise inconsistent or unclear

[4] Hobbes (1962) 146.

moral duties will be placed upon the hearers. Different moral authorities must in effect clone each other: there can be only one rightful moral authority, yet that right can be transferred, and even held by every member of a community, in an ultimate moral consensus where moral authority and moral autonomy do not conflict. In such a case, rightful authority is held, not by a single person, but by a body of persons, a body which is contingently community-wide.

Moral authority is not the same as moral power. Such authority needs moral legitimation. Only one thing, it appears to me, can *morally* legitimate the claim to moral authority, and that is that the moral judgments made should be true. The claim to authority is then self-validating. The legitimation of a claim to moral authority is therefore epistemological.

The problems of the epistemology of morality have been difficult ones for analytical philosophers. A categorical contrast is assumed between statements of fact and statements of value; hence the charge that a *fallacy* is involved in the so-called 'naturalistic fallacy'. Hume argued that we cannot derive an 'ought' from an 'is'. Whatever statements of fact we produce, they imply nothing about what ought to be the case, and any attempt to derive value from fact is bound to involve a logical error. Hume meant by this, and is standardly taken to mean, that there is a difference of category between 'descriptive' and 'evaluative' statements.

Certainly we do, in philosophy or English grammar, classify statements into 'descriptive' and 'evaluative', just as we classify statements into 'analytic' and 'synthetic', and there is some practical point to this. But categories as such have no place in a purely empiricist philosophy. I shall assume empiricism, and my question will then be whether an *epistemological* contrast can be drawn between the descriptive and evaluative categories of statements.

One way in which the contrast might be drawn is by holding that moral judgments are not statements at all: they are not the kind of thing that can be either true or false. They cannot be known, and therefore do not form part of the subject matter of the theory of knowledge. The epistemological contrast between descriptive and evaluative statements is not then a contrast *within* epistemology, but between what is and is not a part of its scope. Hume sometimes speaks as if this were his view: 'Morality', he said, 'is more properly felt than judg'd of.'[5] Perhaps feelings of approval are involved.

But Hume also states that the 'ought' relation is an *affirmation*, and thus that we do judge of it. Morals must be discoverable, in his view, by means of some impression or sentiment which the ideas of vice and

[5] Hume (1888) 470.

virtue occasion to us; in particular, 'virtue is distinguished by the pleasure, and vice by the pain, that any action, sentiment or character gives us by the mere view and contemplation'.[6] Morals cannot be derived from reason, because they have an influence on the actions and affections, which reason alone cannot do. It is important to note that pleasure and pain here are impressions—that is, experiences. They thus form part of that same epistemological source from which we derive non-moral beliefs. Very simply, some of our beliefs are moral beliefs; they can be true, and, given empiricism, if we know them, then we know them on the basis of *experience*.

I take 'true' here seriously, such that a true statement is one taken to represent reality. I share, although less hesitantly, the view John McDowell holds of Bernard Williams' *Ethics and the Limits of Philosophy*.[7] Objectivity, as Williams says, consists in the relatively stable conviction that a belief answers to reality. This requires that there be a prospect of convergence on the belief, such that the best explanation of the convergence would involve the idea that things are as the belief represents them. Williams says that we have that prospect in science but not in ethics. McDowell points out the possibility that the best explanation we can find for some convergences (no doubt limited, he says) on ethical beliefs might be in terms of the excellence of the reasons which persuade people into the beliefs. I add that it may well be that the one way of making sense of that 'necessity' which Kant observed to attach to moral imperatives is to allow the possibility of there being a relatively stable conviction that a moral belief answers to reality.

If moral claims share, as for the empiricist they must, the same kind of experiential warrant as do non-moral or factual claims, then the epistemological contrast which is sought between descriptive and evaluative statements must, if it exists, derive from a contrast between different kinds of experiential sources. Hume could properly assume this because he was an atomistic empiricist: he believed that experience and thought were complexes with simple parts, such that each part was what it was regardless of how it was associated with other parts. There was supposed to be a direct relationship akin to copying between experience and thought. Broadly speaking, on this view, we must distinguish between external impressions and certain sorts of internal impressions or moral experiences. This Hume did.

However, the kind of empiricism which I propose to assume here is one which accepts that we have failed to make sense of the piecemeal warrant of knowledge by experience. My view is a holistic empiricism distantly derived from F. H. Bradley and W. V. Quine, and it requires

[6] Hume (1888) 475.

[7] McDowell (1986) 378.

no more detail here than the familiar assumption that, while experience is the only source of knowledge, the total body of our beliefs is underdetermined by experience. The usual metaphorical way of expressing this is to say that our claims to knowledge meet experience as a whole and not in piecemeal form.

Our claims to knowledge include moral claims. It follows, in accordance with the epistemological position argued so far, that moral beliefs are either true or false. They form part of our total set of beliefs or claims to knowledge. They are supported epistemologically just as any other statement is supported epistemologically. Since the entire system of beliefs is supported by experience, then the moral beliefs are similarly supported by experience. But although the moral beliefs are supported by experience, they are supported in a holistic way. In particular, they are not supported by experiences characterizable, *independently of the rest of our beliefs*, as moral experiences.

I shall comment here upon the supposed distinctive nature of evaluative judgments. My main thesis at this point is that evaluative and descriptive statements are *epistemologically* identically founded. This does not preclude the view, for example, that evaluative statements are, while descriptive statements are not, standardly action-guiding. But while such views are consistent with the holistic position adopted here, I see no particular plausibility in them. 'There is a missing rung on the ladder', said to a person about to climb it, is as descriptive and yet as action-guiding as one could wish.

Let us allow that there are, subject to these *caveats*, 'evaluative' statements, and that they are frequently (though not necessarily) action-guiding. Still this says nothing about any distinct epistemological status. Moreover, the very concept of 'action-guiding' marks no distinct realm here: the instruction 'make *p* true' may be obeyed in many ways. One way is, given that the entire body of beliefs is to be preserved, to act so that a state of affairs obtains which is, given that body of beliefs, properly described as *p*. Another way is to persuade one's community to revise the body of beliefs (which may, again, require the revision of a moral belief) so that *p* comes out true, perhaps with a quite different action, or even no action at all. Action is merely one of many ways available to us of re-evaluating and re-ordering experience. The distinction between understanding the world and changing it, between the man of ideas and the man of action, is not a philosophically fundamental one.

Quine has held that all the statements in our theory are at epistemological risk in the face of recalcitrant experience. Any belief may be held true come what may if enough adjustments are made elsewhere in the system, and no belief is immune to revision.[8] I add that

[8] Quine (1961) 43.

moral beliefs are similarly at epistemological risk. Neither morality nor, if we follow Quine here, the laws of logic, have epistemological special status. But the fact of epistemological risk does not entail that revision of certain factual statements, moral judgments or the laws of logic is readily available. It does not follow that we have what may be called complete freedom of the will to revise beliefs or hold them immune as we choose. Thus certain principles of logical inference, certain principles of morality, certain factual statements, may be *indubitable*. Indubitability here does not imply necessary truth, for it is a psychological and not epistemological notion.

Psychological doubt is required to query those principles of inference or moral judgments which we accept come what may but which are at risk epistemologically. In practice such doubt may not be psychologically possible. If it is to be possible to doubt some belief, we need to envisage an alternative belief; and our actual view of the world, expressed in our particular community's totality of beliefs, may not give us any such alternative.

Given this conception of the epistemological identity of foundation for both descriptive and evaluative statements, a certain characterization of moral argument becomes possible. An elementary example is provided by Morton White:[9]

1. Whoever takes the life of a human being does something that ought not to be done.
2. The mother took the life of a foetus in her womb.
3. Every living foetus in the womb of a human being is itself a human being.
4. Therefore, the mother took the life of a human being.
5. Therefore, the mother did something that ought not to be done.

Independently, we may feel that the mother did not do something here that ought not to be done. We are then required to hold the conclusion of the argument false. We are then (unless we revise logic, which I shall not deal with here) required to deny some premise which was involved in reaching the unacceptable conclusion. We might choose to deny that every living foetus in the womb of a human being is itself a human being. A descriptive statement is here being revised to save an evaluative statement.

This simple example shows how there can be moral or other evaluative constraints upon the ways in which we theorize or select factual descriptions. Appeals to simplicity or elegance in science are a version of the thesis put forward here. Since there is room for moral and other evaluative constraints upon our descriptions and theorizing, it is not

[9] White (1981) 30.

surprising that issues of a quasi-political kind should surface. It is sometimes held that we have a duty to be conservative of the existing belief system. Quine himself merely observes that we have a 'natural tendency' to preserve the existing system,[10] and we may note that new information has a cost. These conservative tendencies involve holding that what requires justification is not belief but change in belief. Knowledge is not justified true belief, therefore, for to suggest this would be to hold that what requires justification is belief itself, rather than just change in belief. These contrasting positions may be compared with two contrasting notions of justice: first, that of Robert Nozick,[11] according to whom justice consists in any state of affairs that is justly achieved; and second, that of John Rawls,[12] where justice is determined by an independent criterion against which any given state of affairs is measured. On my account truth is analogous to Nozick's conception of justice, and consists in any system of belief that is the consequence of a justifiable series of variations upon an earlier set of beliefs accepted as true. We are not to ask by what title truth was originally claimed. The justification of truth is thus partly historical. Any quasi-political requirements should not be seen as calls for a check of the existing system against some independent evaluative standard, for the standard itself is a part of the system, and itself at risk of revision.

Thus we see that evaluative constraints like appeals to morality or simplicity or conservatism may properly exist in our theorizing. These standards have no special status, however, and may themselves be revised if the overall theory requires it. Notice that we need not be concerned here only with very general evaluative beliefs. In the example of abortion provided by Morton White, a particular judgment 'this is not a wrong act' may be used to constrain our belief as to when an entity is a person. The constraint may also work the other way, of course: neither this hypothesized moral judgment nor our theory of the person are so well founded in our total system of beliefs that it is easy to tell which should constrain which.

Only one thing, I suggested earlier, can morally legitimate the claim to moral authority, and that is that the moral judgments made should be true. The claim to authority is then self-validating. The legitimation of a claim to moral authority is therefore epistemological, and the epistemological form of this legitimation assumes a holistic empiricism. We have to achieve an equilibrium in moral judgment and factual judgment, not just within the realm of the moral or just within the

[10] Quine (1961) 44.
[11] Nozick (1974).
[12] Rawls (1972).

realm of the factual, but across the entire system including both. Evaluative or moral matters can thus rightly constrain our choice of factual description, and vice versa. The truth in morality, as within the rest of our beliefs, is warranted in a revisable fashion by the totality of experience together with the rest of what we believe.

Who, then, has moral authority? Knowledge being conceived as a whole, any person who studies a *particular* discipline, necessarily against a background of unquestioned presuppositions, is concentrating on a part at the expense of the whole. The person who has moral authority is the person who has an overview of the whole. A special skill which it is the duty of philosophers to develop is not their analytical ability but their ability to *synthesize*. The philosophical and moral dilemmas, the big questions of life, are not distinctive because they have to be answered in some special way, but simply because they are *big*. They make demands on ranges of experience and expertise which transcend the barriers between the particular disciplines. Questions such as those about the nature of man, his relationship to God and to his fellow men, and what ought to be done, are so big that everything we claim to know is up for revision. No student of a *particular* discipline, as such, has the training or knowledge to deal with this. Philosophers who have thought through the implications of our moral beliefs for the rest of our understanding, have thought through the implications of the rest of our understanding for our moral beliefs, have revised as appropriate and achieved a sound synthesis, are not giving just another opinion, to be weighed equally with any other. The philosopher's synthesis gives him or her moral authority. This is the foundation of philosophical confidence.

On Applying Ethics

JAMES M. BROWN

I

Applied ethics work seems to me to be of three main kinds. There is participatory work, where a person whose specialism is ethics participates in a process leading to ethical judgments or decisions. And there are two kinds of teaching work where the teaching objective is to make learners better placed to participate in such processes; one kind of teaching work relates to matters which are specific to the future occupation of the learner, the other kind relates to matters which are not specific to it.

Ethics—or moral philosophy—is a branch of philosophy. If applying ethics differs from doing what moral philosophers do anyway, it differs only in ways that are entailed by its being done with reference to specific matters of practical decision. In this, applying ethics is much like applying mathematics or applying psychology.

However, I wish to dwell for a while on a more limited idea, namely that of dealing with matters of practical decision by applying a body of ethical theory. Moral philosophers have spent a lot of time developing and arguing for ethical theories. Some of these theories are theories of right and wrong conduct. Deriving practical recommendations or prescriptions from a theory which has been developed and argued for would certainly be applying ethics; in much the same way, in familiar examples of applied science, practical recommendations or prescriptions (technical imperatives) are derived from well-confirmed theory. Deriving practical recommendations or prescriptions from a theory may, but need not, be a matter of obtaining a specification of a course of action which leaves room only for trivial variations.

What I shall call the fruits-of-theory model of applied ethics is characterized by the thesis:

(a) Applied ethics is application of ethical theory.

When I talk of the fruits-of-theory model, I shall be referring only to thesis (a). But there is a further model, called the engineering model, in which the fruits-of-theory model can be embedded, although it is distinct from it. One natural concomitant of the fruits-of-theory model is the notion expressed in a second thesis:

(b) There is one body of sound, well-grounded ethical theory waiting to be applied to practical problems.

Another natural concomitant is the assumption of a division of labour whereby non-philosophers (or persons in non-philosophical capacities) supply problems for applied ethics treatment and philosophers, having already equipped themselves with the well-grounded body of theory, bring the relevant part of it to bear on the problems supplied and characterized, and obtain authoritative outcomes which the non-philosophers do well to accept. We may summarize the division of labour assumption in a third thesis:

(c) Non-philosophers supply the problems, and philosophers supply and apply the theory.

Since those with the task of identifying and characterizing the problems are the non-philosophers, the body of ethical theory will be quite general and will not contain elements which are specific to problems of health care, say, or business. Accordingly, medical ethics is ordinary ethics applied to medicine, business ethics is ordinary ethics applied to business, and so on. This point, generalized, can be expressed in a fourth thesis:

(d) Professional or occupational ethics is just ordinary ethics applied to the profession or occupation in question.

Now we have arrived at something very like what Caplan calls the 'engineering model' of applied ethics and something very like what MacIntyre calls the 'dominant conception' of the relation of ethics to applied ethics.[1] With its help we can readily say what should go on in the three kinds of applied ethics work previously mentioned. Affirming recommendations or prescriptions which have been derived from a well-supported ethical theory can constitute contributions to practical deliberation, to the training of professionals insofar as that involves ethics, and to the civic education of citizens insofar as that involves ethics. All three kinds of work can be seen as based on the production of theory-backed practical recommendations and prescriptions.

However, there are reasons for thinking that the whole thing is a bad idea. Thesis (d) is questionable: it is not at all clear that professional or occupational ethics is just ordinary ethics applied to the work of the profession or occupation. The division of labour expressed in thesis (c) is assailable in both its parts. It seems undesirable for non-philosophers such as doctors to have complete control of identification and characterization of problems to be solved. And treating philosophers as

[1] Caplan (1982/3) 314; MacIntyre (1984) 498–9.

authoritative in the supplying and applying of theory is something that commends itself only if thesis (b) is accepted. But it is pretty plain that thesis (b) is false: far from there being some body of well-grounded ethical theory, there are extant rival theories which differ in practically significant ways and there is no decisive way of reducing the number to one. Finally, the very idea of ethical *theory* being a desirable thing to have has been called in question. If even thesis (a) has to be dropped, nothing remains of our model of applied ethics, and some different understanding of applied ethics work is needed.

I shall comment on each of these theses and shall suggest that, shorn of theses (b)–(d) and of its claim to being the whole story about applied ethics, the fruits-of-theory model reflects part of the truth.

II

A great deal of applied ethics work is directed at problems which confront professionals. Thesis (c)'s division of labour gives control of the applied ethics agenda to the relevant profession. This may lead to the agenda being unduly restricted or bestowing undue prominence on some items.[2]

It is a commonplace that the salience of problems depends on the perspective of the viewer. The people most knowledgeable about activities of a certain kind are likely—through weakness, inadvertence, perspectival limitations or even ill-will—not to bring forward for ethicists' attention all the problems which might be solved as a result of that attention. Since the proceedings and findings of applied ethics are influenced by the agenda, giving some limited group excessive control of the agenda is giving that group some control over the proceedings and findings. If applied ethics is not to be unacceptably interest-group-bound what is needed is some standpoint-neutral way for items to get into the agenda tray and be treated in the same way as acknowledged problems.

Onora O'Neill has suggested that we need to be able to pick out and characterize moral problems in ways that start from but do not simply endorse the identifications and characterizations which the agents mainly involved would give.[3] Let me list some procedural rules that suggest themselves:

—that it not have to be shown that an item is a problem before it is regarded as eligible for consideration.

It is plain that any theory which delivers a conclusion about what is to be done in a problem situation will also deliver conclusions about what

[2] Cf. O'Neill (1984).
[3] O'Neill (1984).

is to be done in situations which present no problem. So something's not being a problem does not make applying ethics to it impossible. Moreover, applying theoretical considerations to a situation may bring to light a hitherto unnoticed disagreement or raise practical doubt where previously there was ethical assurance. In this way the envisaged rule can enrich the agenda.

—that items for consideration be sought from those with specialist knowledge (such as health care professionals) and from those with whom they deal (such as patients and families of patients);
—that a person's not being in one of those groups not disqualify her from proposing items of agenda;
—that an item's merely being regarded by members of one or other of those groups as not a problem not be a reason for its non-consideration (no veto rule);
—that philosophers working in applied ethics should be ready to pursue items that occur to them as potentially interesting items for attention (you may speak without being spoken to);
—that items be sought from a wider rather than a narrower range of sources (and not just from philosophers and physicians, for example);
—that characterizations of given items be sought which others can be brought without coercion to share. (The philosopher has a special responsibility to try to grasp what others are getting at and to bring different persons' prior characterizations of an item into relation with each other.)[4]

The upshot of this is that no one group should be viewed as authoritative on the matter of what ethics is to be applied to. Neither someone's proposed problem nor her characterization of it is to be disregarded merely on the strength of someone else's claim to be in charge of problems. With luck, people working in applied ethics will develop an enhanced perceptual capacity to spot problems so that, after the effortful work of coming to see as problems things which, unprompted, they would never have come to see as problems, they will then find some such things striking them as problems at first encounter.

Now consider the second part of the division of labour, the part which assigns to philosophers the tasks of supplying and applying theory. To illustrate the problem, let us take the case of medical practice. Caplan warns us against supposing that ethics specialists are 'on a par with other consultants and experts who are present in medical settings'. Since propriety seems to require experts to stay out of one another's spheres of expertise, this would tend to inhibit moral con-

[4] Cf. O'Neill (1986) 25–6.

tributions from non-ethicists and to discourage ethics specialists from giving 'close attention to the realities of illness and anxiety for patients and their families'.[5] This is a general point about co-operation between experts that would hold even if thesis (b) were true. Its falsity makes things worse for the division of labour. It means there is no reason to attribute special authority to ethics specialists in the matter of bringing the appropriate principles to bear on a given case. If the philosophers are not to be authoritative in the matter of bringing theory to bear on problems, who is? Perhaps those in whose area of special competence the problems arise. Thus it may be suggested that the best ethical guarantee is the doctor's conscience. Now a doctor who is conscientious and perceptive is no doubt more likely than anyone else to come up with good ethical proposals. Nevertheless, doctors' ethical hunches remain hunches even when informed by great clinical experience and conscientiousness. However conscientious the doctor, it is not at all unlikely that, when thought through in the way that philosophers are trained to think things through and doctors are not, some of her hunches will turn out to fit ill with others. This suggests that there may be something even better than the doctor's conscience, namely the doctor's conscience plus scope for improvement through criticism.

It thus seems that the work of applied ethics is not to be divided in the manner envisaged in thesis (c). This is not to say that the special knowledge and skills of good health care professionals and of good philosophers count for nothing. What they count for is the expectation that their possessors' input into collaborative applied ethics work will be good even if not authoritative and final.

A possible obstacle to applied ethics work, as thus conceived, is that philosophers may not want to co-operate with members of appropriate professions or that the latter may not be willing to pay any attention to philosophers. This would not matter if applied ethics work were not worth doing. But it does matter. However, there are philosophers and professionals who talk to each other; and, unless it were to become fashionable to believe that applied ethics is not worth doing, I should expect this to become more rather than less common as, on both sides, an uneasy awareness that one ought to be co-operating grows.

III

There is reason to doubt thesis (d). Different occupations have their characteristic virtues or rankings of the virtues. The things that seize a teacher's attention about a situation will often not be the things that

[5] Caplan (1982/3) 318; see also Maxwell (1980).

particularly strike a soldier; in some situations the immediate responses of a good teacher will be different from those of a good soldier. And there are cases where a journalist ought to keep secret something which a similarly placed lay-person ought not to keep secret. Such differences reflect differences between the ethics of one occupation and the ethics of another, and between the ethics of a special occupation and general ethics.

But this does not mean that the ethics of a profession has to be left to the members of that profession. While professional ethics may diverge from general morality, they have to be continuous with each other in that they should be reachable from each other by intelligible deformations. Part of the task of applied ethics is to assist with the process by which prospective members of professions become ethically equipped for membership.

The newcomer to professional training is likely to bring with her various dispositions to respond to situations of various kinds. In health care the responses of a lay person to blood, faeces, wounds, nakedness, convulsions, etc., are often not appropriate.[6] In learning to be a lawyer one must learn to be prepared to set aside pre-professional feelings of fairness or natural justice. It is not clear that disconnection of one's pre-professional spontaneous responses can be piecemeal. Since some pre-professional responses are clearly inappropriate, they all come into question. Part of the business of becoming a professional is coming to know which of one's pre-professional responses—including pre-professional moral responses—one can trust in and which to inhibit until such time as they stop occurring or become integrated with the others.

Becoming a member of a certain profession involves coming to be able to think as members of that profession think, to be able to decide as they are able to decide, to have the priorities of a member of that profession. To the extent that there are ethical aspects of the profession's work, it involves coming to have the ethics of the profession. And this involves coming to be sensitive to certain features of situations (those features which have to do with a professional's conduct being ethically proper), coming to see situations as calling for certain kinds of conduct or as calling for the avoidance of certain kinds of conduct, coming to have a second nature such that it is natural to behave in certain ways, to have certain thoughts and perhaps certain affective responses or not to have them.

What is second nature to a professional may be strange to the person who is taking the initial steps towards becoming a professional. In particular, the ethical responses which come naturally to a professional may be significantly different from the pre-professional ethical

[6] Cf. Thompson *et al.* (1983) 16–20.

responses of the future professional. If, when the professional responses are acquired, they are to be *ethical* responses they have to be in some way an extension of the pre-professional ethical orientation of the person. The possibility cannot be ruled out that professional responses will be at odds with pre-professional ones. If the professional responses becoming second nature is not to be experienced as an abandonment of ethics (as though health care workers had to regard the demands of their calling as overriding ethics) then the professional response has to come to be experienced as rooted in and continuous with pre-professional ethics. It is for this reason that part of the work of teaching applied ethics is to develop the links between the ethics of the profession and the existing moral responses of the learner. It may involve considering formulations of professional ethics and exploring justifications in general ethical terms for those formulations. It may involve taking cases where the demands of professional ethics seem at odds with those of general ethics and seeking to show that the reasons which are taken to be decisive in such cases are already present—although not decisive—in the extra-professional cases. The pre-professional felt moral responses have to be drawn upon (rather than disregarded) and brought to bear on professional work situations. Suppose this succeeds. Then the learner will eventually come to have certain feelings about the courses of action that are indicated by professional ethical guides (whether or not these are formulated as explicit universal principles). These feelings will be akin to—and will have developed from—the feelings which the learner had earlier about courses of action which she or he saw as morally required. Part of the aim of this process is to prevent the fragmentation of the ethical. Professional ethics does not have to be seen as a special case of ethics in general, but it must not be seen as utterly discontinuous with general ethics either.

Attempts at justification can backfire and raise doubts about justifiability. Where a profession's accepted codes of ethics or current practices in ethical matters resist attempts to establish continuity between them and pre-professional moral responses, alert learners may be bringing with them into the profession a sense of a need for improvement. In any case, as changing circumstances produce novel situations some of which call for ethical decisions, there are bound to be situations where reaching a conclusion about ethical conduct is better understood as *enriching* or *adding to* the profession's ethics rather than just bringing the old ethics to bear on a new case. To the extent that this is true, the profession has to be seen as inventing its ethics as it goes along. And the process of learning to be a professional appropriately includes getting into the way of sifting out moral considerations, elaborating ethical hunches, and relating them to more general traditions in ethical thinking. The questionable character of thesis (d) is far from leaving applied ethics with nothing to do.

IV

I take it that thesis (b) is false. Granted that, is there any point in applying ethical theories to problems and in teaching them to students?

There are problems of such a kind that they arise only if there is good reason to think a solution is available. If we have in mind only problems of this kind then it will seem to us that contested theories cannot properly be applied since contested theories give no assurance that solutions exist. But problems of another kind come without any accompanying assurance of a solution. Such a problem comes because something has to be done, and the problem is to find something concerning which one can reasonably accept that that is what has to be done. If a person has a malignant tumour or schizophrenia something has to be done. There are various kinds of treatment in current or recent use. Not every procedure that anyone might suggest is tried. Only those procedures are used which are prompted or backed up by some theoretical conjecture or hunch about what underlies the disorder. Problems of this second kind, if they are urgent and do not fall within the scope of some uncontested theory or technique, are the targets of a variety of applied theories. Ethical problems are often like this. So the falsity of (b) does not rule out the application of theory to them.

Part of the aim of applied ethics teaching is to develop students' ability to think articulately and critically about ethical issues. Plausible-looking bad reasons have a knack of acquiring currency in society at large, and it is part of the task of applied philosophy not merely to criticize them but to put criticism of them in places where it is likely to be taken up and to receive comparable currency to the bad reasons criticized. One way of endeavouring to carry out the task is to try to acquaint a significant proportion of our new graduates with those criticisms. Another is to place the criticisms at the disposal of members of the professional groups whose work concerns the matters to which the bad reasons relate.

It might be thought that teaching students different ethical theories and pointing out that they yield different practical conclusions is likely to induce moral scepticism.

> We have set out to produce in our students a willingness to challenge old beliefs, to pursue the implications of principles further than they naturally would, and to look at alternative beliefs. . . . But most of us do know, by casual observation or by sessions with distressed students, that it can unsettle and upset, and it can also produce moral

> skeptics and even cynics. Part of our own faith, it seems, is that anything, even a moral skeptic, is better than an unconscious moral dogmatist.[7]

I do not think that student distress should be discounted as just showing an immature person's unreadiness to take on the burden of intellectual integrity. It surely has to be reckoned as a cost when someone is distressed who would otherwise not have been distressed. And perhaps we cause more distress than we are aware of; perhaps we should be devising or seeking non-intrusive ways of finding out how much distress we cause. For my part, I have been only rarely made aware of distress associated with ethics courses. No doubt a person who has good circumstantial reason to see the world as rather bleak will sometimes find that the lack of philosophical consensus on the foundations of ethics provides a suitable idiom to express how she or he currently sees things. And it may be that an ethics course sometimes overtaxes a person who is ethically overbrittle and who would have been overtaxed sooner or later anyway. But it does not seem to me likely that distress or scepticism is being caused on such a scale that ethics courses are doing more harm than good. (Indeed, a recurring task in first-year ethics courses is that of shaking someone's faith in the correctness of a glib scepticism or relativism.)

What grasping different theoretical conceptions may do is equip the learner to recognize, and perhaps know how to respond to, arguments proceeding from those standpoints. Utilitarian arguments can be very hard to resist, especially if you do not even know they are utilitarian arguments. One thing that a person who has completed an applied ethics course ought to be able to do is recognize as utilitarian a utilitarian argument when she meets it. And if resisting it is what on reflection she would have wanted to do, the course will have benefited her by leaving her better placed to do that. Another thing that grasping different theoretical conceptions may do is inspire the learner with a sense that some approach (perhaps even an anti-theoretical one) is promising and that there must be a way of sustaining it against the objections. This in turn may lead to fertile, imaginative, new ethical thinking. The student's study of approaches other than the one that fires her intellect gives her some measure of insurance against wasting time re-thinking old thoughts and against being beguiled by an approach whose intellectual appeal is only superficial.

If a discussion that has been going on a long time has reached a stage where the parties can only give uninspiring repetitions of tediously familiar aguments then it is to be expected that newcomers will walk

[7] Baier (1985a) 240.

away rather than want to join in. If all moral theory had to offer were theories that are clumsily wrong or over-cautiously right, scepticism would be an apt response. To be worth spending much time on, an ethical theory has to give an enduring sense of being on to something and of being illuminating even if it is faced with massive objections. It seems to me that we are in possession of such theories. Utilitarian, Rawlsian and Kantian theory are examples.

Moreover, whatever else ethical theories might be, they are utterly different from inarticulate feelings. Showing that moral thinking can be eloquent and closely reasoned can do a lot to combat a cluster of ideas about the privacy of the ethical: that everyone is alone with her own private moral feelings; that there is no better or worse in ethical deliberation, no good reasons and bad ones, and thus no scope for articulating reasons and discussing them with others; that, since my decision is ultimately my own, there can be no contribution that another can usefully make to my deliberations. What applied ethics courses can show is that, while moral theory will not make deliberation and decision superfluous, it is also not true that there is nothing to be said for or against a choice of action or a reason for action.

V

I suppose an ethical theory is at least a structure of propositions or principles giving a fairly comprehensive and fairly unified account how persons should act or how persons should be or what is worth setting store by. Do we want ethical theories at all? It might be thought not. For, other things being equal, generality and simplicity are virtues of theories; but what the ethical improvement of society calls for is rather ways of thinking that seek shared understandings in diverse local conditions and that are hospitable to diversity and richness of ethical concepts.[8] However, this last is a point more against expecting too much simplicity and generality than against theory. And a Feyerabendian proliferation of theories can cope with any amount of diversity and richness.[9]

While theory is not everything in moral thinking, it is important. Pulling diverse things together, seeking underlying unity, producing conceptual enrichment, seeking to make different parts of our ethical views fit together well rather than badly and to learn things that we did not know before (which involves coming to have a view on something on which we previously had no view or coming to have a view contrary

[8] Williams (1985) 117.

[9] Feyerabend (1968) 14–15.

to some view that we had before)—all these things have a place in ethical thinking, whether this is a social or a solitary activity.

Explanation-seeking has a place in ethical thought as elsewhere. Brewers may seek to explain why beer sometimes turns out sour. Someone may seek to explain why some retaliation is good and some not. The search for an explanation may lead to reconsideration of the *explananda,* as when a thinker finds herself forced to the conclusion that punishment is not morally justifiable after all. An explanatory hunch might turn out not to be capable of being satisfyingly incorporated into a body of ethical attitudes and beliefs that reflective people are able to go along with; it would thus be found unsatisfactory in a way which would not have come to light had such incorporation not been attempted. Ethical theorizing need not be directed on every occasion at facilitating deliberation or adjudicating between different proposals for action; it might be directed at explaining something we do not understand. But it can still be practical. It is because brewers wanted to avoid brewing sour beer that they were anxious to have an explanation for beer's turning out sour. It may be because we want to bring up our children well that we are anxious to know why child-striking is sometimes all right.

There is clearly a role for quasi-speculative ethical theorizing. There can be point in people thinking through a position, elaborating it, seeing where it will lead, while suspending judgment on it. Part of the role of philosophers is to put ideas to the test of argument—including imaginative thought-experiment—without being yet committed to trying them out in the real world. If morality is a matter of conventionally continued practices, the practices may need to change from time to time. If over a given interval what they are shifting towards is something already explored in imagination and argument by philosophers, the fruits of such exploration can be introduced into the deliberations of the society, and may lead to people preferring to halt the trend or preferring to add momentum to it. Thus, even if we think of morality as more a matter of civilizing practices than theory-implementation,[10] philosophical theorizing has a role.

VI

I have tried to argue that most of the shortcomings of the engineering model of applied ethics are due to aspects of that model other than its core, the fruits-of-theory model. I have suggested that there is nothing wrong with theory as such, or with philosophers developing theories.

[10] Baier (1985b).

We do lack authoritative solutions to ethical problems, and it looks as though we shall continue to lack them. This is a reason for not doing anything that can be done only where authority is to be had. It rules out philosophers acting as ethical Red Adairs, flying in in helicopters to bring raging ethical problems under control. It rules out philosophers acting as ethical consultants if that means handing down rulings on the ethical acceptability of this practice or that research project.

On the other hand there is every reason to suppose that ethical discussions and deliberations, to which philosophers contribute along with others, have a chance of being better than otherwise similar ones to which philosophers do not contribute. Part of the task of philosophers is to help to improve public debate on pressing moral issues and, together with those involved in or affected by the work of specific occupations, to contribute to the articulation, development and assimilation of occupational ethics. A goal of applied ethics teaching is to supply future professionals and other citizens with a vocabulary and an enrichable set of concepts and distinctions for thinking about and discussing ethical problems; another goal is to heighten people's sensitivity to shortcomings of argument and foster a climate which is inhospitable to bad argument. Another task for philosophers is presented by the fragmentary and often conflicting ethical hunches that people have. In the first instance contrasting hunches may look equally plausible or implausible. Philosophers are well equipped to take up such hunches and to show which are capable of development and which are not. This work can put people in a better position to judge—no doubt in the light of things that philosophers say about those developed versions—which of the original hunches they want to cleave to and which not. The philosophers themselves are among the people who may judge what developed hunches they want to cleave to, but their judgment is not especially authoritative. But, that aside, the philosophers' role is not, I think, a merely clarificatory one. In developing a hunch (her own or someone else's), a philosopher can invite us to see things a certain way, and the invitation is quite likely to be one that a non-philosopher could not have initiated.[11] Here again, though, the philosopher's proposal is not authoritative. That it is made by a philosopher does not oblige the hearers to accept it. Making a non-authoritative imaginative proposal is quite different from exercising specialist analytical skills in, say, separating two concepts which had become confounded. It may be that philosophers are not preachers; but, when a community or society deliberates, those of its members who are philosophers do not have to doff their philosophical hats in order,

[11] For a good example, see the paper by Barrie Paskins in this volume (pp. 95–116).

without impropriety, to contribute to that deliberation. (What *would* be improper is using sophistical tricks to gain personal advantage or advantage for their favoured option of those being considered.)

Thus philosophy has an applied ethics role, although not a role in which the philosopher's special abilities are best deployed in isolation. Rather the applied ethics activities are in the main ones that involve active co-operation between philosophers and others, and in which philosophers do not have an especially authoritative position. Indeed, part of the task, I think, is to raise awareness of value questions among people at large and recruit them too into the applied ethics enterprise.[12]

Societies—like individuals—do well to reflect on their goals and values, and on the ways in which and the extent to which their arrangements are in accordance with those goals and values. Seeking to articulate values in a disciplined way, without being discouraged by their resistance to convenient and easy expression, is part of the co-operative task. Another part is to subject those values and goals to critical scrutiny. Social and technological change make it unlikely that things which there is good reason to try to achieve now are things that there will always be good reason for trying to achieve. If a society becomes unreservedly committed to goals that are only transitorily worth having, the society is unprepared for the time when those goals' time is past. The philosophers' task requires that they and those on whose co-operation they depend can maintain a critical distance from prevailing values. Thus the work of applied ethics needs not only non-co-opted philosophers but also non-co-opted engineers, physicists, pharmacists, and so on.

In short, there is an applied ethics role for philosophers, but applied ethics should not be left to philosophers alone.[13]

[12] Maxwell (1984) has argued that the exclusion of value-articulation and value-scrutiny from natural science has cost science dearly in rigour and self-understanding.

[13] The present paper restores some material (mainly in section III) omitted from the version read at the Belfast conference, and also makes some minor changes from that version, some in response to comments by the conference participants and subsequently by my colleague Terence McKnight and, more recently, by the editor of the present volume, for which I am very grateful.

Philosophy in the Nuclear Age

BARRIE PASKINS

I have chosen this title to set myself the task of commenting on the practice of philosophy in the light of my work as a philosopher in a university postgraduate department of war studies. I shall begin with some general remarks on how we are to understand 'philosophy', then discuss a neglected one-sidedness in the commentary which philosophers have attempted on such topics as the problems of the nuclear age.

The Practice of Philosophy

Professional philosophy in the English-speaking world (as also in European centres) is dominated by an esoteric set of self-generated questions, and the principal function of courses in the subject is to train the next generation of professionals. I shall refer to this institutional embodiment of the love of wisdom as Phoenix Philosophy in order to emphasize its supposed capacity to regenerate itself from its own ashes. Phoenix Philosophy is extremely difficult and demanding intellectually, and those who make the grade show every sign of being as prodigiously clever as professional mathematicians or high-flyers in the natural sciences.

Phoenix Philosophy faces at least two practical problems. One is what to do if it destroys itself from within, by demonstrating to itself that the project upon which it is engaged is a dead-end. If that happens, the intellectually ambitious will presumably be quick to go elsewhere, and the subject will die. Richard Rorty is one highly regarded professional who has argued in some detail that philosophy as we have long understood it has indeed reached the point of self-defeat, though he is unwilling to draw the obvious conclusion, and offers the following reassurance, if that is the right word:

> A nation can count itself lucky to have several thousand relatively leisured and relatively unspecialized intellectuals who are exceptionally good at putting together arguments and pulling them apart. Such a group is a precious cultural resource. As we keep saying on our grant applications, the nation would do well to have analytic philosophers advise on public projects.[1]

[1] Rorty (1982) 221.

> The useful kibitzing they can provide . . . is made possible by their familiarity with the historical background of arguments . . . punctuated by stale philosophical clichés which the other participants [in inter-disciplinary discussions] have stumbled across in their reading, but about which professional philosophers know the pros and cons by heart . . . In any case, the need for teachers who have read the great dead philosophers is quite enough to insure that there are philosophy departments as long as there are universities.[2]

This makes piquant reading in President Reagan's England, and I am unable to judge whether its condescending arrogance is meant ironically, but Rorty is worth citing as illustration of one problem which can arise within philosophy as it is currently conceived.

The Phoenix's other problem concerns students who are not going to become professional philosophers. What do you teach them? What value for them can there be in anything that you are equipped to offer? How do you keep them acquiescent enough from generation to generation to sustain staff-student ratios that are favourable to the training of the high-flyers who are your real preoccupation? How in hard times do you demonstrate the need for your discipline in the university?

Useful Philosophy

Let me suggest an alternative conception of philosophy, in order to indicate the extent to which I am, and am not, sympathetic to the Phoenix. I do not deny that philosophy has some self-generated and profoundly important questions within itself which can be investigated adequately only at the highest level of sophistication. But *at least as important,* I shall argue, is what I shall call Useful Philosophy. Consider any reasonable enthusiastic and able person who applies him- or herself to the study of philosophy for a large part of a year or more. Suppose that study to be such a person's primary access to philosophy, which will shape their understanding of the subject and be their lifelong guide whenever they try to carry their philosophical studies further. Suppose it will probably be the only formal schooling in philosophy that they ever receive. Then they will have gained Useful Philosophy if and only if what they have learnt will be of use in doing something other than philosophy, something with its own organizing priorities, of use in straining against those priorities towards a closer approximation of the rational ideal of selecting that which is best all things considered, and in a direction for which the person accepts whole-hearted responsibility.

[2] Rorty (1980) 393.

It is immediately obvious that Useful Philosophy is not prey to the Phoenix's problem of what to do with students who are not going to become professional philosophers: on the contrary, it is focused on the contribution of those students to the community at large. Nor is it likely to face the possibility of final self-immolation that Rorty is not the first to prognosticate for the Phoenix. For it seems wildly unlikely that philosophers devoted to uncovering and developing the value of their students' philosophical potential in other parts of life will find themselves blocked on all sides at once by anything that might happen *in philosophy*.

What might Useful Philosophy look like? Notice that every structured activity into which the student might go necessarily has its own organizing priorities, which are what make of it a structured activity. War studies in a university, war planning elsewhere, teaching for an examination, deciding how to set about architecture or town planning, bringing up children, campaigning for a political party, deciding the likeliest number of dimensions to be attributed to physical reality, all have their own organizing priorities; and these determine which is to be considered the most straightforward and which the less possible options without settling the question of what we are to do *all things considered*. Wherever the student may go, he or she will necessarily face the question of what should be done all things considered in the light of priorities which are for all practical purposes given, but which leave some space for thought about where to lean, within or against the given framework. How we are to think *all things considered* has been a basic issue throughout the history of philosophy, and it would be surprising if there were any human activity to which our great tradition could make no constructive contribution. The problem is not the tradition's vacuity or self-exhaustion, but to get the right insight to the right person in the right place.

I defined Useful Philosophy in terms of straining against the given constraints *in a direction for which the person accepts whole-hearted responsibility*. I emphasize this because I have in mind something other than the relatively easily taught skill of devil's advocate. Of course every philosopher should be able to argue any cause when that kind of stimulus is needed. But I am wishing to direct attention to a much more intimate kind of involvement in the given activity, one in which the person who has profited from his or her philosophical education can make himself or herself useful as whatever-it-may-be-and-philosopher. For this, the activity must be re-made in the philosopher's own person, and so must the philosophy. An original act of synthesis, one might say, must precede every analysis.

To design a course in Useful Philosophy would be to act under conditions of considerable uncertainty. One would not know the future niches of one's students, and would need therefore to implement a highly adaptable syllabus. Rorty reports on philosophy teaching in America in horrifying terms:

> Training in philosophy turned into a sort of 'casebook' procedure, of the sort found in law schools. Students' wits were sharpened by reading preprints of articles by currently fashionable figures, and finding objections to them. The students so trained began to think of themselves neither as continuing a tradition nor as participating in the solution of the 'outstanding problems' at the frontiers of a science. Rather they took their self-image from a style and quality of argumentation. They became quasi-lawyers rather than quasi-scientists—hoping an interesting new case would turn up.[3]

For all I know, this is an over-statement encouraged by Rorty's sense that the Phoenix is dying. Clearly, Useful Philosophy would have to be organized in such a way as to emphasize that which is of abiding value, so that the student would regard himself as learning something to be pondered wherever he may find himself, confident of its long-term power of illumination. The frontiers of science image is no more encouraging than the law-school analogy in this regard, and the phrase 'self-image from a style and quality of argumentation' is very strongly suggestive of a new breed of sophistry, antithetical to regarding philosophy as shaping that to which one can give whole-hearted commitment. Plato would have to count for a great deal more than the latest preprint in the teaching of Useful Philosophy.

Practical exercises would be an essential part of teaching Useful Philosophy. One might, for example, get hold of material that architects take seriously and get students working on the question, how would you, required to make yourself useful as a philosopher, contribute to the discussion of THIS? And how would you, as philosopher and teacher of sixteen-year-olds, handle THIS part of the curriculum? Etc. Clearly, not-too-tame architects, savage school-children, etc., would be invaluable partners in the exercise.

Style would surely emerge as a vital and perhaps a substantive issue. Inescapable problems would certainly include 'You will not be understood if you . . .', 'What about strengthening the confidence of the weakest pupils?', 'What conception of the heart's reasons or of citizenship, would you be conveying if you confine yourself to . . .?' Nor can it be obvious that these are contingent issues, mere tactics, once we remove the simplifying and far-too-long unexamined assumptions of Phoenix Philosophy.

[3] Rorty (1982) 227.

Plato's *Republic* as Illustration

It might be objected that I am proposing to reduce philosophy to the much-feared status of a service subject; or engaging in unjustified arm-waving about something that is done already, the low-level activity of popularization; or conflating philosophy with the history of ideas—witness my give-away reference to Plato. I think that all of these objections rest on a single mistake, which can be made plain by considering a novitiate's encounter with Plato's *Republic*.

When we first read *The Republic,* and for a long while afterwards, there is no distinction to be drawn *by the student* between a historical, a literary, and a philosophical approach. It would be a fatuous historical or literary study of the work which proceeded without any struggle with the ideas it contains, and the struggle with those ideas simply is the activity of philosophy. Of course, the work can be taught by different people whose several specialities involve different incapacities for a fully rounded response to Plato. But that is the teachers' problem, and a difficulty for the student only to the extent that his teachers are unable to overcome their limitations. The book is challenging to the whole person, heart and mind. The challenge is obviously historical in part, to acquaint oneself with the differences and similarities between Plato's world and one's own. It would be a wretched kind of historical study that did not make the reading of *The Republic* into, among other things, a searching enquiry into the history of the present! The challenge is evidently literary in part, but again it would be a pathetically inadequate literary response that avoided entry into the questions of truth. Similarly, a philosophical reading that is deliberately abstracted from the historical and literary, especially one that confines itself to the validity and truth of Plato's argument to the exclusion of all discussion of how we feel about Plato's vision and sensibility, would be—indeed *is*—assailable on philosophical grounds, as an exercise in false abstraction, false because unexamined.

The Republic is such an obvious choice for any humane education largely because it returns us to the fullness of our intellectual and emotional being; this is why it is so vital a part of so many now separated disciplines. If there is any serious doubt about this, it is perhaps to be found more in the humanities than in the sciences, so let me give a humanities example. English Literature is an extremely popular and vitally important part of education. Let us assume for the sake of argument that the novels of D.H. Lawrence are (still) an important focus of Eng. Lit., and let us set aside the fashion for French-style 'theorizing' which poses such a grave threat to that minute attention to particular, good texts which is the sole reason why Eng. Lit. matters in the first place. Lawrence challenges his reader to reflect upon a variety of types of character, and to return a heartfelt judgment guided by the stories that he tells. How are we to judge him? I submit that no educated judgment of his work is possible that is returned without a proper awareness of what Plato's *Republic* tells us about the nature of man. Plato is no more decisive, perhaps, than Lawrence, but to throb with Lawrence, and to fire shaft upon shaft against the 'rational' man whose head is at war with all that is vital in us without ever having come to grips imaginatively with *The Republic*—this is mere ignorance. Of course, such a claim makes Eng. Lit. a rather difficult subject, for it involves us in trying to interrelate our own world and those of Plato and Lawrence. But this is no objection, for Eng. Lit. *is* a difficult subject.

Rorty thinks it so obvious as to be beneath discussion that 'the need for teachers who have read the great dead philosophers is quite enough to insure that there are philosophy departments as long as there are universities'. But wrongly: doubtless historians will need to go on reading snippets of Plato as long as taste continues to confer value upon anything nurtured in neo-Platonic schools of thought. But it is one thing to need to know about Plato as a reference-point in an enquiry for which his inwardness is of minimal significance, quite another to sustain his presence in all good reflective thought and feeling. Phoenix Philosophy leaves Plato perilously isolated by claiming that his philosophical content is adequately defined by present and future states of the Phoenix. I expect he is robust enough to shift for himself, but my example from Eng. Lit. and history suggests that the ascendency of the Phoenix impoverishes our response to Lawrence.

It might be thought that I protest too much because the kind of claim that I am advancing is perfectly well met by the elementary requirement that every educated person must have dipped into Plato. It is true that to pick up a few scraps of information, so that one can essay a few well-informed remarks about the forms and their critics is not difficult for those who are so inclined; and we can all get a good digest of *The Open Society and Its Enemies*. But there is more than this to *The Republic*'s being a living presence in the thoughts and feelings of all educated people. To teach the book in such a way that it can form a part of our students' permanent stock of ideas is, to put it mildly, difficult. If it is to be done at all, there is a need for a great deal of intellectually demanding work.

The objections I mentioned earlier were: reducing philosophy to a service subject; arm-waving towards low-level popularization; and confusing philosophy with the history of ideas. As regards service, I am assuredly not proposing that we philosophers make ourselves into passive purveyors of what our colleagues in other disciplines think they need their students to know about philosophy. My example shows this. Nor am I proposing any remotely easy popularization. It would not be unchallenging to attempt a serious account of, say, the relations between *The Republic* and *Women in Love*. As regards the separation between philosophy and the history of ideas, there is of course a place for the kind of historical scholarship which strives to set aside the present and to concentrate on Plato in his own time. But that is obviously a minority specialization, and it is simply question-begging to set up some deliverance of the Phoenix as drawing the line between what is philosophy and what is a quite different thing, the history of ideas. 'What can the nuclear age learn from the age of Plato?' is a philosophical question, however unilluminating about it may be the current preoccupations of Phoenix Philosophers.

Meaning and The Whole

However appealing my argument, it would I suppose fail of conviction if Phoenix Philosophy were in the process of delivering something to compare with the Theory of Relativity, or Gibbon's *Decline and Fall* . . . or *The Republic*. Rorty is one witness that it is not doing anything of the kind, but of course his argument is the subject of in-house debate at the usual high level among Phoenix Philosophers. I have neither space nor competence to contribute; but it is to my purpose to say, however inadequately, why I think the Phoenix is only part of philosophy. This will indicate that I have a rather basic philosophical reason for counterposing Useful and Phoenix Philosophy.

What, we might ask ourselves, is the basic unit of meaning? Is it, for example, a sentence, a statement, a proposition, a thought, etc.? This is a convenient question for me here because so many philosophical positions use it as a point of self-definition. I want to say that the basic unit of meaning is actually communication between whole persons, from which any abstraction must be made only with critical caution. Consider, for example, the child learning the meaning of words with whom Wittgenstein begins *Philosophical Investigations*. Augustine is cited there as an illustration of the naming theory of meaning, against which Wittgenstein pits an elaborate set of arguments to draw attention to the learning of rules, criteria and conventions, which he argues to be necessarily interpersonal. I have no doubt that meaning is at *least as complicated* as Wittgenstein argues it to be. But let us notice that his emphasis is intensely impersonal—that 'interpersonal' as he discusses it is something which gets established among persons considered in abstraction from whatever may flow from their personalities. Common sense alone cannot establish anything in philosophy, but there is a hint from common sense to be heeded here. We surely know perfectly well before we philosophize that learning almost anything, and certainly anything of any difficulty, involves the perceived character of the teacher. Before this is dismissed as contingent psychology, let us consider at least one possible speculation about it.

Why should the personality of the teacher be such a potent force for learning and non-learning? One obvious general answer is that a person thinking hard about the meaning of what he is being told scans that which he is trying to understand for its whole meaning, as much for what the communicator is, and is trying to do, as for that extra-personal thing to which the communicator is gesturing. A commonplace at least worth pondering in this connection concerns the acute (or fabled) perceptiveness of children about the atmosphere in which communication takes place. We are in our present lives, and as likely as not were in our biologically formative condition, vitally interested in the whole being of one another, as necessarily curious about the speaker as about what he is trying to tell us. The teacher with a passion for his subject communicates its value through the infectious quality of his enthusiasm, unless some other factor intrudes, whether part of the speaker's or the hearer's character, or something else. Any sort of communication that is in any way taxing has us scanning the attitudes of the speaker, for what he really thinks and feels about it, and how it fits into his life, what this utterance makes him into. It will not do to exclude all this by unexamined definition, any more than it can be right to remove Wittgenstein's critique of the naming theory of meaning by exclusionist definition.

Clearly, what I have just gestured at in a couple of paragraphs requires hard-working discussion on a large scale. Lacking the space for it here, I shall hurry on to a fairly obvious consequence of anything that might be philosophically important in the area I have pointed to. I shall outline this consequence in two overlapping connections, of which the second will be the dichotomy between Phoenix and Useful Philosophy.

First, a comment on a familiar problem in methods of teaching. It is well known that one can legitimately teach almost anything, and especially anything that has a controversial content, in either of two sharply contrasting ways—either as impersonally as possible, withholding one's own attitude to the greatest possible extent in order to focus students on the question and their attitude to it; or in a much more open way, allowing one's own views to become apparent on the ground that the students are entitled to know where one stands. Clearly, the choice of method is largely tactical. Neither is propagandist. The age and aptitude of the students, the teacher's personality, the topic being studied, the atmosphere of other studies by these students with this and other teachers—all these are among the factors that will rightly govern the tactical decision. But some generalization seems to be possible. In any subject that is in any way controversial (i.e. in any subject!) it would surely be highly peculiar if all the teachers withheld their own attitudes all the time. For the students would then be deprived of important material for their developing thought on the matters in question. Those who teach them do so by some measure of greater competence in the subject. The attitudes of these more competent persons, and what the persons with these attitudes are like as persons, is worth knowing.

There is something which we as philosophers would like to believe which makes this hard to take. Our ideal is that the stronger argument should defeat the weaker, and that contingencies such as the enthusiasms of one teacher and the deadness of another should be dismissed as accidental to the essential description of what counts as an argument. We are emphatically right to cleave to this ideal in a world in which the easy and normal thing is to trade on one's character and authority, using every resource to dominate. The abstractions which separate validity and truth from what will please are vital throughout human life, and the Useful Philosopher has a special responsibility towards them. But we human beings are legitimately interested in what the teacher, as a whole person trying to make sense of life and of his own life, makes of the material that we are grinding at. What he, with truth and validity to the fore in his life, and fallibility a manifest characteristic, makes of it, and what this priority makes of him, is well worth knowing in our necessary day-to-day computation of the value of minute particulars. This is something for philosophy to understand, not to exclude by definition.

The Phoenix Needs Useful Philosophy

This brings me back to the dichotomy between Phoenix and Useful Philosophy. Phoenix Philosophers tend to be insistent that the meaning of their utterances is determined by their chosen context of operation. How their words are taken up and misused outside the academy (if they are!) is accidental. The meaning of 'Liberty, equality, fraternity' is to be gleaned from the philosophers' writings, according to this view, and not from what it has come to mean on the streets. Any words can be twisted in any way, and it is simply destructive of the enterprise of philosophy to encroach upon the philosopher's freedom with any suggestion that he has a wider responsibility than to pursue the truth. In contrast to this, I do not want to say that absolutely every twisting of a philosopher's arguments should be laid at his door. But the other extreme, of picturing the philosopher as a disembodied author of disembodied arguments, is equally unrealistic. Let me give a couple of examples of where I think the correct middle position is to be located. With Nietzsche's philosophy, one unavoidable question surely concerns the kinds of risk of misunderstanding that he was prepared to contemplate and/or ought to have anticipated. For example, did he think it seriously possible that he would be read beyond a very narrow circle of sophisticates who would grasp the full complexities of his irony? Ought he to have done so in view of his historical situation? With Wittgenstein's philosophy, and the intense interest and massive influence which he knew himself to be exercising, one wants to ask what he thought he was doing in relation to his readership. Why did he deploy such an elusive style, and why was he silent on social and political questions, thereby implying that there could be no fruitful discussion of them? In both of these cases, the author's attitudes and personal purpose are legitimate objects of enquiry because they affect the meaning, the overall thrust, the bearing upon how we should enact our love of wisdom, of the writings of these two great philosophers.

Any philosophy owes us an account of what it would mean for people to take the thing on board as a part of their supposed wisdom about life. One great weakness in Nietzsche's writing is, it is widely agreed, the almost complete practical vagueness of his notion of the superman. He owes us some sort of insight in these matters and fails utterly. The position with Wittgenstein is less subject to agreement. An earlier generation was eager to confine discussion to detailed arguments, abstracting entirely from the extraordinary style and irony of his writings. Another generation is perhaps now moving in to claim his 'overall thrust' for their own. (Rorty does this, for example.) The question of his style is glossed over as before. Before one can assess the adequacy of Anscombe or Kripke on Wittgenstein, one needs to know what he was up to: his portentousness and obliqueness are essential issues here.

By this measure, it is obvious that the Phoenix cannot ever hope to deliver, alone, anything near to what we rightly require of it. However good by its own criteria, Phoenix Philosophy is systematically silent about its own human meaning. The very impersonality on which it prides itself, by which it approximates or even trumps mathematics and the natural sciences, guarantees this. The damaging one-sidedness of any achievement it may attain derives from something completely general, which I have tried to indicate in terms of theories of meaning. When anyone comes out with a difficult utterance, we struggle with the impersonal meaning of the words but equally, and for good reasons, we want to know what the person is, and what he is doing (in a sense of 'doing' that is personal, beyond impersonal speech acts). What Phoenix Philosophy needs to overcome this one-sidedness, so far as possible, is systematic encouragement to become aware of the human meaning of its own activity, to become articulate (by criteria of real understanding between real people) about the meaning for us of its utterances. In short, what it needs is Useful Philosophy, which is tailor-made to get the philosopher out and about, and into the business of examining how he is understood.

You will see, then, that I am in a way more sympathetic than Rorty to the traditional aims of Phoenix Philosophy. He thinks it can be shown to have completed its project, and that we must now contemplate a post-Philosophical age. I suspect that his characterization of the supposedly single project of philosophy since Descartes is much-too-neat, a charge which will not dismay those sympathetic to his avowedly polemical approach. Leaving that aside, I am most concerned here with what he proposes to put in its place. He thinks that in 'a post-Philosophical culture', philosophy comes to look

> much like what is sometimes called 'cultured criticism' . . . the literary–historical–anthropological–political merry-go-round . . . The modern Western 'culture critic' feels free to comment on anything at all. He is a pre-figuration of the all-purpose intellectual of a post-Philosophical culture . . . He passes rapidly from Hemingway to Proust to Hitler to Marx to Foucault to Mary Douglas to the present situation in South-east Asia to Gandhi to Sophocles. He is a name-dropper . . . His speciality is seeing similarities and differences between great big pictures, between attempts to see how things hang together.[4]

We should look for the future of philosophy in '[t]he life of . . . inhabitants of Snow's "literary culture", whose highest hope is to grasp their time in thought' uninhibited by fear of 'a life which leaves nothing permanent behind'.[5]

Intentionally or not, the invocation of Snow invites commentary in terms of Leavis's discussion of the two cultures. It will be obvious from my juxtaposition of Lawrence and Plato that I am far from wishing to underwrite Leavis's conception of the primacy of the English school. But what is most dreadful in Rorty's scenario is focused by his idea of passing rapidly from Hemingway to Proust, etc. A large part of the vital purpose of Eng. Lit. is to oppose the reduction of great texts to counters in some game of cocktail parties and television chat shows, by showing in practical criticism the value of detailed, loving scrutiny of something that proves to be worth the effort. Rorty seems to want philosophy to scramble into the business of manipulation, as much in his remarks on the culture critic as in his emphasis on committee kibitzing, quoted earlier. Against this nightmare, I want to say philosophy can and should play its part in the counter-culture of educated people who are striving to make sense of their lives and roles within the traditional resources imparted by such disciplines as Useful Philosophy.

[4] Rorty (1982) xl.
[5] Rorty (1982) xli.

Aristotle and the Bomb

Let me now try to give some substance to these generalities through a kind of argument to which I find myself increasingly drawn in my attempts to do Useful Philosophy in a department of war studies. Nuclear weapons are an obvious point of departure. They offer a relatively uninviting topic for philosophical analysis, as comparison and contrast with the issue of animal rights can quickly reveal. Philosophers have been able to play a leading role in developing public concern about the rights of animals by drawing upon central philosophical questions of long standing in order to initiate debate. It has been possible to show that cruel practices can be connected with philosophical positions, and that these intellectual underpinnings can be subjected to very damaging criticism. In proceeding thus, philosophers have been on strong professional ground, for the relationship between human nature and the nature of animals is unquestionably philosophical. Anyone who wants to take a serious interest in the treatment of animals, even as an apologist of a big food company, must in the nature of the case tangle with the philosophers.

The nuclear weapons problem is different in that the concepts underlying it are of recent invention, and of unexplored relation to established philosophical concerns. At times, 'the strategists', as I shall call them, have stuck out their necks in a direction suitable for surgery. For example, such writers as Herman Kahn and Thomas Schelling, contributors to what is now called in Washington 'the golden age of nuclear strategy', made the incautious claim that their policy advocacy was scientific. This laid them open to the devastating critique visited upon them by Philip Green in *Deadly Logic*.[6] But this was a rather exceptional development. Some of the most distinguished of the strategists—for example, Bernard Brodie in the United States, Sir Basil Liddell Hart in the UK, and Raymond Aron in France—never succumbed to such philosophically convenient pretensions. Their earthy yet sophisticated thought offers no obvious hostages to philosophical fortune.

Furthermore, much contemporary strategic writing—shall we call it 'silver age'?—is so manifestly tied to policy advocacy, so little concerned with anything which the plain man would call 'the philosophy of deterrence', that the broad concerns of philosophy are very difficult to connect with it. An extreme example is Colin Gray's *Strategic Studies: A Critical Assessment*.[7] Gray makes so light of dispassionate argument, is so 'robust' about the fact that he is pleading a cause, as to make any attempts at textual criticism look naive. What does Socrates do when

[6] Green (1966).
[7] Gray (1982).

Thrasymachus answers all his questions with jokes addressed to the pit? Gray *is* extreme, but a study of current problems which is admirably moderate by current standards, such as Michael Nacht's *The Age of Vulnerability: Threats to the Nuclear Stalemate*[8] avoids the larger questions to as great an extent as Gray does. Nacht assumes that Soviet assertiveness and aggressiveness can be held in check only if the United States shows itself ready to compete in every side of the arms race, and moves on at once to narrow technical questions, despite a broadness of mind which is obvious in his opening chapter. It is difficult to resist the conclusion that this narrowing of focus in the literature is expressive of a development in the political culture. Since nuclear weapons and deterrence are a political phenomenon, the philosopher is hard pressed to know how to begin when the political culture seems so radically resistant to philosophizing.

This difficulty has not silenced us, of course. We have tended to concentrate on those parts of the debate into which we can gain confidently professional entry. Above all, philosophers have focused on ethics. This has enabled them to connect established philosophical issues with public debate. Consequentialism versus absolutism, the principle of double effect, the issue of conditional intentions, the question of what decision principle to use in weighing up the risks of nuclear war and of Soviet domination—all these are controversies within our professional competence. And the ethical questions are an important factor in at least two real-life political controversies: that between defenders of strategic orthodoxy and 'the peace movements', and that between advocates and opponents of 'limited nuclear options', i.e. of adding more discriminating targeting options to Western capability and planning. The politically important struggle for the hearts and minds of the churches is an obvious example of the way that the focus upon ethics gives philosophy a role in the debate.

It is certainly appropriate that our contributions to debates about the bomb and other aspects of the nuclear age should be focused on ethics.[9] But I feel that the way we typically formulate the ethical questions is one-sided. One of the principal tasks of Useful Philosophy is to expose and challenge one-sidedness; so this issue should help me to make clearer the shift of emphasis that I am proposing within philosophy.

In the history of philosophy, there seem to be at least three main emphases which are possible for the handling of many central ethical questions. The current, well-developed favourites are consequentialism and deontology. The other, neglected tradition derives from Aris-

[8] Nacht (1985).

[9] This includes, of course, arguments such as that of Williams (1984) *against* making much of the ethical input into public debate.

totle. He says that particular problems are so difficult and uncertain that ethics can do little if anything to illuminate them: we must expect men of good will to differ about them. But there remains something which ethics can do, he maintains: it can develop an outline of the moral and intellectual character which it is good and rational for us to cultivate in ourselves and in others. And are we not likelier to hit the target, he asks, if we have something to aim at? What little has been written recently within this tradition has concentrated almost entirely on private individuals rather than on public life and politics, with the exception of MacIntyre's *After Virtue,* on which I shall comment as we proceed.

The significance of what I am calling the Aristotelian tradition may become better appreciated if we can find a suitable label for its leading idea. We need some term comparable with 'consequentialism' and 'absolutes' and 'rights', which shall be near enough the mark to avoid misleading yet sufficiently close to ordinary English to attract and promote sympathetic attention. The best I have managed after many failures is the term 'anthropological ethics'. This seems to me inviting for the non-professional, and useful in directing attention to Aristotle's concentration on aspects of the whole life of man, such as the virtues and the vices. 'Consequentialist, absolutist, rights-based, and anthropological ethics' seems to me a list of ethical approaches which does well in avoiding on one side the off-putting mystique of 'deontology' and 'aretaic ethics', and on another side the switch-off of sympathy which I find that talk of an ethics of virtue produces in virtually every kind of audience.

In one important respect, Aristotle's own example is unhelpful for envisaging the scope of anthropological ethics. His analysis of the virtues and the vices *of the individual* is not carried over into his political theory, which shares Plato's preoccupation with the just constitution, and thereby gives a boost to the single-minded devotion to rules that I am so uneasy about in contemporary ethics. Anthropological ethics, I want to say, should examine what is excellent and vicious in human life both individual and collective.

Objections from Machiavelli

There are several instructive reasons for being resistant to the very idea of anthropological ethics. They can be epitomized by Machiavelli. According to Quentin Skinner, Machiavelli is a transitional figure. He inherits a tradition of political writing which does indeed belong to anthropological ethics. This tradition centres on the question: should the good ruler seek to be loved, or feared? It is, according to Skinner, a somewhat empty game, because the answer is known in advance: the good ruler is to be lovable, and the enquiry is no more than an exercise in elegant arguments elegantly phrased to this pious conclusion. Machiavelli stands it on its head brutally, through his ruthless demonstration of the political virtue of many characteristics which would be abominable in the ordinary citizen. Skinner concludes that Machiavelli has shown the political virtues to be whatever set of qualities it takes to operate the political system effectively. This is why he is a transitional figure. By shifting attention on to the system, and making the virtues and vices wholly derivative, he opens the way to the moderns, from Hobbes onwards.

This fits Machiavelli neatly into the pattern Skinner is weaving with the title *Foundations of Modern Political Thought.*[10] It also encapsulates two kinds of objection to anthropological ethics as an exercise in Useful Philosophy. First, if the virtues and vices are wholly derivative, we must concentrate on that from which they derive, the system, and this brings us back to the exclusive study of rules and constitutions.

Second, Machiavelli's achievement should be a reminder of the modern political dichotomies that harmonize with Skinner's Whig theory of the significance of Machiavelli. Machiavelli was a 'realist' in his marginalizing of the moral factor in politics, in favour of the demands of the system. His 'realist' heirs from Metternich to Morgenthau and Kissinger have struggled to keep the dangerous enthusiasms of the moral to the margin. In American political writing, the alternative to their chilly sobriety is a wildly impulsive, crusading zeal, whose reality is hard to deny in President Reagan's world. Nor is the American example obviously untypical. General De Gaulle was a leader deeply concerned about virtue both individual and national. His 'moralism' may be more deeply serious than the American variety, but one needs to pause before pressing the claims of an argument whose practical implication, if any, may be to legitimize Gaullism as against consequentialism, rights theory, and the rest.

Another kind of objection derives from MacIntyre's *After Virtue.*[11] This rich work deserves extended examination in its own right for which I do not have space here. It must suffice to state what I take to be its overall thrust as to the nature of the virtues. MacIntyre values Machiavelli for reasons antithetical to Skinner's. As a critic of the idea of a predictive social science, MacIntyre praises Machiavelli's lively sense of the role of fate in human life. He thinks fortune is so ubiquitous that the enlightenment project of predictive control of social life must give way to renewed deliberation about the virtues. But he is too much of a historicist to accept Aristotle's implicit belief in a timeless doctrine

[10] Skinner (1978), esp. Vol. 1, 128–38.
[11] MacIntyre (1981).

of the virtues. To talk sense about the virtues, we must place them in their historically contingent social context. MacIntyre avoids making this into a reduction of the virtues to the analysis of social systems by resort to poetry, that is, by arguing that the most searching and realistic studies of the virtues are to be found, not in discursive works of philosophy and the social sciences but in the more intuitive creations of literary and other artists. The best basis for writing a history of the content of anthropological ethics would, for MacIntyre, be centred on a history of literature.

Generosity as a Test Case

I can respond to these and other objections best via an example. There will be little overt dissent in the modern world from the view that one of the virtues is *generosity*. It is, I take it, that largeness of spirit whereby the generous person finds more scope for time and attention to others, and fellowship with them, and if funds permit expenditure upon them, than the mean-spirited would think possible. Generosity comes more naturally to some than to others, as is also true of other virtues such as courage and prudence, and perhaps of all the virtues. But like perhaps all the virtues, we can work at it, strengthening and stabilizing it, becoming generous and more admirably generous by practising generosity. Generosity is emphatically not confined to the wealthy, as Aristotle mistakenly supposed, for even the humblest have choices as to how they will spend their time and energy. Nor is generosity confined to individual human beings. Some companies are much more generous in their dealings with employees and customers than others, and it is far from clear that this generosity is bad for business.

What of states? Historians who are not trying to be artificially simple in their language naturally find themselves saying, for example, that the Marshall Plan was a piece of unprecedented generosity, and that this generosity was far from being contrary to American interest. Similarly, columnists have argued that Mrs Thatcher's gloating insistence upon how little concession she had made to Commonwealth opinion over sanctions against South Africa bespoke a deliberate narrowing of national ambitions. Whether we agree with these particular assessments or not, we can scarcely doubt that they are part of everyday political commentary, that they mean something which is rationally discussable, and that deployment of virtue words and vice words in such contexts is a perfectly ordinary deployment of those terms. The onus of proof is upon those who would wish to hold that we cannot attribute generosity and meanness, and other virtues and vices, to statesmen and to attitudes of states.

The logical shape of generosity is instructive in at least five ways. First, generosity is not readily characterized in terms of rules. There is something of spontaneity about it that needs to be distinguished from the natural place of rule-following in our lives. Second, the merits of generosity cannot be captured in social systems, those main preoccupations of political thought since Hobbes. It may well be that generosity makes life in a social system easier to bear, but generosity is compromised, less than generous, if this is its only motive. What the generous person does is to extend a hand of friendship beyond what is naturally and automatically possible. Part of the importance of his action is precisely its being a gesture towards something that the system cannot capture. 'Would that your position and our relation were better than I, rooted in life where I am, can make it' says the act of generosity. It is a symbolic gesture against the exclusions without which we cannot live.

This brings me to a third instructive feature of generosity. Machiavelli makes his paradoxical doctrine of political virtue plausible to us by confining attention to a peculiarly insecure kind of regime. Perhaps there is little or no space for the normal virtues in that extreme environment, but the condition nowadays of the states in which we live is in the sharpest possible contrast, in at least two ways. First, and very often remarked in this connection, is the fact that our states are very far from being one dagger thrust from destruction. Second, and equally important, the normal virtues which Machiavelli presupposes as a foil for the dark genius of the prince may have been secure in his world altogether apart from the state, but in our world they are not. Private and public interpenetrate in so many ways that it is problematic in the extreme to assume, as modern realists do, that the state can live one kind of life while its citizens live an entirely different one.[12] The state is, for example, so deeply enmeshed in our being so much better off than the poor of the world that a mean-spirited attitude of our governments to poverty diminishes us as individuals. Perhaps, therefore, there is a way in which we should take Machiavelli more seriously than Skinner appears to do. Perhaps we need to learn from the wide range of *differences* that separate his world from ours.

A fourth feature of generosity concerns MacIntyre's historicist interest in imaginative literature. True generosity does indeed require the subtleties and privileges of imaginative literature to be identified. Because it comes from the heart, and can be polluted by so many imperfections, the nearest that we can come to its presentation is in a form of discourse as free as imaginative literature is to probe head and heart, thought and deed, together. A journalist, biographer or historian

[12] Morgenthau (1972) 3–15 is a classic statement of modern realism. I discuss it further in Paskins & Dockrill (1979) 277–85.

able to be penetrating on such matters is, we readily say, in need of all the gifts of the novelist.

This requirement is compatible with Aristotle's idea that a doctrine of the virtues is best conceived as a piece of target-setting. Ethics determines the target, literature's subtleties may be needed to determine the extent of our hits and misses. In this regard, MacIntyre's emphasis on literature is eminently Aristotelian. But what of his anti-Aristotelian historicism? If the example of generosity is any guide, then one should perhaps infer that MacIntyre is as over-schematically historicist as Aristotle is over-schematically essentialist. A quick, over-cheap historicist point to make would be that Aristotle does not recognize the virtue of generosity. But then we must ask whether this is a limitation in him, to be explained in terms of his philosophy and specific class condition, or a fact about the Greeks as a whole. In this particular case, I suspect that the impulse of Plato and Aristotle but not Socrates towards god-like self-sufficiency is more relevant to understanding Aristotle's failure, as I would put it, to grasp the nature and merits of generosity than the character of the Greek mind. The Greek concern for hospitality bespeaks a seriousness about outsiders which could well be brought to bear to argue this case. I doubt that there is any sound basis for having settled convictions about the extent to which the virtues are historically conditioned, and can see no necessity for *a priori* historicism in MacIntyre's sensible attempt to combine a suitably modest sense of the possibilities of social science with a sociologically inquisitive interest in the imaginative arts.

Fifth, let us notice that generosity is a virtue which is ill-assorted to the horrors of a moralizing foreign policy. Making the demands that it does, it requires a thoughtful and sincere public. It is the failings of American foreign policy to sustain the high standards exemplified by the Marshall Plan—failings as much of shrill, self-deceiving moralizing as of *Machtpolitik*—that prevent us from being able to say that modern America is generous by nature. Of course, the concepts central to anthropological ethics may be misrepresented and abused, but that applies to every position, and the record does not suggest that one position is less amenable to travesty than another.

Implications

To what extent, and how, might we generalize from this example? First, what of the relation between rules and virtues? I submit that anthropological ethics is peculiarly well placed to encourage intelligent curiosity about the form and limits of rules in the good life of the individual and the collective. Justice is, to a large extent, the virtue of discovering or inventing just rules, and following, popularizing and enforcing these rules. But forgiveness cannot be captured in rules in anything like the same way. And there is a comparable point which should make more impression on realists. We must remind them of one of the most important lessons for which thoughtful people value Clausewitz. This is his insistence on the vital necessity in war of something that cannot be captured in rules, something which in its highest manifestations he calls genius.

Leadership and the virtues of good followers (such as obedience, loyalty, initiative, and good counsel) are another set of qualities in which the interplay of rules and spontaneity is interesting and practically important, as in European–American disagreements about the recent bombing of Libya.

My second specific point about generosity concerned its universality, the way it transcended particular social systems. Here, too, I think, the point can be generalized to cover the other virtues. Faced with some candidate which depends for its merits exclusively on one highly controversial social ordering, we are bound to be sceptical. For example, some Victorians, and some moderns, appear to hold that selfishness is a virtue because of its economic utility. Change the economic conception but a little, and this quality returns to its traditional place among the vices. The apostles of greed were and sometimes are to be heard criticizing generosity. The very fragility of their argument for selfishness, depending so exclusively on one controversial variable, makes the 'virtue' for which they are contending singularly unfitted to appear in any *outline* of the good life of the sort envisaged by Aristotle.

My third point about generosity concerned the extreme and untypical narrowness of the political environment that makes sense of Machiavelli's paradoxical teaching about the political virtues. The general point here, it seems to me, is that states and people want to see their lives as *at least innocent* and preferably recognizable as positively good by others. The American public, for instance, would not be at all easy with the thought that the exclusive object of American foreign policy is to preserve and if possible increase the wealth and security of Americans. The myth of the innocent American is, indeed, best understood as protection against such a view. The well-meaning Republic makes mistakes, according to this story, by being forever innocent of the wicked ways of the world. It is not in its own right yet another of the grubby players for power and interest. *They want to be respected and liked among the nations, and are not unusual in this.*

Now here is a question which should be illuminating about the virtues: what qualities does a nation-state require, to be respected and liked among the nations? An immediate part-answer suggests itself which is of direct application to foreign and military policy. To be respected and liked, a nation-state must be capable of, and working at, friendship among nation-states, friendship *as against mere clientage*. The relative independence, the scope for independent thought and speech and action, which are typical of friendship are a pre-condition of something that nation-states typically want. Now of course it may be that they cannot have it, and arguments to this effect are not wanting. But the point I am after is that the desire to be recognized as innocent and preferably good in the world has relatively definite policy implications. If this is what you want, unless you are convinced you cannot have it and must talk a different language entirely (giving up the innocent American), then you must concentrate on developing real friendship and the elimination of client relationships. To do that you must act and be a certain kind of way.

I have already generalized my fourth point about generosity, the need to complement social science with literature. My fifth point concerned the horrors of a moralizing foreign policy. It should now be plain that the kind of discourse about anthropological ethics that I have in mind is more attuned to the criticism of foreign policy than to the exigencies of ideology.

Conclusions

How, then, at a level of generality sufficient to be called 'philosophical', should one set about what I have been calling anthropological ethics?

First, we should work from the assumption that Useful Philosophy is at least as important as Phoenix Philosophy. We cannot say what this would mean for the overall shape of philosophy because we do not know how it would change our sense of the subject. But we can be sure that it would make us much easier with the presence to us of immediate practical concerns in a way far different from what will be delivered to the moral philosopher trying to fit his work into a discipline dominated by the abstractions of Phoenix Philosophy.

Second, what is the basic unit of analysis in philosophy? Here I have sketched a case for two positions. (a) The bearer of meaning is the whole utterance, including not only the proposition and the impersonal speech act but also the whole person of the speaker. This brings with it reinforcement of the instinct that the philosopher is one who should be especially open about his striving to make sense of life as a whole, though from a particular location, which may well not be primarily that of a professional philosophy department. The wholeness of word and deed also affects our sense of the relationship between altruism and egoism. It is not isolated piety to say that the American people want to be respected and liked in the world. To be valued among people is necessarily a universal concern among the kind of compulsive communicators that we are. Ethics is not out on a limb in emphasizing that we are all members one of another.

(b) I have assumed that individual and collective can be treated in the same terms. We inherit a situation in which one set of traditions, which might broadly be called 'liberal', would have us think about collectivities in rigorously impersonal terms, as the product of contracts among the only real people, who are individuals. The state is a chilly *Gesellschaft*. On the other hand, we know historically that this tradition is very problematic, that states are typically dependent on nationalism or some other feeling which invests them with something much warmer than a contract, *Gemeinschaft*. We can of course take sides in this great quarrel, but I am suggesting that we explore the implications of cutting across that set of polarities, and explore the implications of peoples' talking about the state, etc., in intensely personal terms. Let us by all means heed every argument aimed at unmasking this personalist idiom, but let us equally be open minded about the possibility that when people speak of the state in personal terms, they mean what they say. After all, there is at least one pretty general reason for thinking of the state as a person. It is so much the agent of my wishes in so many ways—for example, so much the determinant and vessel of my attitudes towards the poor of the world—that it is only by a very questionable kind of self-privatization that I can separate its conduct and character from the actions and character of something that is unquestionably a person, namely myself.

Third, an obvious Aristotelian resource is to collect the widest possible sense of the place of the virtues and vices in individual and collective life in many times and places. Do we need any particular guidance for handling such data? We must certainly give a particular importance to our own sense of priorities. Ethics is a practical enquiry. Our own values are not, therefore, to be viewed as mere contingencies. If our attitudes differ from others, then that is a practical issue, not a mere datum for relativism. Do we need something further, beyond the realization that ethics is this practical enquiry, to do anthropological ethics? I think we certainly need MacIntyre's sense of the complementarity of social science and imaginative literature. But his historicism seems to be as unnecessary a presupposition as Aristotle's essentialism.

Does this not give us enough to do? Perhaps after many years of Useful Philosophy grappling in a vast variety of contexts with the demands of anthropological ethics, we will be in a position to essay a grand synthesis. I must also confess that I already have a kind of grand synthesis in mind, and suspect that it would be less than human not to have. Let me conclude with this thought. The various examples that I have assembled in this paper have been designed to suggest some of the many ways in which reflection on the virtues and vices is germane to rendering the moral reality of the nuclear age. I am not trying to disparage well-developed debates about the consequentialist versus deontological deliberation of nuclear deterrence. But it is now a commonplace that the bomb is above all a political phenomenon, and I have been trying to suggest that the moment we turn from relatively abstracted discussion of deterrence to reflection upon the foreign and military policies that place the bomb in our world, then we come face to face with anthropological ethics, the Aristotelian quest for an outline of the good life. That is a necessary but neglected position from which to edge forward towards a less one-sided philosophical representation of the nuclear predicament.

Justice, Exploitation and the End of Morality

ALAN RYAN

This paper is a small contribution to two large subjects. The first large subject is that of exploitation—what it is for somebody to be exploited, in what ways people can be and are exploited, whether exploitation necessarily involves coercion, what Marx's understanding of exploitation was and whether it was adequate: all these are issues on which I merely touch, at best. My particular concern here is to answer the two questions, whether Marx thought capitalist exploitation *unjust* and how the answer to that question illuminates Marx's conception of morality in general. The second large subject is that of the nature of morality—whether there are specifically *moral* values and specifically moral forms of evaluation and criticism, how these relate to our explanatory interests in the same phenomena, what it would be like to abandon the 'moral point of view', whether the growth of a scientific understanding of society and ourselves inevitably undermines our confidence in the existence of moral 'truths'. These again are issues on which I only touch if I mention them at all, but the questions I try to answer are, what does Marx propose to put in the place of moral judgment, and what kind of assessment of the horrors of capitalism does he provide if not a moral assessment?

Marx and Morality

It is a feature of Marx's work that he seems at one and the same time to be dismissive of morality and yet full of what most people would describe as moral indignation.[1] Take perhaps the best known of all Marx's prophecies:

> Along with the constant decrease in the number of capitalist magnates, who usurp and monopolize all the advantages of this process of transformation, the mass of misery, oppression, slavery, degradation and exploitation grows; but with this there also grows the revolt of the working class, a class constantly increasing in numbers, and trained, united and organized by the very mechanism of the capitalist

[1] Lukes (1985) 4–5.

> process of production. The monopoly of capital becomes a fetter upon the mode of production which has flourished alongside and under it. The centralization of the means of production and the socialization of labour reach a point at which they become incompatible with their capitalist integument. This integument is burst asunder. The knell of capitalist private property sounds. The expropriators are expropriated.[2]

It is hard to deny that terms such as *usurpation, slavery, degradation* and the like are terms of moral condemnation, and implausible to think that Marx employs them in less than a wholehearted way. Cohen's claim that whether he knew it or not Marx attacked capitalism for its *injustice* rests on the plausible point that Marx uses terms such as 'rob' and 'usurp' in their plain sense, and does not so to speak bracket them or place them in inverted commas; Marx condemned theft, not 'theft'.[3] Yet, Marx's scepticism about ethical appeals is well known. When he wrote to Engels about his *Address* to the International Working Men's Association, he observed, 'I was obliged to insert two phrases about "duty" and "right" into the Preamble to the Rules, and also about "truth, morality and justice" but these are placed in such a way that they can do no harm'.[4] In the *Manifesto,* Marx mocks the believers in eternal moral truths, and seems at least to suggest that the Marxist conception of ideology relegates ideals of all sorts to an epiphenomenal status:

> When people speak of ideas that revolutionize society, they do but express the fact, that within the old society, the elements of a new one have been created, and that the dissolution of the old ideas keeps even pace with the dissolution of the old conditions of existence.
>
> When the ancient world was in its last throes, the ancient religions were overcome by Christianity. When Christian ideas succumbed in the eighteenth century to rationalist ideas, feudal society fought its death battle with the then revolutionary bourgeoisie. The ideas of religious liberty and freedom of conscience merely gave expression to the sway of free competition within the domain of knowledge.[5]

The task, then, is to see whether Marx has a consistent position on all this.

The starting point is Marx's antipathy to writers who stressed the role of ideas—moral and other—in social life; it has two sources, neither of them particularly surprising. In the first place, Marx's so-called 'materialist conception of history' is very largely an 'anti-

[2] Marx (1976) I, 929.
[3] Cohen (1983) 443.
[4] Marx and Engels (1962a) 139.
[5] Marx and Engels (1962b) I, 52.

idealist conception of history'. Marx, writing in opposition to his former friends and colleagues, was eager to insist, as he had done in his critique of Hegel's *Philosophy of Right,* that what happened in social, economic and political life was not to be explained as the result of an Idea implementing itself.[6] Greater economic equality was not caused by Equality manifesting itself in the phenomenal world. Demands for justice did not arise because Justice embarked on a campaign of self-realization. Whether Marx was right to think that his Idealist contemporaries believed in the efficacy of the Ideal in quite so literal a fashion is not a question we need pause for, though we ought to recognize the passion with which he assaulted all appeals to *verités eternelles.* It is enough to see that a man who denies that ideas owe their effectiveness to the operations of the Idea is not denying that ideas make an important difference to what happens. Marx, indeed, tended to over-estimate the importance of ideas—intellectuals usually do; a man who thought ideas had no impact at all would hardly have spent twenty years in poverty and ill-health writing *Capital,* nor would he have been so concerned to destroy the erroneous views which, as he thought, the Lassalleans put into circulation in their Gotha Programme. All Marx seems to have believed was that for ideas to make a difference, they had to be *somebody's* ideas and to make a difference to how they acted. Moral ideas may make a difference, but not in virtue of reflecting the demands of Morality; they make a difference by making a difference to the way individuals behave. As Cohen emphasizes in another context, when norms are cited in a causal explanation it must be by way of the effect on behaviour of *adherence* to those norms.[7]

Secondly, however, Marx evidently believed that moral demands were intrinsically dubious in a way other kinds of practical demands were not. There are two or three different things at stake. The first is that Marx thought that in politics mankind is mostly moved by self-interest; so, where people profess ideals, they will act against them under the impulse of self-interest, or they will interpret them so as to reconcile them with self-interest. It is thus inept to ask people to do for purely altruistic reasons anything very much opposed to their interests. Ethical socialists were asking employers and members of the ruling classes to behave 'justly' or 'fairly', with no reason to suppose this would affect their behaviour.

The second point is not a matter of sociological, but of philosophical scepticism; although it is harder to elucidate, it is intellectually more fundamental. Marx followed Hegel in disbelieving in the existence of a

[6] Marx (1975) 60ff.
[7] Cohen (1978) 217–25.

realm of the *ought* which stood opposed to the *is*.[8] Hegel's objection to the Kantian picture of a noumenal realm of values which contrasted in all ways with the phenomenal realm of the merely factual strikes a chord with many twentieth-century readers. It starts from the objection which occurs to many readers on first taking up the *Grundlegung*—if men are moved in fact by phenomenal desires but are supposed as a moral matter to be moved by the moral imperatives of the noumenal self, it is impossible to see how the noumenal self gets the necessary grip on the phenomenal self. The point is not restricted to the most impressive or serious aspects of morality; an opening batsman who is going out to face what Len Hutton aptly called 'the nasty short-pitched fast stuff' in the fading light may reasonably feel fairly frightened, but he cannot quell his fears by issuing himself with injunctions to be brave or not to be frightened. Unless he already desires to be an unflinching opening batsman, nothing will come of addressing any number of imperatives to himself. In putting forward this view, Hegel and Marx were anticipating views recently defended by Mrs Foot and Professor Williams, both of whom have argued that all reasons, moral reasons included, can only *be* reasons for persons who have pre-existing aims to which those reasons are relevant.[9]

Thirdly, Marx also thought, as many other writers have done, that there was something epistemologically dubious about moral judgments, or, more mildly, that they were not on all fours with factual judgments. A man who, when it is raining, *believes* that it is raining will best explain his beliefs by appealing to the fact that it *is* raining; the truth of what he believes features in the best explanation of the fact that he believes it. Marx's theory of ideology *may*—though I think it does not—imply that the truth of a belief is *never* an adequate explanation of our holding that belief. In the case of moral beliefs, however, Marx certainly holds that we are always to look for an explanation of someone's moral beliefs elsewhere than in their truth. His sociological analysis of morality, though utterly undeveloped, at least implies that 'morality' belongs with law as part of the machinery by which class-divided societies preserve order in the face of conflict of interest. The features which Kant ascribes to morality—its coercive character and its independence of self-interest above all—reflect in a mystified fashion the social function of the institution of 'morality'.

Exploitation

It is in this perspective that what follows is written; before plunging into the main topic of exploitation and justice, I should say that the

[8] Marx and Engels (1975) IV, 37.
[9] Williams (1981a); the same thought runs through Williams (1985).

above sketch of Marx's position is not intended to pre-empt discussion of a familiar view (put forward as persuasively as I have seen it, by Steven Lukes in his *Marxism and Morality*) to the effect that Marx had no time for the morality of rights, obligation and justice, but espoused what one might call an ethics of liberation.[10] I think that this is a misleading way of stating the case, and one which does some violence to Marx's insistence that he preached no ideals, not even that of liberation. To my mind, the interest of Marx's stand on the status of morality is this: he repudiates any suggestion that his condemnation of capitalism rests on ethical or moral considerations, and he looks forward to the day when we shall dissolve all forms of appraisal in the one category of the 'practical'. I shall argue for this view at the end of this paper, however, and do not mean to beg it now. For the moment, I want only to rest on the familiar fact that Marx both appears to condemn capitalism as unjust and immoral and to repudiate moral assessments as practically futile and intellectually worthless. It is to the dissolution of this paradox that I now turn.

The best recent discussion concludes that Marx thought that capitalist exploitation was unjust; some writers who hold this view go on to claim that Marx had what can properly be characterized as a theory of 'needs-based' justice, epitomized in the famous slogan 'from each according to his ability, to each according to his needs'.[11] I do not suggest—some writers have done so, however—that Marx thought that capitalist exploitation was just; my claim is that Marx thought that it was not in an *absolute* sense just or unjust because there is no such sense. On Marx's account, capitalism was and had to be just-in-appearance according to prevailing notions of justice, but it was and had to be unjust-in-reality according to those same prevailing notions. The assertion of a gap between appearance and underlying mechanism is a familiar feature of Marx's analysis of capitalism (Cohen's essay on 'The Withering Away of Social Science' usefully explains why)[12] but it raises the question whether Marx believed that capitalist exploitation was *really* unjust. This turns out to be a bogus question because it presupposes what Marx denied, that there is a trans-historical standard of justice which can be applied to the case. His position is not unlike that of the post-Copernican astronomer who readily speaks of the sunrise and who yet understands the nature of the phenomenon quite differently from his Ptolemaic predecessor. The astronomer denies that the question 'does the sun really rise?' has a firm answer, and Marx in the same way denies that the question 'is capitalist exploitation really

[10] Lukes (1985) 27.

[11] Elster (1985) 229–31; Geras (1985) esp. 60–5.

[12] Cohen (1971/2).

unjust?' has a firm answer. The proper response is neither yes nor no, but an account of why we talk about the world in the way we do. Marx's denial of eternal moral truths, and of *justice eternelle* along with them, makes the status of his own distributive principle (first enunciated in so many words by Louis Blanc, apparently) 'from each according to his ability, to each according to his needs' problematic. Is it a principle of socialist justice? My answer is that it is not—or, to put it differently, that Marx certainly thought it was not, and had compelling reasons for so thinking.

The question of exploitation arises for Marx in the following way. It is apparent that in pre-capitalist societies a lot of unpaid labour is done by, say, peasants working their lords' fields three days a week, or by slaves working at the absolute pleasure of their owners. If we ask how the surplus product generated in such societies finds its way—is '*ausgepumpt*' in Marx's graphic term—from the labourers to their superiors, a story about the exploitation of the direct producers comes naturally. Those who produce the product work for nothing; they perform unrequited labour for their feudal superiors or their owners or whomever. But, we might say that the question whether they are *exploited* needs a further premise in addition to the premise that they perform unrequited labour. This is that they perform this unrequited labour on an unjust basis; this proposition may be supplied by, or run in conjunction with another premise, viz. that this labour is *forced labour.*

It is debatable whether the fact of coercive extraction is an indicator, rather than a constituent of injustice. On the view that it is a constituent, we begin from the premise that seizing goods or labour from another is *prima facie* unjust, either because it is a violation of the proprietorship of the victim or because it is an unwarranted invasion of his freedom. The contrast between coerced and uncoerced labour marks the distinction between a free gift, which raises no questions of justice, and forcible taking which does raise such questions. On the 'indicator' view, it is some other notion of justice which explains the injustice of the taking; the fact of coercion is itself explained by appeal to the unlikelihood that the victims would consent to unjust treatment. If we were to set as the criterion of justice the view that the labourer should receive goods equal to the market value of his efforts, it would be neither here nor there whether workers were forcibly parted from the difference between that standard and what they actually got. If they were induced by some sort of religious enthusiasm to accept an exploitative bargain, it would still be exploitative. We might, however, expect to find that *most* exploitation was backed by coercion just because ideological blandishments work badly if they have to work on their own. My own view is that Marx is not absolutely clear on this, but that his settled position is that it is the coerced quality of the labour that is objectionable. On any view, we may certainly say that when one man labours unrequited for another, and does not do so voluntarily—that is, when he is not giving his efforts as a gift—the question of injustice is raised. Marx was impressed by the way capitalism's apologists pointed to the contrast between the visibly coercive nature of feudalism and slavery and the contractual nature of capitalism, and to the contrast between the visibly unpaid nature of slave labour or feudal services on the one hand and the paid labour of the worker under capitalism on the other, as the features which make capitalism non-exploitative and intrinsically just. To their apologia, he had two powerful replies. The first is that within slavery and feudalism there was a standard of justice which slavery and feudalism appeared to meet.[13]

The slave-owner was entitled to the product created by the slave because the slave was the property of the owner; there was no more question of the slave having entitlements over the product than of the plough or the spade he wielded having entitlements over the product. Since the slave was the owner's slave, so was the slave's labour, and so was the slave's product. With his functional account of moral ideas, Marx was committed to the thought that in some sense the slave system *had* to have a legitimating theory which allowed it to survive; if slaves more or less met the conditions the theory demanded—were captured in war, were foreigners rather than former citizens, or whatever it might be—the social order could operate smoothly enough. It goes without saying that slaves do not like being slaves; but the point of all theories of justice is to allow us to think that what people do not like doing, they may rightly be compelled to do, if the coercion simply enforces just entitlements. *Mutatis mutandis,* the same story applies to feudalism; the theory of justice required is not one which turns the direct producers into the property of the exploiting classes, but one which depicts them as related in a hierarchical system of mutual obligation and benefit. Once again, there must not be too great a gap between the legitimating theory and the apparent operations of the society; Marx seems to think that this presents few problems until the social system is ripe for dissolution.

A qualification to my denial that Marx holds an absolute standard of justice must now be made. Marx is in no doubt that the standards of right which emerge as slavery gives way to feudalism, and as feudalism gives way to capitalism, are 'higher' standards. He is, in this, a good pupil of Hegel, holding as Hegel did that the perception that 'men as men are free' is one of the achievements of the modern world. This is not, however, because Marx thinks that at the end of the road lies a state

[13] Marx and Engels (1962b) I, 426, 429 (*Wages, Prices and Profit*).

of affairs in which we know what justice really is and finally create a society which realizes justice. At the end of the road lies a society which has left justice behind. To see this, we need to move on to the question of how Marx's account of the operations of a capitalist economic system relates to his ideas about justice and exploitation. The basic elements of the story are the same as before, but their employment is interestingly more complex.

The concept of exploitation features in Marx's second reply to the apologists for the capitalist order; its technical role belongs to Marx's account of the generation of surplus value and thus as part of the explanation of the capitalist's profit, but that account also demolished the apologists' understanding of how the capitalist was entitled to his profit. Marx faced a problem which baffled his predecessors. If the capitalist buys all his inputs at full value, and sells his product at no more than its full value, where does the 'extra' come from that the capitalist can pocket as his profit? That he has to pay the full price for his inputs is guaranteed (on average) by the existence of competitive markets; anyone dissatisfied by his offered price can move elsewhere. By the same token he can ask no more (on average) than the full value of his output. Marx hit on the solution when he decided that what the capitalist bought from the worker was a special kind of commodity, namely 'labour-power'. Labour-power is special because it is the one commodity which, when it enters into production, creates more value than went into its production.[14] 'Labour-power' is the worker's capacity to work, and when the capitalist buys it, what he buys is the right to set the worker to work for whatever time it is the labour contract lasts, and to appropriate whatever value the labour actually done adds to the other inputs.

The question arises whether the worker is 'robbed'. The difficulty is that Marx appears to say both yes and no. The worker certainly does unpaid labour; as Marx insists, only a part of the worker's time is used to repay the cost of his subsistence, the rest going gratuitously to the capitalist. But Marx equally insists that the capitalist acts 'with full right'; the fact that he gets a better deal out of the worker than the worker intends or understands is neither here nor there—any more than it is when you sell me a horse you believe to be ill-tempered and feckless and I turn it into a Derby winner.[15] One way of resolving this apparent contradiction is to beat one's way through Marx's vast *oeuvre* looking for a definitive view. The difficulty with that approach is that it is easy to impugn the status of much of what Marx wrote, and we are still left to decide which texts represent (what would have been) his

[14] Marx (1976) I, 270ff.
[15] Marx (1976) I, 301.

considered position. The other way is to put together what appears to be the most coherent account which is tolerably consistent with what he says over many years; this is what I shall do now.

So, we must revert to the question of how we are to decide on the justice of the process whereby the worker sells his labour-power for its full value—which is, roughly, subsistence wages—but gives surplus value to the capitalist. Bourgeois justice is based on the thought that everyone ought to receive a return equal to his or her contribution; this is the principle of market exchange, that equals exchange for equals, and it displays the kind of equality and impersonality to which bourgeois society aspires.[16] There is no space here to go into the interesting question of how this standard relates to another basis for the capitalist's assertion of a right to his profit, namely his insistence that his capital is *his*, just as the worker's labour-power is the worker's, and whatever happens *after* the bargain is struck makes no difference to the legitimacy of the bargain. Marx certainly takes this claim seriously, as we have seen. The obvious thought is that Marx intends, first, to employ this kind of argument *ad hominem* against socialists who found their socialism on the idea that workers *own* their labour, and second to show how vulnerable capitalism is to an inquiry into its origins. If capitalism began in forcible expropriation, the current generation of capitalists cannot claim that the resources they control really are 'theirs'. If the system began in robbery, it must go on being robbery, just as it would only be an elaborate form of robbery if I stole £50 off you by first seizing your bicycle and then selling it to you for £50.[17] Quite how the attack on the pedigree of current titles of ownership bolts on to the *ad hominem* demonstration of capitalism's injustice is hard to say. For my purposes, it is enough to notice that at least it provides Marx with yet another opportunity to insist that what the workers ultimately want is not justice but the abolition of private property.

'Equals for equals' is a very different standard from that which underpinned slavery and feudalism: under capitalism, 'freedom, equality and Bentham rule'. At the level of exchange, claimed Marx, this principle did, generally and on the whole, govern proceedings. Some employers cheated their workers, paid them with dud coin, made them buy their food in the employer's shop and then watered the milk—but these were exceptions, and the existence of profit did not depend on the existence of crooks. Indeed, magistrates and judges from the same social class as these criminals were perfectly ready to use the law against them. Social stability demanded that most people believe that justice was enforced, and justice had to be enforced to induce that belief.

[16] Marx (1976) I, 280.
[17] Elster (1985) 222–3.

At the level of exchange, where the operations of capitalism were visible to the untutored eye, equals exchanged for equals. There was a known standard, and wages revolved around it. The worker whose employer would not pay the going rate could leave and work elsewhere; the employer could truthfully say that he *could not* pay more than the going rate—if he did, his prices would rise, he would lose his trade, and he would go out of business. There was thus no question of exploitation being a matter of personal wickedness on the part of capitalist employers, a fact Marx insisted on when he explained how capitalists appeared in the pages of *Capital* only as the bearers of capitalist relations.[18] Some capitalists were decent, good-natured men, and some were perfect brutes who abused their wives and children along with their employees and their servants. That was beside the point. The point was that *qua* capitalists they were all locked into the same exploitative relations with their employees, and that their relationship had to be, and was, compatible with bourgeois standards of justice at the surface, unreflective level.

It is important to take this insistence on detaching the question of surface justice from the moral evaluation of individual capitalists at its proper weight. In part, it amounts to nothing more than Marx's reminder that the task of the social scientist is not to judge but to explain—we do not rebuke Odysseus for his superstitions, for he could not be expected to rise above the intellectual level of the age, and we do not rebuke capitalists for behaving as their position in the economy forces them to behave. If it is true that in the usual sense of freedom, capitalists, having more resources than their workers, are therefore much freer than they, it is also true that Marx sees all of them so caught up in the workings of the capitalist economy that he regards it as futile to ask whether the capitalist is 'free' to cease being a capitalist. Marx does not suppose that capitalists wish to injure their workers, and he does not suppose that capitalists have eccentric views about the desirability of overwork, bad housing and bad food; what they suppose, and largely correctly, is that they cannot under capitalism do anything about it.

Marx's impatience with moralizing is more than an insistence on that point. It reflects, if it is not itself an argument for, his holistic view of the social and economic order, both his explanatory holism and his evaluative holism. It is a requirement of capitalist production relations that the transactions which appear as an exchange of wages for work should be compatible with conventional ideas about justice, and however we are to explain the origins and acceptance of the bourgeois conception of justice, its interest for Marx is almost wholly exhausted

[18] Marx (1976) I, 92.

by its role in the system. Marx's interest in justice does not descend to the level of injustices done to or perpetrated by individuals, even though, as the long extracts from the Blue Books and elsewhere in *Capital* make clear, it is the effects of the capitalist system upon individual welfare—overwork, fear, destroyed health, destroyed family life, pervasive misery—that make capitalism repulsive.[19] In explanatory terms, it is the abstract and impersonal nature of the capitalist system which is distinctive. Individual capitalists are but the agents of capital which governs them—more comfortably, to be sure—just as it governs the workers. Marx's thought is exceedingly hard to set down simply, but it is at least that while the systemic properties of the whole society depend upon the thoughts and actions of its individual members, they also confront individual members as an external fact.[20] It is worth writing in terms of 'the capitalist mode of production' only because it is simultaneously a network of individuals interacting according to their own aspirations and beliefs and a system which dictates to those individuals what aspirations and beliefs to adopt.

The heart of the analysis, in Marx's own eyes, lies in the analysis of the productive system. He was full of contempt for economists who distinguished, as Mill did, between the laws of production and the laws of distribution.[21] He was even more full for contempt for 'distributivist' socialists who thought that all the ills of capitalism could be cured by tinkering with distributive mechanisms in the name of 'fairness'.[22] On Marx's account, production determines the distributive system. So, it is not surprising to find that Marx looks for the truth about the exploitation of the labourer in production not distribution. Marx claimed that the surplus was *created* in production, not distribution; it was only realized in exchange. It is not because goods are bought at less than their value or sold at more than their value, but because a surplus appears in the course of production that the capitalist can appropriate a profit. The process is simple enough; the capitalist buys his inputs, including labour-power, then sets them to work; all inputs other than labour-power simply add their existing value to the output. When labour-power, bought at its full exchange value, is turned into labour—which is a use value—the divergence between what goes into the worker's labour-power and what the labourer can add to the product's value appears, and there is the surplus value waiting to be appropriated.[23]

[19] Marx (1976) I, 370–416.

[20] Anthony Giddens's concept of 'structuration' is intended to accommodate this double perspective; see his (1976).

[21] Cohen (1978) 108–11.

[22] Marx and Engels (1962b) II, 21 (*Critique of the Gotha Programme*).

[23] Marx and Engels (1962b) I, 430–1, Marx (1976) I, 268–70.

The merits of this account as an account of the generation of profit are not very great; happily they are no concern of ours here. Three aspects of the account are important, however. In the first place, Marx's account locates the source of profit only in 'living labour'; the great contrast which Marx insists on is that between capital considered as 'dead labour' and the worker's activity, which is 'living labour'.[24] The metaphysical horror of capitalism is that dead labour sets living labour to work; and the worker's efforts go to reinforce the power of dead labour over himself. The driving force of capitalism, says Marx, is capital accumulation; dead labour demands constant additions to its strength, and neither the worker nor the capitalist can resist it. This is in part a matter of imagery and rhetoric, but it is important imagery and rhetoric, since it is the natural embodiment of Marx's sociological perspective on the capitalist economy. What Marx says is that capital itself appears like a vampire, death in life, sucking the life blood of its victims. The sociological holism of his explanatory theory generates an evaluative (but not a moral) holism, for the implication is that capitalist society is 'inverted' and the curious combination of slavery and freedom embodied in capitalism results in a society where the absolute freedom of everyone to buy and sell in the market is at the same time the enslavement of everyone by an impersonal, even a dead, force.

A second and equally important, if less dramatic, feature of the argument is that it shows how Marx can both assert and deny that capitalist exploitation is consistent with justice. In buying labour-power the capitalist does not violate the rule of 'equals for equals'; in *using* labour-power, he does.[25] 'Robbery' does take place, but it does not take place where any previous critic had thought it took place. This, incidentally, is one reason why Cohen cannot be quite right in arguing that Marx's theory of exploitation can be detached from the labour theory of value.[26] Under capitalism the surplus exists only as surplus *value*. With rents in kind, forced labour, or the ownership of slaves the workers' forced contributions to the wealth of the exploiting classes is based directly on the products of their labour, but capitalist exploitation only works at all because the way in which it works is veiled by its expression as the appropriation of value rather than things. It is none the less true for Marx that exploitation is always the same thing, namely the forced performance of unrequited labour. But, Marx's contrast between what goes on visibly in exchange and invisibly in production now shows why there is no straightforward answer to the question whether capitalism is unjust; the elaborate but only satisfactory answer

[24] Marx (1976) I (appendix), 1006–8.
[25] Marx and Engels (1962b) I, 429.
[26] Cohen (1978/9).

is that capitalism is in contradiction with itself, forced to produce in ways that violate the principle of justice which it is simultaneously forced to profess.

It must be noted that Marx is not as some commentators have thought, arguing that capitalism is just by its own lights and unjust by socialist lights. In so far as capitalism is unjust, it is unjust by capitalism's own lights, not by some socialist standard of justice. Indeed, there are no socialist standards of justice. For the third thing to observe about Marx's analysis of exploitation in the production process is that it leads on very naturally to what he says in the *Critique of the Gotha Programme* about the fatuities of the Lassalleans and the true contrast between capitalism and socialism.

The Lassalleans had demanded a fair day's pay for a fair day's work, and had propped this demand up with the claim that since labour was the only source of value, the labourers were the only people entitled to share in it.[27] Marx regarded this as utter nonsense; the value of whatever is produced depends on much more than the labour that goes into it, and, in any case under any system of production the total product will have all sorts of claims on it—for depreciation, research, new investment, and the education of those too young to work and those too old or too ill to work. To suppose that 'the whole product of labour' is there to be consumed at will by the labourers is completely absurd. Moreover, appeals to a fair day's wages compound the folly by supposing that there could be such a thing as fair wages; the only rational demand is for the abolition of wages. And it is to this that Marx turns his attention.

In doing so, he makes his famous distinction between the lower and the higher stages of socialism, arguing that under 'stage one' of socialism, 'bourgeois standards of right' will prevail in the sense that what workers receive will vary according to their contribution to the social product; only under 'stage two' will society be governed by the principle 'from each according to his ability, to each according to his needs'. The interesting issue concerns the status of stage one. In stage one workers are paid in proportion to their contribution; and at this stage, we find that exploitation ceases and (bourgeois) justice is achieved. For, in the absence of capitalists, nobody can take off an income simply because he happens to own the means of production; the workers as a whole get the whole product—over a lifetime, of course, not in the wage packet each week. For, between what they get through the social wage—education, pensions, sick pay and so on—and their ordinary

[27] Marx and Engels (1962b) II, 18–20.

wages, they get everything there is to be had. That is one purpose of getting rid of the capitalists.[28]

But as between one individual and another, justice requires that those who contribute more should receive more. As Marx says repeatedly, equal right creates unequal results;[29] returning what is contributed means that those who contribute more get more. Thus, over a lifetime, the more productive receive more than the less productive, though neither loses anything to the unproductive classes who have now been expropriated. Marx plainly regards this stage as a second best; so do writers such as Roemer and Elster who are committed to 'individualist' accounts of justice and might therefore be expected to regard it as the end of the road to justice. In fact, all three concur in their scepticism about the idea that greater contributions *entitle* those who make them to greater rewards. Elster and Roemer are partly motivated by scepticism about the whole idea of desert, partly by the thought that those who do the most productive work frequently have the most interesting occupations and therefore hardly need added reward. Marx does not go into details, but seems to hold something of the same view as Rawls—that desert may well be illusory, but that differential rewards are an economic necessity. It is worth stressing that it is only because of economic necessity that 'bourgeois' justice still gets a look in.

After that stage, we reach the end of the road. Here, on my view, there is no justice, because there are no rights. There is, however, a principle distributing work and resources, the famous principle of 'from each according to his capacity, to each according to his need'. This is not a principle of justice in Marx's eyes—and mine—because it does not ground claims of *right*. There is no question of its imposition on the members of the communist society; there is no question of anyone being forced to work on these terms. Not only is it not a principle of justice, it is not a moral principle at all. It will be understood by everyone, not as a moral principle but as a practical or rational principle. It does not have the mystified standing of what are nowadays passed off as moral principles; that is, people who adopt that principle will understand that they have chosen it because it expresses the way of life they wish to live, not because it is a 'dictate of morality'.

Sceptics will not wish to take my word for it that this is Marx's view. They may be persuaded if they consider what Marx says in his early *Critique of Hegel's Philosophy of Right*. In that essay, Marx defends two views, the first that Hegel is quite wrong to suppose that the modern state is a rationalized constitutional monarchy, the second that a truly

[28] Marx and Engels (1962b) II, 22–3.
[29] Marx and Engels (1962b) II, 24.

democratic society would abolish the state entirely. The status of this second claim is exceedingly unclear, but there seem to be two elements in it, the first that there would be no distinctively 'political' institutions in such a society, the second that social decisions would not issue in 'law'. These two thoughts are connected; Marx thought that republican theory, as found in writers like Rousseau, emphasized the public-spirited role of the citizen, and the general-interest directed nature of the state precisely because the actuality of bourgeois society was competitive, individualistic, and directed at private interests only. The Rousseauist state had to be simultaneously a moral ideal and a repressive reality, because it demanded the sacrifice of men's real interests for the sake of imposing an external order on the war of all against all which raged in civil society. Paradoxically, Marx came to think that there was a hidden harmony to be elicited in capitalist society—production was co-operative and social—even though he held as strongly as anyone that in practice bourgeois society was riven with conflict. This allowed him to think of the institutions of a socialist society as so to speak emanations of the collective life of that society, not as something imposed in the name of a political morality. That rational institutions *are* such emanations was something else he learned from Hegel; as a very young man he seems to have thought that law might be this even in his own Prussia. Thereafter, he held the view we always associate with his name—the view that law is essentially coercive and class-interested, but a society free of conflict would have rules which were non-coercive, and by our present standards not really 'rules' at all.

An illustration is his treatment of representation. Real representation is a matter of real needs; so the butcher and the baker are my real representatives, they mediate between myself and nature. Political representation is illusory; there cannot be any such process as that of licensing another person to bear my moral or political will and commit me against my actual empirical will. There can, and under any conceivable scheme would have to be, some way of delegating decision-making. The authority such decision-makers would have is not moral or political authority. It is, so to speak, only as much authority as the facts and our wishes between them will generate. It would be a *practical* matter, and their authority would be in the same sense only a practical authority. They would serve my need to delegate decision-making in the same way the butcher and the baker serve my need to delegate the process of getting food.

Critics of Marx have often mocked his apparent belief in the possibility of a society in which there was simultaneously absolute freedom of choice for every individual and absolute unanimity in collective decision-making. It is certainly true that he offers not even a sketch of the decision-making process by which the freedom of each was to be reconciled with the decisiveness of all. It is equally true that he owed his readers some account of the process, since it is plain that the two chief planks in his account of socialism are its concern for individual freedom and its commitment to a form of economic rationality which transcended the 'anarchy of production'. I do not have anything to add to this argument, save for a suggestion about the proper framework for its conduct. That framework is holistic and historicist, and is roughly as follows. Like Hegel, Marx sees history culminating in freedom and reason; capitalism is in some ways the most perverse of social and economic orders just because it offers so much liberty in the sense of *laissez-faire* and demands so much rationality in the sense of means-end calculation and yet operates under the sway of blind necessity. It is this latter fact which is decisive. Marx contrasts what one might call our mastery of nature with the social system's mastery of us. This is Marx's naturalized version of the Hegelian notion of alienation, and it is what underlies the Marxian conception of freedom. It is a concept which only makes sense in a holistic context, one in which the subject of history is the human species; the mechanisms of alienation are capable of reconstruction in individualist terms, however, and the species' misfortunes fall, of course, upon individual human beings.[30]

At this point it is possible to put the argument together. The horrors of capitalism are, of course, horrors—misery, overwork, ill-health; they are not, however, moral horrors. That is, they are not be laid at the door of anyone's wickedness or misbehaviour, and they lead to no conclusions about who is to blame. Nobody is guilty of the crime of constructing capitalism. They are, so to speak, natural disasters like cancer or consumption, plainly disastrous but not the results of wickedness. This is wholly consilient with the view that we are the victims of capital, not masters of our productive abilities; it is also consilient with the view that freedom and necessity are compatible where the necessity is that of the natural connection between means and end—and that they are not compatible when the contrast is between being constrained by needs you would rather not have as opposed to needs which stem from goals you choose. In saying this, I am not conceding that Marx does after all have a moral view, one founded on freedom. It is not a moral view; freedom is not an ideal, and we are not morally obliged to seek it. Like freedom from ill health, it is a natural good and its pursuit is a practical, not a moral imperative. This is not to say that *very* much hangs on whether we follow my view or that put forward in Lukes's *Marxism and Morality;* I do, however, think that my view has the advantage of lining up more exactly with what Marx said and with what

[30] Marx (1975) 189.

motivated him. Against Lukes, my reading makes it more intelligible that Marx should insist so vigorously that the communists preach no ideals.[31] It also makes Marx an interesting precursor of, for instance, Bernard Williams. Like Williams, Marx denies the existence of specifically and specially *moral* considerations; though he does it in different terms, he also—following Hegel—sees the difference between Greek, or more specifically Aristotelian, ethics and modern forms of ethical thinking in the impact of non-teleological natural science and in a resulting ability to analyse the judgments made with so-called 'thick' concepts into a descriptive and an evaluative component.[32] What Marx adds is a sociological hypothesis about why we have the mystified concept of 'morality'—I readily concede that what Marx omits is a careful account of where the boundaries lie between 'moral' and non-'moral' evaluation.

Is it worth insisting on the extreme position I have been pursuing? It is not a question to which a wholly conclusive answer can be given, but there are some considerations I find very persuasive. It might be said that Marx leaves open exactly what Bernard Williams leaves open, namely, the debating of alternative conceptions of the good life, 'ethics' if not 'morality'. This, however, cuts across two distinctively Marxian concerns. In the first place, although Marx was avowedly attracted to the Greek world in something of the same way that Schiller was, he was insistent that mankind had grown out of that stage of life. If we try to say that Marx had an 'Aristotelian' conception of ethics as opposed to a Kantian conception of morality, we have to acknowledge that Marx himself would have insisted that in the modern world one could not be an Aristotelian without qualification. In the second place, Marx's concept of the practical goes beyond Aristotle in supposing that we might conflate *all* separate forms of assessment in the one category of the practical. Critics of Marx as well as enthusiasts for the intellectual bravado with which he conducts his case will surely wish to emphasize the divergence of his case from common sense as well as from Aristotle.

Similarly, it might be argued that Marx's insistence on the need to move beyond assessments of justice and rights makes him some sort of a utilitarian. Here again, I think Marx's insistence that decision-making under socialism would not issue in rules, would not involve concepts such as blame, would not rely on inner sanctions such as the conscience pulls him so far away from moral theory as ordinarily understood that we do better both in terms of moral theory and in terms of an accurate grasp of intellectual history, to emphasize the difference between Marx's enterprise and anything more orthodox. Indeed, I think we

[31] Marx and Engels (1965) 47.
[32] Williams (1985) 143–5.

ought to side not only with Bernard Williams's sharp contrast between morality and ethics but with Geoffrey Warnock's earlier insistence that it is intellectually coherent to deny the claims of morality, and that writers such as Nietzsche did so.[33] On my reading, Marx did not do that; rather he bracketed the claims of morality and went on to characterize capitalism and its alternatives in different terms. That leaves it an open question whether he was wholly wise to do so; I hope I have suggested that he was not, but I should emphasize that I have certainly produced no conclusive arguments against his enterprise.

One last point needs to be made. There is one sense in which Marx might be said to have an ethic. The imperative to rise up and overthrow capitalism is a practical, not a moral imperative. Nonetheless, if it is to be followed, there are various qualities of mind and character which men must possess if they are to do it. The sick patient who is either cowardly or self-deceived may in a sort of way know that he must have a painful operation or submit to a disciplined course of medical treatment, but he will not be able to bring himself to do it, or will always find some half-believed reason for not doing so. So with the proletariat; what it needs above all else is a combination of intelligence, vitality and courage. Sentimentality and self-indulgence will do no good—as Marx told Weitling with some heat as far back as 1846.[34] These are what one might call military virtues; they are, again, instrumental rather than moral, but no harm is done by calling them virtues. As always with Marx, and with many other thinkers for that matter, there is some question whether he does not in fact value the qualities of cis-revolution man so highly that he really has less enthusiasm for the trans-revolutionary than he claims to have. Anyone who has spent any time in an art gallery will remember the contrast between many artists' detailed and enthusiastic treatment of this world and the inferno on the one hand and their insipid depictions of what purports to be paradise. That, however, is another topic and one which would take us very far from the narrower topics of this paper.[35]

[33] Warnock (1971).

[34] McLellan (1973) 157.

[35] I am indebted for discussion to Onora O'Neill, Stephen Clark and the other participants at the Royal Institute of Philosophy Conference in Belfast, also to Steven Lukes, Jenifer Hochschild and Jim Griffin, and to the Balliol Cerberus Society and the Politics Department at Princeton University. From the vast literature on all aspects of Marx and Marxism I would single out as particularly helpful Buchanan (1982), Elster (1985), Roemer (1982) and (1986), Lukes (1985) and Wood (1981).

Acting According to Conscience

DESMOND M. CLARKE

We have inherited from the history of moral philosophy two very different proposals about how we ought to behave.[1] According to one view, we are required to do what is morally right; on the alternative formulation, we are required to do what we believe to be morally right. Unless these twin demands on our moral decision-making can be made to coincide by definition, it is inevitable that in some cases our beliefs about what is morally right may be mistaken. In such cases, it is not clear what we are morally required to do. Are we obliged to follow our conscience in every situation, i.e. to act according to our moral beliefs, or is it sometimes permissible not to act according to our own moral beliefs?

If we are never allowed to reject our moral evaluation of an action without incurring moral fault, it seems as if we are providing a philosophical justification for fanaticism; on this view, each person would be obliged to do what he believes he ought to do, no matter how mistaken his beliefs may be, and he would be held morally blameworthy if he failed to act as he believed he ought. On the other hand, if it is permissible not to follow our moral beliefs in action, there is a complementary danger of undermining the effectiveness of moral beliefs in guiding human behaviour to the extent that, for any particular moral conviction we may hold, we may always wonder whether we should implement that belief in practice or suspend action while we reconsider our moral duties.

As already mentioned, the choice between what the moral law requires and what our beliefs about the moral law require has a lengthy history. For example, Aquinas discussed the question of following an erroneous conscience or acting according to mistaken moral beliefs in the *Summa Theologiae*, where he came to the conclusion that conscience is always binding, even in the case of an agent who is mistaken about the morality of a given action. 'We should state quite simply that every act of will against reason, whether in the right or in the wrong, is always bad.'[2] In other words, when our moral evaluation of a proposed

[1] The problem goes back at least to Aristotle's ethics. See Aristotle (1915) E1, 1129b. (I owe this reference to J. D. G. Evans, who discusses the text briefly in his (1977) 87.)

[2] Aquinas (1966) 63 (IaIIae, q. 19, art. 5).

action concludes that it is right, then we ought to do it; and if we conclude that it is wrong, then we ought not to do it. It is always morally wrong to act against our own moral judgment.

This discussion in the *Summa* has been traditionally understood to mean that an agent has a moral obligation to follow his conscience even when it is mistaken, as long as the agent is not aware that his conscience is mistaken. John Finnis seems to have adopted this standard interpretation and made it a part of his theory of natural law, when he says that

> One should not do what one judges or thinks or 'feels'-all-in-all should not be done. . . . If one chooses to do what one judges to be in the last analysis unreasonable, or if one chooses not to do what one judges to be in the last analysis required by reason, then one's choice is unreasonable (wrongful), however erroneous one's judgments of conscience may happen to be . . . Practical reasonableness is . . . an aspect of personal full-being, to be respected . . . in every act as well as 'over-all'—whatever the consequences.[3]

The final phrase here, 'whatever the consequences', suggests that this rule is not subject to review even if extremely unacceptable consequences result for the agent or for others who are likely to be affected by his proposed action. Following one's conscience takes priority over other possibly conflicting sources of moral guidance.[4]

Before considering the various options available to the moral agent, it may help the subsequent discussion to give an example from one of the traditional sources of the debate of an erroneous conscience at work. Aquinas uses the example of someone who makes a morally wrong decision as a result of his ignorance of a relevant fact, where the ignorance (in Aquinas' view) is not blameworthy:

> Say that an erring reason tells a man that he ought to seek intercourse with another man's wife, then his will consenting so to act will be bad, for the fault arises from ignorance of a law of God he ought to recognize. But say the mistake lies in his imagining that the appealing woman who lies with him is his wife, then his willingness to have intercourse is exempt from evil, since his mistake arises from ignorance of a circumstance which excuses and renders his act involuntary.[5]

[3] Finnis (1980) 125–6. See also D'Arcy (1961) for a full exposition of Aquinas' theory of conscience.

[4] Finnis (1980) 133 (note V.9) recognizes that it would be reasonable for the agent to reject his own moral evaluation of a proposed course of action and to 'bow to contrary advice or instructions or norms', if he were aware of having formed his practical judgment 'inadequately'.

[5] Aquinas (1966) 67 (IaIIae, q. 19, art. 6).

On first reading it looks as if Aquinas thinks it is easier to be ignorant of the identity of one's spouse than of what the law of God requires, and that the former ignorance is involuntary whereas the latter is not! The text might be charitably understood so that it is concerned, not with a false belief about the identity of one's sexual partner, but with a false belief about the legal status of someone whose identity is well known. Thus it is possible to believe mistakenly—on the basis of having gone through a marriage ceremony and having had a family with one's sexual partner—that one is married, whereas for reasons unknown to either partner the marriage is null and void. If understood in this way, Aquinas' example suggests that it is morally good for a man to have sexual relations with someone whom he mistakenly believes to be his wife, even though it is morally wrong for the same man to have marital relations with someone who is not his wife (the same lady in each case).

Thus, if the action of having sexual relations with a particular person is modestly described as *R*, and the indulgent husband is called *H*, Aquinas' moral theory implies two inconsistent conclusions:

(1) It is morally wrong for *H* to *R*

and

(2) It is not morally wrong for *H* to *R*.

This type of inconsistency is not a logical inconsistency in the original theory. It is closer to what Bernard Williams called a 'moral conflict', when inconsistency in moral beliefs is generated as a result of a false factual belief.[6] In Williams' terminology, a pair of beliefs may be said to conflict if they are logically consistent and if there is a true factual belief which, when added to the original pair, will make them inconsistent.[7] In a similar way, Aquinas' moral theory implies that it is wrong to have sexual relations with someone who is not one's spouse, and it is morally right to follow one's conscience. These are consistent beliefs. However, if the relevant agent has a false factual belief about the legal status of his sexual partner, Aquinas' theory implies that it is morally right—and also that it is not morally right—to have sexual relations with a given individual. Since Aquinas cannot consistently endorse both conclusions, he chooses the opinion which favours the individual's conscience and says, in effect, that the agent is morally right in following his mistaken moral belief.[8]

[6] Williams (1973).

[7] Williams (1973) 167.

[8] Brenda Cohen (1967) discusses the inconsistency involved in claiming that some action is morally wrong and, at the same time, that it is morally right for others to act in that way. (I am grateful to Jim Brown for bringing this and other relevant material to my attention.)

This brings the discussion quickly to the main point at issue. What does Aquinas or Finnis mean by 'following one's conscience'? And in cases where the deliberations of an individual's conscience conflict with the moral law, why do they endorse one of the conflicting pair of moral beliefs (the one favouring the individual's conscience) rather than the other? Why grant supremacy to conscience as a general rule?

First, what is meant by following conscience or acting according to conscience? The standard example of not following one's conscience is where an agent believes that something is morally wrong and, despite that, decides to do it or, believing himself obliged to do something, he decides not to do it. It is important to acknowledge that failure to follow one's conscience in both of these ways is not only possible, but is presumably an everyday occurrence in the lives of many people. Otherwise there is a temptation to claim that it is not possible not to follow one's conscience, that acting according to conscience is tautologically necessary in the sense that whatever one eventually decides to do—possibly after many considerations and changes of mind—is precisely what is meant by conscience, so that an agent (by definition) always follows his conscience. We can avoid this kind of conclusion by distinguishing between what an agent decides to do and what he decides it is morally right to do. This distinction can apply in the case of specific actions; and conscience is the judgment of a particular individual about the *morality* of a specific action, or the belief of an agent (at a particular time) about the morality of a particular action. Thus an agent should be said to be 'following conscience' when his actions coincide with his moral evaluations of various proposed actions.

As long as an agent's moral evaluations coincide with those implied by our preferred moral theory, it is left unclear why we describe his corresponding actions as morally good or evil; it may be because, by following conscience, he also happens to do what the moral law (in our estimation) requires and by not following conscience, he fails to do what the moral law requires. Aquinas opens up, but only slightly, this neat coincidence between the moral law and the moral judgment of individual agents by considering the case of an agent who believes mistakenly that a certain action is morally right and who is not aware of any reason to believe otherwise. There is obviously no conflict within such an agent's beliefs. He believes that he ought to do something and then proceeds to do it. But what about those who know (or merely believe) otherwise? For those who believe that the agent in question ought not to act as he proposes, what should they say about the morality of his behaviour?

Aquinas apparently thinks that there is no serious problem here, and he might resolve the apparent conflict by saying: objectively, the agent has one obligation, but subjectively he has another. However, the agent should follow the subjective interpretation of his duties. This assumes that both the prospective agent and those describing his behaviour agree on what is required by the moral law. Indeed, Aquinas seems to think that one could not be involuntarily ignorant of what the moral law requires in serious cases, so that any mistaken beliefs about its requirements would involve moral fault in the agent. At the same time, Aquinas could hardly demand that fallible human beings should never hold false factual beliefs which might compromise their implementation of the moral law. Hence problems about erroneous consciences are of limited significance for Aquinas. They are confined to cases where the implementation of an objective moral principle is compromised by a false factual belief; for Aquinas, one could never be mistaken inculpably about the immorality of something which Aquinas regards as intrinsically immoral.

One can complicate Aquinas' example further and open up a bigger gap between individual conscience and the so-called moral law in two ways: by allowing agents to be inculpably ignorant of the moral law or, even more seriously, by allowing rational agents to disagree about the 'objective' morality of fundamental issues. We then have the following situation.

A moral theory *T* implies that doing *A* is wrong. But the agent *P* does not agree, not simply because of mistaken factual beliefs on his part which are relevant to applying the relevant moral principles, but because he does not even accept the general principles on the basis of which *T* implies that *A* is wrong. In this case, what does *T* say about *P*'s proposed action? We might even imagine a conversation in which a proponent of *T* encounters a dissident agent who openly plans to do what *T* says he ought not do. Should the proponent of *T* talk as follows: 'I believe that *A* is wrong and that you should not do *A*. However, I realize that after due deliberation you have come to the conclusion that you ought to do *A*. In the light of this, I think you should do *A*.' This makes moral disagreement impossible. It could be translated into a general principle to the effect that, according to any moral theory, a particular action is wrong unless an agent believes (mistakenly) that it is right; in that case, it would be morally right for that agent to act according to his own moral beliefs.

H. A. Prichard considers an example like this in his essay on 'Duty and Ignorance of Fact',[9] where he takes the case of an agent who is convinced that he ought to torture heretics for their spiritual benefit. Prichard comments:

> . . . Provided the would-be torturer remained, in spite of all we had said, in a very high degree confident that torturing, and torturing

[9] Prichard (1966).

> only, would save the heretic, he would be bound to inflict the torture. No doubt we also think that we should take steps to prevent him; but here there is no inconsistency. And in fact we not infrequently think ourselves bound to do some action which will prevent someone else doing something *which he is bound to do*. Indeed, if this were not so, few would fight conscientiously for their country [italics added].[10]

There is no inconsistency in the torturer's beliefs, but there is something wrong with our beliefs if we describe the torturer as being bound morally to do something which we believe he ought not to do. This is the conclusion to which Prichard is driven by his argument. He believes that torturing is immoral, that the agent in question is morally obliged not to torture the heretic but, because of the agent's moral beliefs, that he is also morally 'bound to inflict the torture'. This is the same kind of moral conflict which emerged from Aquinas' text.

Thus both Aquinas and Prichard, despite the difference in the reasons offered by each, are equally committed to saying that an agent is morally obliged to do what he thinks he ought to do; both are therefore unable to avoid describing the agent who is genuinely mistaken about a moral issue as being morally obliged to do what he ought not to do. If this conclusion is unacceptable, as I assume it is, it may be possible to find an alternative resolution of the dilemma which gives rise to this unpalatable conclusion, by examining the reasons offered for endorsing the agent's conscience over the demands of our moral theory. Prichard addresses the issue directly as follows: 'If a man has an obligation . . . to do some action, does the obligation depend on certain characteristics of the situation in which he is, or on certain characteristics of his thought about the situation?'[11] If our duties depend on objective features of the situation in which we find ourselves, since we are sometimes incapable of knowing (with adequate certainty) what these are, especially when the knowledge required involves making predictions about the likely consequences of our actions, it follows that we might have duties which we are incapable of discovering. 'Indeed . . . we are driven to the extreme conclusion that, although we may have duties, we cannot know but can only believe that we have; and therefore we are even rendered uncertain whether we, or anyone else, has ever had, or will ever have, a duty.'[12] The extreme conclusion follows, for Prichard, from his claimed inability ever to know that any action he takes could be guaranteed to have the effect which he intends; and if his duty is defined in terms of bringing about a certain effect (rather than attempting to do what he

[10] Prichard (1966) 56.
[11] Prichard (1966) 41.
[12] Prichard (1966) 48.

believes he ought to do), he can never be sure whether he has a duty to perform one action rather than another because of the unpredictability of the results of his efforts. The rest of the argument is straightforward. Since we cannot have a duty to do the impossible, and since it is impossible for us to know what our 'objective' duties are, it follows that we cannot be obliged to perform so-called objective duties. We can only be obliged morally to do what we believe we ought to do.

Unfortunately, Prichard's analysis leads to the conclusion already quoted about the moral obligations of the misinformed torturer: it leads Prichard to claim that the would-be torturer is morally obliged to do what he ought not to do. This inconsistency in Prichard's description of the torturer's moral status is even less acceptable than the apparent implications of what he calls the objective view. If we have to choose between these two options it may be more promising to reconsider the difficulties in the so-called objective view and to see if it could be amended to avoid what Prichard calls the extreme conclusion of never being in a position to know what one's duties are.

This reconsideration can be approached in two stages. In the first place, it is not clear what is wrong with saying that we may have some duties of which we are unaware and that, as a result, we are not able to perform them. The apparent strangeness of this implication derives from the connotations of blameworthiness which are associated with the term 'duty', and which are much less evident if our duties are expressed in terms of what it is good (morally) to do. Thus, there is nothing immediately odd about saying that there are some things which it would be good to do but I am not in a position to identify them. While it may be odd to blame an agent for not doing what he could not know he ought to have done, there is nothing odd about claiming that it would have been good had he done something which he was not in a position to identify as his duty.

Thus Prichard's conclusion can only be sustained if he can show that we are *never* in a position to know what our duties are. However, this part of the argument is not adequately supported by the sceptical doubts about our ability to know the likely effects of our behaviour. While we may not be able to know with certainty what will happen as a result of each of our directly caused actions, there is nothing paradoxical in saying that we have a duty to do or refrain from doing certain things because of their usual consequences. Our moral duties are not specified with respect to the unpredictable consequences of action tokens (which cannot be known), but with respect to types of actions the normal consequences of which are known with enough certainty to warrant commending or forbidding them. The second stage in reviewing Prichard's argument, therefore, is to deny the 'extreme conclusion' that we can never know what our duties are because they depend on objective characteristics of particular action tokens. Our moral rules apply directly to certain types of action which should be done or avoided, and it is not required that we be in the impossible position of being able to predict with certainty the unpredictable consequences of particular proposed actions before we are ever justified in acting morally.

This suggests that the arguments against the objective view of duties are not as strong as they might have initially appeared, and that the argument against the subjective view—that it implies that one is morally obliged to do what ought not to be done—is strong enough to justify a reconsideration of the objective view of duties. If this position could be sustained it would force us to change the way in which we describe the moral duties of people other than ourselves. When we find an agent who, in our opinion, is acting immorally we would have to say that he is acting immorally or that he is morally obliged not to act as he does even if he has genuinely held moral beliefs which lead him to conclude that his behaviour is morally acceptable. From our point of view, his moral beliefs are simply mistaken and the behaviour which results from those beliefs is, despite his good intentions, immoral. This modification in our description of other agents would provide a simple, coherent way of describing those who hold (in our opinion!) mistaken moral beliefs; it would involve adopting the opposite view to Aquinas or Prichard, both of whom describe the behaviour of others as dutiful or morally good even when it is against the moral law.

This may restore coherence to our descriptions of the moral obligations of others, but it gives rise to a whole further series of complementary problems when we adopt the first person perspective and try to give corresponding descriptions of our own moral deliberations. It also seems to sharpen the issues which arise in the context of tolerating behaviour in others which, according to this proposal, should be described as immoral.

When I adopt the first person perspective and attempt to identify my moral duties, I can consider the morality of a proposed course of action for a finite amount of time and then I must reach some decision about its moral status. Once I have reached this point, I could apply Aquinas' suggestion and implement my moral belief in practice. Indeed, Aquinas' discussion suggests that I have only two options at this stage: to act as I believe I should (which is morally required), or to fail to implement my moral beliefs in action (which is morally wrong). However, this fails to take account of my fallibility, even in moral matters, and it fails to address a serious problem about the degree of confidence which I am justified in having in my moral views. This point can be made by first considering the case of an agent other than myself, and then applying the same conclusion to my own case by a simple transposition.

If we consider the factual beliefs of an agent *P*, we usually require some appropriate evidential basis or at least some reason to trust *P*'s authority in a particular matter before we would endorse those beliefs. Of course, if we are not being asked to believe them and if his beliefs affect no one else to their detriment, we would probably not be too concerned about what *P* believes. The question of justification arises if we are asked to endorse *P*'s beliefs and, more seriously, if others apart from *P* are likely to be affected by *P*'s holding the beliefs he espouses. Even if we cannot decide what to believe ourselves, the mere fact that others hold contrary beliefs automatically counts against *P*'s beliefs. The two parties cannot both hold true beliefs if they are inconsistent.

In the case of moral beliefs, there is no similarly easy way in which we can argue, *a priori*, that at least one member of a pair of inconsistent moral beliefs must be wrong. Nevertheless, as long as opposing moral beliefs have plausible support, there is clear force in the idea that *P* should be less confident about the status of his moral beliefs when he encounters equally well-founded, different moral views in others.

If we add to these considerations about the justification of moral beliefs the extra qualification that, in some cases, the implementation of one's moral beliefs in action is likely to cause someone else harm, we have serious reasons for doubting some moral beliefs; we have good reasons, in fact, to wonder about the source of the moral confidence which a prospective agent claims to have in his own moral views.

These are the kinds of remarks which are unexceptional when made about others. We should make exactly similar comments about ourselves, and should wonder how it is possible for us to be so confident about our moral views—especially those which impinge on others—when we have no similarly unqualified confidence in our factual beliefs.

The general principle to the effect that I should follow my conscience, right or wrong, suggests that I should make my own moral judgment about issues as best I can and that I am morally obliged to implement these moral judgments in action no matter what the consequences. This seems to be a perfect recipe for fanaticism, because it underpins the individual moral judgment of each agent with a generalized endorsement to the effect that we ought to do what we believe, mistakenly or otherwise, should be done. If this general endorsement of conscience is withdrawn and if we substitute instead the principle that we ought to do what is morally right (rather than what we believe is morally right), then it is possible to find ourselves in the following situation.

> I have considered the morality of *a* and come to the conclusion that it is morally right. On the other hand, I realize that it would cause harm

> to others if I did *a*; I also realize that others hold a contrary moral view, and it is not clear how I can justify the kind of confidence in my own moral judgment which seems to be required in order to reject the moral wisdom of recognized authorities. In the circumstances, it may be better not to do *a*, and I have no way of resolving the matter definitively. So, while I still believe that *a* is morally right, it seems as if I could refrain from doing *a* without incurring moral fault.

Of course this might still be described as following my conscience in the sense that I did what I thought should be done when all the relevant circumstances had been considered. However, there is an interesting sense in which this is also a case of not implementing my moral evaluation of a situation and of repudiating my own moral judgment; in other words, of not following my conscience.

This comes close to challenging the autonomy of moral judgment or, in different terms, the duty of each individual to decide moral matters for himself. There is a logical sense in which it is impossible not to decide moral issues for oneself; even if we accept the guidance of a moral authority, this is still an example of deciding what to believe in moral matters. In this almost trivial sense, anything we decide to do results from our own decision! However, it is also patently obvious that we can decide not to act according to our moral judgments and, as already indicated above, this is a frequent occurrence in the lives of those whom we regard as immoral. The question which emerges at this stage is: whether it is possible, *without moral fault*, not to follow our own moral judgment about a proposed line of action.

From the point of view of others who describe my behaviour or relative to the demands of a particular moral theory, what I ought to do is to do what is morally good. However, from my own point of view as I deliberate within the limited time available for making a decision, it does not resolve the issue nor provide any definite guidance to be told that I should do what is morally good. I have to deliberate and make up my own mind. One of the implications of the earlier part of the discussion is that I can no longer rest content at any stage in my deliberations in the comfortable assurance that, mistaken or otherwise, what I ought to do is to act according to my own moral beliefs; so that, even if it turns out in retrospect that I was mistaken, it was still my duty to have done what I thought I should have done. This provides a little space in which doubts about my own moral judgment may lead me, in some cases, not to implement my moral beliefs.

Even a limited scope for conscientiously not following my own conscience seems to open up the kind of floodgates the fear of which may explain Aquinas' unqualified backing of conscience. If I can decide that *a* is morally evil and, because of my doubts about the judgment, still do *a* with moral impunity; or, less worryingly, if it is possible to come to the conclusion that I ought to do *a* and, for similar reasons, I can fail to do *a* without incurring moral fault, is there not a serious danger that moral rules will become unhinged from human behaviour at precisely that point at which they should be connected, viz. in the judgment of individual moral agents and the application of rules to particular cases? Might it happen that a pervasive lack of confidence in my moral decision-making would effectively reduce the moral life to sceptical pusillanimity so that all efforts to reach difficult moral decisions are undermined by consideration of 'maybe this' and 'maybe that'?

This suggests that there should be three options rather than two available in moral decision-making, and that the scope of the new option, while possibly wider than we might have traditionally wished, does not completely exclude the other two. In Aquinas' schema, as in the deliverances of Kant's pure practical reason, the human agent reaches a moral decision with relative ease and the only two options available, at that stage, are: (a) to act according to one's moral judgment, which is morally required; or (b) to reject one's moral judgment, which is morally wrong. The third option which seems to be required by the complexity of moral decision-making and the limited powers of most fallible intellects is: (c) to reject the conclusion of my own moral deliberations and not follow my moral judgment about a proposed action, and to do this for reasons which are morally commendable. This involves believing that something is morally right (or wrong) and, despite that, not acting accordingly.

This is not an example of making a moral *decision* and not implementing that decision, or (what would be incoherent) deciding not to do what one has decided to do. The logical space required for not following conscience lies between the moral beliefs of the agent and the decisions to act or not act in certain ways. Not following one's conscience occurs when one decides to act in a way which conflicts with one's moral beliefs. The decision not to implement my moral belief in action results from a review of its epistemic status, and also from considerations of the impact on others of acting as I had planned. What makes this an example of acting against my conscience, rather than just changing my mind, is that I may continue to hold the same belief about the morality of what I proposed to do but, in the light of other considerations, not implement it. If this third option were not available, it would appear that I must hold all my moral opinions with a kind of unqualified certainty and clarity which is rarely achieved by fallible agents who are even minimally conscious of the scope for genuine disagreement in moral matters.

Something similar to this moral ambiguity is also relevant in explaining the possibility of being a tolerant person. Any worthwhile theory of tolerance will require that some moral agents refrain from doing what they think ought to be done. The conflicting demands of being faithful to one's conscience and, at the same time, of being respectful of the moral demands of a wider community may not be capable of reconciliation in some cases. But it is important that these be presented as conflicting demands on the conscience of the moral agent, and not be resolved by any general principle which says: 'follow your conscience no matter what the consequences'. Nor is it possible to resolve the moral dilemma involved in tolerating immoral behaviour by describing the tolerant as holding inconsistent beliefs about the morality of a given course of action. It is not possible to believe consistently that an action is morally wrong but that it is morally acceptable for others to act in that way. If I believe that a certain type of action is morally wrong, then I must also believe (if I am to be consistent) that it is wrong for anyone to act in that way. The issue of tolerance only arises when I consider allowing others to do what I regard as morally objectionable.

However, the issues that arise for the tolerant are not quite as acute as those which apply to the moral agent who fails to implement his own moral beliefs. The reason for this is that it does not follow immediately from the fact that I consider some type of action morally reprehensible that I have a corresponding moral obligation to restrain others from acting in that way. I cannot without inconsistency describe as morally good or morally neutral the behaviour of other people which infringes the moral rules which I accept. However, it does not follow that I have a moral obligation to interfere in those of their actions which I describe as immoral. Tolerance involves restraining myself from interfering in their behaviour even when I regard it as immoral. The task of giving reasons for doing this, without exposing myself to the charge of moral cowardice, presents difficulties which are analogous to the reasons I need in order not to follow my own moral beliefs in certain cases.

On all these issues, Aquinas' way out seems to be too simple. It assumes that well-informed agents will not disagree about what the moral law requires, and it also suggests that those cases where the moral beliefs of a particular agent are mistaken can be explained simply in terms of false factual beliefs which are relevant to implementing an agreed moral principle. This model of moral decision-making fails to take account of human fallibility, even in moral matters; more fundamentally, it is totally inadequate to the complexity and ambiguity which are unavoidable features of most decision-making in human affairs in which irreconcilable moral ideals may preclude the possibility of any satisfactory action in a particular set of circumstances.

Apart from the assumption about the ease with which we can reach agreement on important moral issues, the other reason why Aquinas endorses individual conscience at the expense of moral norms seems to depend on a very inclusive understanding of what it means to follow one's conscience. Aquinas' argument is, in brief: 'To maintain this position [i.e. that it is wrong to follow a mistaken conscience] is unreasonable (*irrationabiliter*)'.[13] In a similar way, Finnis argues that it is 'unreasonable . . . if one chooses not to do what one judges to be *in the last analysis* required by reason . . .'.[14] The phrase 'in the last analysis' suggests something like 'when all relevant considerations have been taken into account'. But one of these relevant considerations might be that one's moral judgment differs seriously from that of other reasonable people whom one independently respects, or that one's proposed action would cause serious harm to many people. In those circumstances, one may be justified in rejecting one's personal moral belief in favour of one which avoids causing harm to others.

The kind of issue which is almost emerging at this point concerns our model of what an ideal moral agent looks like. If one supports a very individualistic picture of an autonomous moral agent who makes up his own mind on moral issues and, as a man of principle, 'sticks to his guns' in the face of moral pressure from others in the community to revise his moral opinions, one might encourage the moral resilience of this type of agent with the slogan: 'follow your own conscience'. However this too easily commends for our emulation the behaviour of Cromwell in Ireland, the dutiful torturer of Prichard's example or the single-minded dedication to an evil plan of other social or political reformers who use murder or torture in the pursuit of their misguided objectives.

The alternative image of the moral agent is much less simple. Where it differs from the first image is in the lack of clarity and certainty in the agent who is sorting out his moral beliefs. This may be uncomfortably close to the jesuitical probabilist whom Pascal repudiates in his *Provincial Letters*. There is something immediately attractive about the religious and moral single-mindedness of the Jansenist in contrast with the calculating casuistry of the contrary position; however, there is nothing within the first image to protect it from fanaticism, and any suggestion to the effect that one should always follow conscience no matter what the consequences seems to give an unqualified theoretical support to that position.

The alternative image of the moral agent includes the possibility that one may hold moral beliefs which, for morally acceptable reasons, one

[13] Aquinas (1966) 60 (IaIIae, q. 19, art. 5).
[14] Finnis (1980) 125–6.

chooses not to implement in action, and that one may do this without incurring moral fault.

The extent to which we should blame agents who fail to act according to our concept of the moral law and those who fail to act according to their own moral beliefs is a major issue which is not directly addressed here. As long as we demand that they always act according to their own moral beliefs, even when they are (in our estimation) mistaken, a number of odd results seem to follow. Those who mistakenly believe that some morally right action is wrong and fail to act accordingly would be blamed even though they did something which (in our estimation) is morally right;[15] and those who mistakenly believe that a wrong action is right and who act accordingly would be considered blameless even though (in our estimation) they did the most evil things. If following conscience is always required, the agent himself should say in retrospect that he acted as he ought to have done and that his behaviour was morally commendable. However if we give up the principle that one should always act according to conscience, we could say of the misguided agent that he did wrong; in retrospect, that he should not have acted as he did. Besides, as Williams points out, we should be able to make sense of an agent's regret if he acts as a result of a mistaken moral judgment;[16] and it is difficult to make sense of such agent-regret if there was an unambiguous principle which required him to act as he did.

In summary, the general moral principle which requires agents to act 'according to conscience' may involve a moral theory in describing a particular action by a given agent as both moral and immoral at the same time. It would undermine one of the most important functions of a moral theory if this conflict were resolved by assuming an implicit qualification on every moral rule to the effect that 'one ought (ought not) to do *a*, unless the agent sincerely believes otherwise'. For those who accept a particular moral theory, it is not possible consistently to believe that some action is morally wrong and that other moral agents have a moral duty to act otherwise. This does not resolve the fundamental issues which each agent must face in trying to accommodate his moral autonomy to the moral demands of the community at large. At the same time, the tension between these two is too casually removed when the moral demands of the community include the qualification that, ultimately, each person should follow his own conscience.

Whether or not we should blame those who fail to observe what we regard as morally required is a separate issue. The analogy with the law may help here, in so far as we do not make the legality of actions depend

[15] Cf. Aristotle (1915) H2, 1146a27–31.

[16] Williams (1973) 172ff., and the discussion of agent-regret in his (1981b).

on the beliefs of the agent about their legality. It is not normally accepted that the mistaken belief of an agent about what is legal or illegal will change the way in which his actions will be described in a given jurisdiction. On the other hand, we make provision in the law for blaming people more or less for their failure to observe the requirements of that law. This allows us to say that an action is illegal, but that the agent involved need not be held blameworthy.

In a similar way, we should describe the behaviour of those who act (in our estimation) immorally as immoral behaviour, even in those cases where they believe otherwise. From the point of view of the individual agent who is deliberating about the morality of a proposed action, it is a dangerous exaggeration of the autonomy of moral agents to assume that we have a right or a duty to do what we believe should be done, irrespective of the beliefs of others and despite the consequences for all those who may be affected by our actions.

Leisure

ELIZABETH TELFER

Although the theme of these papers is 'Contemporary Moral Problems' my paper is partly about Aristotelian ideas. I had originally intended to apologize for this, but I find there is no need: many other contributors have found Aristotle to be timelessly relevant, as I myself have.

The Everyday Concept of Leisure

Let me begin by explaining what I take the concept of leisure to be, in ordinary thinking. It is natural to oppose leisure to work, and define it as 'that time when one is not working'. But this would not be appropriate for all senses of 'work': where work is equivalent to effort or struggle or undertaking a demanding task, it is quite compatible with leisure. Thus a person can speak of spending leisure time *working* in the garden or say of a strenuous hill walk 'That was hard work'. The kind of work which is contrasted with leisure is, rather, what is referred to when a person says that *his* work does not leave him much leisure, or that he has now stopped working and is a man of leisure.

We might assume that the sense of 'work' which is to be opposed to leisure is that of 'gainful employment'. But we should not jump to this conclusion, for at least two reasons. First, a housewife or househusband is not regarded as being at leisure when looking after children or other dependants, although he or she is not paid for doing this. Secondly, and conversely, a person can earn money through what is nevertheless called a leisure pursuit: if, for example, his hobby is making something which he then sells, or playing in a band at local functions. Leisure is typically contrasted, then, with work in the sense of 'occupation'—what is mentioned in answer to the question 'What do you do?' when asked of a new acquaintance. But although work in this sense is often contrasted with leisure, it would not be right to say that a person's leisure consists of all the time he does not spend on his occupation: for example, time spent sleeping or getting one's food is not normally regarded as leisure time. The reason seems to be that leisure is concerned with choice and opposed to necessity. Time spent on earning a living, or on eating and sleeping, is not leisure time because it is necessary for subsistence. Again, time spent looking after dependants is not leisure time because it is spent meeting obligations; it is time which one is not free to choose to spend otherwise. Time spent on lucrative hobbies, however, can count as leisure time insofar as they are an optional extra, subsidiary to one's main source of income.

The conceptual connection between choice and leisure is borne out in many familiar ways. One is that the same activity, apparently with the same role in a life, can be regarded as a leisure activity by one person and not by another. Thus one person might describe daily visits to his elderly parents by saying 'I spend quite a lot of my leisure time with my parents', another by saying 'I don't get much leisure—I have to spend a lot of time visiting my parents'. The difference seems to be that the first person regards visits to his parents as something he freely chooses to do, the second as something laid upon him. A second familiar point is that a person can choose to spend extra time and care on preparing and eating meals, or on clothes and toilette, and if he does, these activities can be spoken of as in part leisure activities, as when someone says 'Cooking is one of my hobbies'. (In this sphere, needless to say, an activity which one person or group regards as an extra or pastime, such as baking one's own bread, is regarded by another person or group as a necessity of life.) Thirdly, an activity can cease to be a leisure activity through a change not of attitude but of circumstances: thus a person who earns money by a leisure activity will start to regard it not as part of leisure but as a second job if he begins to need the money to meet financial commitments.

I suggest, then, that the best everyday definition of leisure is: that time which a person can use as he chooses, which is free from necessity and obligation. This definition, however, is by no means unproblematic. For example, it might be objected that on this account anyone who chooses his job, or anyone who chooses to work when he need not, is at leisure when he is at work. The same might be said about looking after one's children whom one chooses to have. To this I think I can reply that a job, paid or not, does not become leisure simply through being chosen initially: this is because a job, once entered upon, usually involves obligations which cannot be avoided at will.

Where an occupation or some aspect of it is *not* structured and leaves scope for individual choice, the usual antithesis between work and leisure breaks down and we can speak of being at leisure in one's work. For example, an artist who is given money by a patron to enable him to practise his art as he sees fit, without any strings, might say 'At last I have the leisure to do good work'. In the same way an academic might say that in the vacation he has the leisure to do 'his own work', meaning the research which he himself chooses to undertake. Conversely, a person who volunteers to take on a demanding job such as the secretaryship of his tennis club might claim that he has less leisure as a result;

quite appropriately, given the highly structured and committing nature of the post, even though it is not only voluntary but also connected with his leisure activities.

Can we say that leisure time is time spent not only as one chooses, but also with pleasure? This is certainly mistaken: a person can derive pleasure from his work and fail to derive pleasure from a holiday, party or game. We might try instead to say that leisure activities are those done *for* pleasure, thus leaving room for the possibility that pleasure may not be obtained. But this seems to be either uninformative or wrong. There is one use of the phrase 'for pleasure' which seems more or less to mean 'as a leisure activity': that is to say, it means 'not as a matter of employment or other necessity'. To say then that leisure activities are carried on 'for pleasure' in this sense of the phrase is not informative. But if it means 'in order to get pleasure', it does not exactly apply to all types of leisure activity: for example, to the person who sets about studying the history of his district because he feels he ought to know about it. It may be, of course, that leisure activities *should* be carried on 'for pleasure' in the sense of 'for the sake of pleasure'. To this question I shall return.

The Problems of Leisure

What are the 'contemporary moral problems' about leisure? We have millions of unemployed, who are sometimes described as having 'enforced leisure'. We are also told that because of increasing automation we will never get back to a state of almost full employment; there will be less and less work to go round, and so (other things being equal) greater and greater leisure, which might be more equally shared out than at present but will continue to increase overall. These situations, actual and possible, raise many questions about leisure. (1) What is the proper place of leisure in life: what is leisure 'for'? How should it be used? (2) What training is appropriate to equip people for leisure? (3) What is the optimum amount of leisure from the point of view of the person whose leisure it is? (4) What is the extent of our *entitlement* to leisure? I shall touch briefly on this fourth question at the end of my paper. The bulk of it will be concerned with a discussion of two possible answers to the first question, each of which implies its own answer to the second and third questions.

It might be objected, however, that my account of the everyday conception of leisure implies that the first question does not make sense; if leisure is the sphere in which there are no obligations, can we speak of using it properly or improperly? The answer is that we can claim that there can be better or worse ways of spending leisure without implying there is an *obligation* to spend it in the better ways: we can for example say that a person's happiness, welfare or self-development is bound up with better ways of spending leisure. Similarly, if society undertakes the task of trying to equip people to spend their leisure well, this need not imply a claim on its part to have the right to *dictate* how people are to spend their leisure; it may rather be an acknowledgement of the duty to foster its citizens' welfare in this respect.

It is true that *one* natural answer to the first question (the answer which is perhaps implied by the scope of what is nowadays known as 'the leisure industry') is that it does not matter how people spend their leisure, so long as they enjoy themselves. But even this minimal answer has some implications. Training for leisure, on this view, is teaching people how to enjoy themselves, which will, if unemployment is going to continue at a high rate, include introducing them to things which they can enjoy doing without needing much money. And the optimum amount of leisure will be the most one can have without ceasing to enjoy it—without getting bored; the enforced leisure of unemployment will therefore be too much leisure for anyone whose training has not equipped him to be able to enjoy it on limited resources (this is not of course the only thing wrong with unemployment).

In what follows, I shall not say more about this 'minimal' or 'pure enjoyment' view of the place of leisure. I shall consider two other views both of which claim in effect that it *does* matter how one's leisure is spent: the *instrumental* view, according to which the proper use of leisure is to enable a person to work, and what I shall call the *Aristotelian* view, according to which the proper use of leisure is the practice of activities worthwhile in themselves. Before I turn to a more detailed discussion of these views, however, I should like to touch on a possible challenge to the common factual assumption which brings questions of leisure into prominence: the assumption that increased automation will bring decreasing employment. It might be said that there is a great deal of work such as caring for the old, the mentally ill, the chronic sick and so on, which will always be available because it cannot be automated, and which is not done adequately at present: why should increased automation not bring about a change in the *type* of employment we take up rather than a decrease in its amount, with a greater proportion of people taking on this kind of work? The answer, I take it, is that in theory this could happen and no doubt it should, but it is not very likely to; partly because society is unwilling to pay for these services. But the existence of these tasks which need doing and which are inadequately done is not without relevance to the theory of leisure, as I shall eventually hope to indicate.

The Instrumental View of the Role of Leisure

According to the instrumental view, leisure has value only insofar as it is useful to the worker, refreshing him and enabling him to continue working. It is work which is of more immediate value: in his work a person develops his rational and creative faculties, strengthens his character through discipline and effort, makes his contribution to the community and establishes his own identity and place in society.

It might seem that if leisure and work are conceived in this way the answers to what I called the second and third questions are clear-cut. Training for leisure will involve learning which kinds of leisure activity are most conducive to good work in various different spheres and being initiated into these activities. It may be, for example, that physical exercise during leisure enables an office worker to sit at a desk for long hours without fatigue, or that drama releases a social worker's bottled-up emotions which would otherwise be vented on irritating but innocent clients. The optimum amount of leisure, on the instrumental view, is that amount which enables a person to do his best work; if he has more than that, he has too much. Moreover, a person who does not work at all (for example, an unemployed person) leads a pointless existence on this view, since leisure has no value apart from work: a general increase in leisure is to be welcomed only if we think people at present have insufficient leisure to enable them to work properly.

But these answers are not as obvious as they seem, because the instrumental view, as stated, rests on a confusion. In opposing work to leisure it seems to be concerned with work as *employment*. But the virtues which it attributes to work belong not to work as employment but to work in different senses (such as 'putting forth effort', 'undertaking a task', 'producing an end-product') which are perfectly compatible with leisure activities, as we saw at the beginning. Moreover, the 'virtues of work' may be *more* evident in some leisure activities than in some jobs. Thus, for example, the possibility of developing one's talents in creation may be very difficult to realize in modern, highly mechanized industry, but a person who makes something in his leisure time can plan the project from start to finish. There is the possibility of character-building in the adoption of demanding projects, such as training for a marathon or building a boat. There is the possibility of contributing to society in very direct ways: for example through political activity or local government. Finally there is the possibility of acquiring through leisure a better kind of identity, one which does more justice to the whole person, than that which relates only to employment. A person's job, unless he is very lucky, relates only to some aspects of his personality, but through his choices in leisure he can redress the balance and acquire a more balanced identity.

If leisure is viewed in this way, as an opportunity for contribution and self-development comparable to employment, a well-spent leisure can be regarded as valuable even by those with a strong conception of the usefulness of work. For the suggestion is in effect that well-spent leisure is leisure spent in voluntary work. Training for leisure, on this 'voluntary work' view, becomes training in 'doing things properly' and in awareness of the possibilities of voluntary services of all kinds, and society can help people to use leisure in this way by providing some of the structure within which these activities take place.

The champions of work might now object that the virtues I am attributing to leisure belong not to leisure as such but only to *well-spent* leisure. This is true, but as I have tried to show the virtues of work do not belong to employment as such either, but only to satisfactory employment. It is true that one's job has to be done, whereas the worthwhile activities of leisure do not. But it does not follow that the qualities making a job *worthwhile* are guaranteed and the qualities making leisure worthwhile are not. The difference is that the quality of leisure, according to the 'voluntary work' account of it, is to a greater degree under the control of the person whose leisure it is than the quality of paid work is under the control of the paid worker. As a matter of contingent fact it may be the case that leisure is often not worthwhile, given that people are weak, lazy and undiscriminating. But this is precisely where training for leisure is relevant.

If we are to give an account of an ideal of leisure in terms of voluntary work, however, careful qualification is needed. The word 'voluntary' here, though it implies 'non-employed', does not simply mean 'unpaid': as we saw earlier, some unpaid work, such as looking after one's children, is essentially *non*-leisurely. Rather 'voluntary' means 'non-obligatory' or 'non-mandatory'. But as we have already seen, a voluntary undertaking which involves a very structured commitment can be seen not as part of leisure but as an encroachment on leisure. There is thus a tension inherent in the 'voluntary work' conception of leisure, a tension which is heightened insofar as this ideal of leisure is looked on as something which people *ought* to pursue: if an ideal approaches obligatoriness, it begins to lose its status as an ideal of *leisure*. The 'voluntary work' conception of leisure, in other words, tends to slide into the view that people should *replace* leisure by voluntary work, an idea to which I shall return at the end of the paper.

A related objection to this 'voluntary work' conception of leisure is that it seems to leave no place for what are after all the activities most closely associated with leisure: games, parties, holidays. But this is only apparently true. These things (I shall use the term 'amusements' to refer collectively to them) will still be needed as refreshments, to enable a person to continue to pursue his worthwhile activities. In other words, just as the employment-relative view of leisure saw leisure as a means to the end of work in the sense of employment, so this more structured and positive view of leisure construes amusements as a necessary means to the successful use of leisure as voluntary work. But insofar as leisure allows more choice and variety than jobs usually do, there may be less need of relief from it.

So far I have considered an instrumental view of leisure, and criticized it on the ground that the values which it attributes to work can also be found in an appropriately spent leisure. This rehabilitation of leisure in terms of 'voluntary work' had the advantage of restoring the possibility of dignity to the lives of those who do not work for pay. But precisely because it makes leisure into voluntary work, it might itself be criticized for losing sight of the *distinctive* value of leisure. Leisure, it might be said, is not an opportunity to work more satisfactorily; it is better than work and is the point of work. Aristotle said 'We work so that we may have leisure',[1] and so I shall call the kind of view of leisure which I shall now put forward the Aristotelian view, without wishing to claim that my account is true to all the details of the *Nicomachean Ethics* and *Politics*.

The Aristotelian View of Leisure[2]

At first sight the notion that we work in order to have leisure seems paradoxical; one wants to retort that we *stop* work in order to have leisure. But the Aristotelian idea is that work is valuable as a means, because it provides the necessities of life and so enables people to have the leisure to carry out those activities which they choose and value for their own sakes. Work, in this context, is not necessarily paid work. The unpaid government official or housewife caring for a family is working to provide the necessities of life although he or she does not get paid. What distinguishes their activity from leisure is that it is valued for its *usefulness*, not that it is paid for: and therefore much of what counts as well-spent leisure on the 'voluntary work' account of leisure would not on the Aristotelian account be leisure at all, because it is activity valued for its usefulness. On the other hand, the Aristotelian view does not imply that all activities which are in fact pursued for their own sakes are rightly so pursued. What I earlier called 'amusements' are regarded as appropriate leisure activities by some people, but Aristotle

[1] Aristotle (1915) 1177b4.

[2] Aristotle discusses leisure, its proper content and its role in life, in (1915) X 7 and 8. Wilkes (1980) discusses the role of contemplation in Aristotle's doctrines.

holds that this is mistaken.[3] Amusements are too childish and unserious to be the point of life, and their proper role is as relaxations to enable us to work again, not as leisure activities valued for their own sakes.

Is this a satisfactory view of leisure? There are two distinct questions here. The first concerns the basic Aristotelian conception of the proper place of leisure in our lives, as that time in which people can do what they think worth doing for its own sake and which is properly spent only if their activities really are worthwhile. The second question concerns the content: what kinds of activity can count as worthwhile in these terms? I shall consider the question of content first and conclude by examining the basic conception.

The Aristotelian conception of the best way to spend leisure is basically an intellectual one, and indeed our words 'school' and 'scholar' derive from the Greek word for leisure. Aristotle derives this conception from a consideration of the function or characteristic activity of mankind: the exercise of reason. For brevity I shall accept without argument the validity of this approach, though clearly there are many difficulties to be raised about it. But Aristotle's own account of the content of an ideal leisure is much narrower than its basis would suggest. The one activity which is regarded as an ideal use of leisure is the *contemplation* of eternal, unchanging, necessary truths; and his main reason for holding this seems to be that this is the only exercise of a human being's distinctive endowment of reason which can be regarded as complete in itself, and not as a means to achieving any goal. We might well be sympathetic to the idea of contemplation as an essential part of leisure but feel there are things worthy of contemplation other than Aristotle's necessary truths, such as great works of art and the wonders and beauties of Nature. We thus arrive at a 'time to stop and stare' conception of ideal leisure, a view which has clear implications about the way to equip people to use leisure well and the need to provide them with the means to do so.

But this conception of leisure may strike us as unsatisfactorily *passive*. Why is it ultimately worthwhile to contemplate ultimate truths but not to discover them? Or to listen to a fine piece of music but not to write one? Aristotle's answer would be that if an activity is productive, it is a means to an end (the discovery, the article produced) and so is not itself ultimately valuable. But this claim involves difficulties, especially as regards leisure activities. If I paint a picture as a leisure activity, I do not necessarily do this in order to have a picture at the end. Very often the end is the means to the means in these cases: I produce a picture in order to spend a day painting, rather than spending the day painting in order to produce the picture. Moreover, the activity of painting is

[3] Aristotle (1915) 1176b9ff.

something which can be valued in abstraction from its result; for example, as an exercise of aesthetic capacities which are as distinctively human as reason. In the same way, the activity of finding out a truth might be seen as an exercise of human reason which is valuable in itself even from an Aristotelian point of view. We can thus expand the Aristotelian view to comprise intellectual and aesthetic activity whether contemplative, investigative or creative.

It might seem that by including productive activities in the content of Aristotelian leisure I have broken down the very distinction between the useful and the non-useful which in this conception marked off work from leisure. But this need not happen if we distinguish (roughly) between the productive and useful. Painting a picture is productive but not useful, because the picture does not fulfil a material need but serves as an object of contemplation; building a house, on the other hand, is *useful*, because the house is needed for human survival. This distinction is only rough, because houses can also be contemplated as works of art and pictures used as tests for eyesight; it has to be regarded as a distinction between common ways of seeing the two pursuits, not between the pursuits as such. But it enables us to preserve a conception of leisure as the proper sphere of the non-useful activities which have intrinsic value.

A second omission from the 'stop and stare' model of leisure concerns personal relationships. Clearly these do not belong only to leisure. But there are activities, such as walking, talking or drinking with friends, of which the main point is that they celebrate or further personal relationships. These activities are certainly carried out for their own sakes, so they are candidates for leisure activities, and they are thought of as typically connected with leisure. I do not propose to embark on a defence of friendship here. But I reckon that I do not need to do this, since no one denies its value: Aristotle's reason for preferring contemplation to friendship seems to be that contemplation is a safer bet because friends can let you down, not that friendship is not valuable in itself.

A third deficiency of the Aristotelian account concerns *pleasure*, which seems to be given less than its due. Are we to say that the activities of ideal leisure are to be pursued because they are noble and enjoyed as a bonus, or pursued because they bring pleasure? Aristotle favours the first alternative. But if we look at what we usually value in the sphere of personal relationships, or in the pursuit of the arts and sciences in leisure, I think we will conclude that it is more nearly right, though perhaps misleading, to say that we value the pursuit of these things for pleasure. What I have in mind is this: if a person says he walks in the country or listens to music or studies archaeology because he thinks it is a worthwhile activity, we are tempted to say that he is missing the very thing that *is* worthwhile in such activities, which involves a spontaneous response to the things in themselves. This is even more obvious with personal relationships: a person who says that he forms friendships because he thinks friendship is worthwhile seems to leave out precisely the response to an individual *as* an individual which is what friendship is. Now to want to perform some particular activity or undergo some particular experience because of its own nature, not because of any principle under which it falls or value which it exemplifies, *is* to want to do it 'simply for pleasure'. Because the phrase 'for pleasure' has connotations of trivial pursuits, we resist it in this context, and prefer phrases like 'for the joy of it'. But the point is the same: pleasure in these ultimately worthwhile activities is not a bonus which is won when they turn out to be enjoyable, but an intrinsic element of their being the activities they are.

If this claim is correct, it has implications about training for leisure. We should not bring people up to think they must pursue the arts and scholarship and personal relationships *because* they are worthwhile, in the sense of being noble, worthy of a human being and so on. Such a policy is self-defeating, because the worthwhileness depends on their not being pursued for that reason, as we have just seen. Rather we must try to bring it about that they do these things simply because they want to, for pleasure, without any particular lofty thoughts about them. If we succeed in this we will have initiated them into activities which are worthwhile as well as pleasant.

I have now completed my sketch of the kind of content which might belong to leisure if it is to play the role of Aristotelian leisure: I suggest that it should be spent in the enjoyed contemplation of truths and beauties, the enjoyment of discovery and creation and the enjoyment of personal relationships. I now turn to a consideration of the general place in life assigned to leisure by the Aristotelian view.

The Role of Leisure in Life

The Aristotelian view of leisure is an attractive one from the point of view of present-day problems of increased leisure. We can say that the more leisure the better, provided people are able to fill it with worthwhile activities; and training people for leisure is initiating them into the kinds of activity which we have just been discussing. We might of course wonder whether everyone is capable of Aristotelian leisure. This might have been a difficulty for Aristotle's own austerely intellectual view of the content of well-spent leisure; but everyone is capable of some form of the kinds of activity which belong to the developed version of Aristotelian leisure sketched in the previous section.

But does such a view demote *work* too much? Suppose a person spends all his spare time on some useful voluntary work, such as Meals on Wheels. From the point of view of the Aristotelian conception, this presumably counts as work rather than leisure. But it seems like a very highly valuable activity, more valuable than many leisure pursuits. Or suppose a person has no leisure but devotes his life to some task, such as famine relief, which is obviously useful; does the Aristotelian conception of leisure mean that such a life is pointless, or make it unintelligible to say that such a person 'lives for his work'? To answer these questions we must look again at the Aristotelian arguments for the place of leisure in life.

The Aristotelian idea seems to be about both the intelligibility and the value of our pursuits. We cannot, says Aristotle, do *everything* for the sake of something else, or chains of means and ends would never stop; there must be some things which a person does simply for the sake of doing them.[4] Moreover, since ends are valued more highly than the means to them, these ultimate ends are the most highly valued things; and (unless *everyone* is wrong) they must include among their number those things which are truly of highest value. Now it might be thought (though I do not think that Aristotle himself argues in this way) that a person who has no leisure, who is always working for the well-being of others, has no activity which he carries out for its own sake; his work for others is done for the sake of a separate result, namely their well-being or happiness. It might seem, then, that his life ultimately lacks meaning and value, at least in comparison with the life of leisure.

But these conclusions do not follow. It is true that we cannot do everything for the sake of something else. But it does not follow that each person must do some things simply for the sake of doing them. For the last members of a person's chains of means and ends, those things for the sake of which ultimately he does everything else and in terms of which his life is intelligible, need not themselves be activities; they can be anything which can be wanted for its own sake. If a person can be said to want others' well-being for its own sake, he can be said to direct all his actions to that end. Thus when Aristotle says 'We work for the sake of leisure' perhaps it need not be one's own leisure for which one works: for example, the politician might dedicate his life to producing a world in which *others* can have leisure.

It is true that on this scheme of life what the politician values for its own sake is the well-being of others, rather than his life's work which brings it about. But he need not conclude that his useful life has *less* value than a leisured life. He might argue, for example, that if many leisured lives can be won through the work of one useful life then that

[4] Aristotle (1915) 1094a18–21.

useful life is worth more than any one leisured life, even though its value ultimately depends on theirs; and this is one way in which we might regard the value of the life of the statesman, the teacher who 'lives for his pupils' or the housewife who 'lives for her family'.

But it is not the only way. We can also value useful lives for their own sakes, if we can see the work done in them not only as useful but also as constituting an example of intrinsically valuable activity; similarly, the liver of the life can treat his work itself as his end in life, if he can view it as one of the kinds of activity which can be so regarded. Consider as an example a teacher who is teaching his class poetry. If he is asked why he does this, he might say 'So that they have something to enjoy in their leisure'. But if he is then asked 'Why do that? Why give them something to enjoy in their leisure?' he can say 'I do it to God's glory' or 'I see it as a duty' or 'I love the children' or 'I find it an intellectual challenge' or 'I find it fun'. Each of these descriptions of a useful activity is a way of depicting it as belonging also to a type of activity which people can practise and value for its own sake: worship, morality, personal relationships, intellectual endeavour, 'amusement' (in our previous sense). Earlier I suggested that productive intellectual activities, such as scientific research or aesthetic creation, can also be regarded as good in themselves, if we abstract from the result and consider the nature of the activity employed; I am now claiming that the same move can be made concerning useful activities.

I contend then that although work, in the sense presupposed by the Aristotelian picture, is useful and has a point and justification which lies beyond it, we can nevertheless understand the motivation of the person who devotes himself to his work, in one of two ways: either he wants the good *results* of his work for their own sakes, or he views his work itself as constituting an example of one or more of the kinds of activity which can be practised for their own sakes. Moreover, we can regard a way of life which is useful as valuable in itself by considering it under an appropriate description. (Of course, it can also happen that a person sees his work as pointless and lives only for his leisure, or that, while *he* values it for its own sake, other people think he sees it in a false light; for example, they may think that what he sees as a duty is not required, or even wrong.)

Now Aristotle himself acknowledges, by implication at least, that useful actions can also be seen as worthwhile in themselves. For the activity of a soldier who saves the city exemplifies the moral virtue of courage, and that of the statesman who governs it exemplifies the virtues of justice and practical wisdom; and he holds that the exercise of moral virtue is valuable in itself.[5] But he does think that activities which

[5] Aristotle (1915) 1176b7.

are not useful and which can be valued only for their own sakes are more valuable than those which are both useful and intrinsically valuable. Is this merely like a kind of snobbish objection to trade? I think we can see Aristotle's point more sympathetically if we link it to some of his claims on behalf of contemplation: that we can carry it out more continuously than we can do anything productive and that the life of contemplation is an unwearied life as far as human beings are capable of this.[6] Now activities which seek results, even if they can also be valued for their own sakes, are by nature *jerky*, shaped by a series of achievements or failures; and they include the conflicts arising from the need to make compromises to achieve a purpose. Pure intellectual contemplation is free from these hindrances. But so is the contemplation of beauty in art or nature; even if an aesthetic experience relates to something extended in time, such as a musical or dramatic performance, the experience itself is not a task, completed when the music or drama is over; we go on thinking about it, reliving it, perhaps repeating it, relating it to other things. Personal relationships, at their best, share this timeless quality; nothing is constructed or produced in them, they flow on inexhaustibly.

It is true that what I called productive leisure activities, such as discovering a new fact or creating a piece of art, are less pure cases of timelessness. But where these are *leisure* activities, where there is no need to fulfil a commission or earn a fee or find a vaccine for an epidemic, they share something of the quality; there is no schedule according to which an amateur painter needs to paint pictures like a housewife making meals, nor is there something which can be finished once and for all.

Timelessness, then, is one quality which Aristotle's contemplation shares with other elements in what I called the developed version of Aristotelian leisure. The other important feature which Aristotle mentions is that contemplation is concerned not with our own petty human needs but with the loftiest possible objects. This claim too can be paralleled by the true leisure activities, in so far as they constitute a quest for Beauty or Knowledge or communion with another End-In-Himself. Of course this sounds like (and is) pretentious *language* in which to speak of quite ordinary pursuits; and of course these things can be pursued in a fettered way through useful activities, as I have already said. But the naturalness of describing true leisure pursuits as 'getting away from everyday trivialities to something that matters' or 'being made to feel the unimportance of all my everyday anxieties' should make us see Aristotle's (admittedly narrower) ideal for leisure as less alien than we are apt to think it is.

[6] Aristotle (1915) 1177b22.

In this discussion of the role of Aristotelian leisure I have tried to do two things. On the one hand, I have sought to raise the standing of work (by which I mean in this context useful activity designed to meet needs) from the low level to which an Aristotelian style of argument might seem to assign it: I have suggested that a person who 'lives for his work' is not leading a pointless existence, and that work as well as leisure can be seen as valuable for its own sake. On the other hand, I have maintained that it is possible to show that the pure leisure activities which belong to my extended content of Aristotelian leisure have a special value which is not shared by the useful activities of work, and which can be understood in contemporary terms.

But are we *entitled* to some leisure of this kind, or is there at all times some useful thing which we morally ought to be doing (when we are not eating, sleeping or taking the amount of relaxation needed to enable us to work)? This moral question will arise for more and more people if the amount of employment continues to decrease. For instead of full employment plus just enough time for necessary relaxation, many people will have rather more time at their disposal, which they can choose either to treat as leisure or to commit to some useful piece of voluntary service, doing one of the tasks mentioned earlier which even in the most automated society will otherwise not get done. Can people claim to be morally *entitled* to the leisure which at last they can have, or must they be useful all the time? And does the answer depend on whether they make 'good' (i.e. Aristotelian) use of their leisure?

These questions are really part of the other huge question, whether morality must allow us some measure of life of our own despite the pressing moral claims of other people. I have no space to discuss this baffling question in general. But I will conclude by commenting in the light of what has already been said on two possible claims to a right to leisure. If it is claimed that we have a right to have the opportunity to practise activities which are worthwhile in themselves, then this claim can be rebutted by showing how useful activities can be seen as also worthwhile in themselves. But if the claim is that we all have a right to escape sometimes from the fret of practicalities and enter a realm of timeless values, then this must be seen as a demand for what I have called Aristotelian leisure.

The Right to Work

BERNARD CULLEN

There is widespread agreement that the most serious and debilitating contemporary social problem in the developed capitalist world is the problem of enforced or involuntary unemployment. The growth in mass unemployment in the 1970s and 80s has produced a renewal of the demand by the labour and trade union movement[1] for the implementation of a 'right to work'; presumably in the belief that the official recognition and legal enforcement of such a right would lead to the increased availability of jobs. This campaigning slogan has sometimes emanated from the most unlikely sources. In his introduction to a published account of the 1971 Upper Clyde Shipbuilders occupation and work-in, entitled *The Right to Work,* Mr Harold Wilson (then, significantly, in opposition) declared that 'what the men of the Clyde proclaimed, and what I went to Clydeside to assert, was "the right to work". And that principle cannot, and must not, be denied.'[2]

The 'principle' of a citizen's positive right to be provided with paid employment was enunciated by Thomas Paine as early as 1792: as one of the 'ways and means' of implementing 'the Rights of Man', he proposed that government should use taxation revenue to provide buildings with 'as many kinds of employment as can be contrived, so that every person who shall come may find something which he or she [*sic*] can do'.[3] The concept of a right to work was popularized by the French socialists at the time of the revolutionary upheavals of 1848. A national Right to Work movement developed in Great Britain in the early years of this century, thrived during the twenties and thirties, again in response to mass unemployment, and came to the fore again in the seventies: there was the Right to Work Campaign and later the epic People's March for Jobs. More recently, the miners' strike of 1984–85

[1] This phrase embraces, in Ireland and Great Britain, the Irish Congress of Trade Unions, the Trades Union Congress, their affiliated unions, the respective Labour Parties and Communist Parties, the British Co-operative Movement, the Fabian Society, and other avowedly socialist parties and sects such as the Workers' Party, the Socialist Workers' Party, and the Militant Tendency.

[2] Buchan (1972) 9–10.

[3] Paine (1969) 268. Paine's visionary social security programme (detailed in Part 2, Chapter 5) still makes very interesting reading.

was called by Mr Arthur Scargill in defence of 'the right to work'. This much is well known to anyone who watches the television news or reads the newspapers.

As well as such public proclamations, 'the right to work' is constantly asserted within the labour and trade union movement as a rallying cry, but I have found that it is very seldom analysed.[4] As a socialist trade unionist concerned to promote the development of a genuinely humanitarian society, my worry is that as long as the assertion of 'the right to work' remains at the level of an unexamined and empty slogan it will serve only to damage, among the population at large, the credibility of socialist economic and social policies in general. For a movement that implicitly leans so heavily on the concept of work and that places its hopes for the creation of a more humane, less aggressive and more caring society primarily on 'the working class', it is little short of scandalous that the concept of work itself has received so little discussion among socialists in recent years—and almost no discussion at all on a philosophical or theoretical level.[5] It is the modest aim of this paper to contribute to the beginnings of such a discussion by focusing on 'the right to work'. I shall consider whether there is such a thing as a right to work (that is, one recognizable in terms of the mainstream philosophical literature on human rights[6]); and if there is, what kind of a right it is, what are the needs that underpin it, what is guaranteed by it, and how steps might be taken towards giving it practical effect.

[4] For example, despite its title Buchan (1972) contains not a word of analysis of 'the right to work'. The author contents himself with asserting, by way of conclusion, that as a result of the work-in '"The Right to Work" is now recognized as a basic human right' (146).

[5] Among the few exceptions see Campbell (1983) 171–92, Attfield (1984), Smart (1985). On the general concept of work there are, of course, the many discussions of Marx's theory of alienated labour.

[6] While I shall use, for the purposes of orientation, what I take to be a generally accepted and relatively uncontroversial topography of rights, I must say that I have every sympathy with Locke (1985) when he says 'I do not really know what a right is, or where it comes from; I find the voluminous literature on the topic almost wholly unrewarding, and the manifold distinctions and divisions of rights, into natural and acquired, positive and negative, active and passive, special and general, claims and liberties, privileges and powers, permissions and entitlements, almost wholly unilluminating' (175). An exception to this general charge is the collection of essays in Pennock & Chapman (1981).

I

Article 23 of the Universal Declaration of Human Rights asserts that 'everyone has the right to work, to free choice of employment, to just and favourable conditions of work and to protection against unemployment'.[7] What does it mean to say that these are 'human rights'? As I understand the concept, human rights (as distinct, for example, from legal or civil rights) are rights which people have, solely by virtue of the ontological fact that they are human rather than belonging to some other kind, to be treated in certain ways or, more usually, *not* to be treated in certain ways. Furthermore, human rights must be, by definition, universal. Indeed, the use of the term 'universal' seems quite tautological in this context, since people have human rights precisely because of their membership of the species, because of some distinguishing characteristic or characteristics which they have in common and which are not shared with other species.[8] Different accounts have been given of what these distinguishing characteristics are that define humanity: for example, all human beings are said to be sentient bearers of rationality; or they are said to be all 'children of God' or 'created in God's likeness'. Whatever the definition proposed, however, it generally admits of no exceptions: no matter how hideous, and indeed how inhuman, the crimes someone (such as Hitler) may have committed, he is still human, according to the kind of definition generally proposed by the human rights theorist, and as such can legitimately claim his human rights.[9]

Thus, for example, because all people are human, Article 3 of the Universal Declaration proclaims *everyone's* human rights 'to life,

[7] See Brownlie (1971) 111.

[8] To say this is not, of course, to deny that other animals have rights—only that they have the same rights as humans.

[9] For a traditional 'natural law' approach to these questions see Maritain (1943). The rights under discussion are the kind of rights that H. L. A. Hart has labelled 'general rights', as distinct from the 'special rights' which arise out of 'special conditions' (see Hart (1955)). Although Hart's 'general rights' have moral priority over any contract or convention, the status of 'person' is not, for him, as universal as it might at first appear. For Hart, general rights can legitimately be claimed not by all human beings, but by 'all men capable of choice'. Another adherent of this will-autonomy theory, Stanley Benn, offers a list of requirements of 'autarchy', defined as 'the condition of being a chooser' (see Benn (1975/6) 116). Campbell (1985) discusses this approach and quite correctly challenges it. Such a restricted view of personhood has serious implications for the rights not just of 'mentally ill persons', but also of children everywhere and of adults debilitated by material deprivations such as acute malnourishment. Going on the harrowing television pictures at the height of the Ethiopian famine, I doubt if many of the thousands of inhabitants of the relief camps would have satisfied Benn's requirements of 'autarchy'.

liberty, and security of person'. These human rights bring with them corollary rights to freedom from interference of various kinds: for example, every person has the right not to be killed, 'no one shall be held in slavery or servitude' (Art. 4), 'no one shall be subjected to torture or to cruel, inhuman or degrading treatment or punishment' (Art. 5), 'no one shall be subjected to arbitrary arrest, detention or exile' (Art. 9), and 'no one shall be subjected to arbitrary interference with his privacy, family, home or correspondence, nor to attacks upon his honour and reputation' (Art. 12).[10] This line of argument provides a much needed defence for every single person, on the basis of our shared humanity, against certain kinds of barbaric treatment at the hands of others, whether individuals, groups, or governments. It declares that certain ways of treating others are simply morally unacceptable, no matter what the presumed gain in utility. Despite the sustained attacks on it in recent years, I find it cogent and convincing.

Can 'the right to work' really be said to be a universal human right in this sense—that is, a right to non-interference of a specific kind, due to every human being by virtue of his or her humanity, at all times and in all places? In fact, it would appear to be quite different, in two ways. First, the right to work, as presented in the Universal Declaration and as interpreted by the labour and trade union movement, does not defend, not directly, at any rate, the right to life, liberty, or security of person. Instead, it demands that a positive benefit actually be provided, to wit, work. This difference corresponds to a distinction between liberty rights and benefit rights, or between rights of non-interference and rights of recipience. Thus, the Universal Declaration proclaims that 'everyone, as a member of society, has the right to social security and is entitled to realization . . . of the economic, social and cultural rights indispensable for his dignity and the free development of his personality' (Art. 22). Among the economic, social and cultural rights considered indispensable for the human dignity of each person are 'the right to work, . . . the right to equal pay for equal work, . . . the right to just and favourable remuneration, . . . the right to form and join trade unions for the protection of his interests' (Art. 23); as well as 'the right to a standard of living adequate for the health and well-being of himself and of his family, including food, clothing, housing and medical care and necessary social services, and the right to security in the event of unemployment, sickness, disability, widowhood, old age or other lack of livelihood in circumstances beyond his control' (Art. 25). With the exception of the right to form and join trade unions (that is, the right not to be *prevented* from forming and joining trade

[10] Brownlie (1971) 108–9.

unions), this is really a charter of welfare rights: it is a list of demands that individuals be provided with certain benefits.

That these benefit rights are of an essentially different order from the liberty rights was formally recognized when the United Nations General Assembly sponsored, in 1966, the International Covenant on Economic, Social, and Cultural Rights. The Covenant came into force in 1976, when it was ratified by the requisite thirty-five member states. Of course, it remains to be seen what effect it will have in practice. In any case, according to Article 6(1), 'The States Parties to the present Covenant recognize the right to work, which includes the right of everyone to the opportunity to gain his living by work which he freely chooses or accepts, and will take appropriate steps to safeguard this right'.[11]

The second way in which the right to work is significantly different from a traditional universal liberty right (such as the rights to life and to liberty) is that it cannot sensibly be said to be universal: that is, a right due to every human being by virtue of his or her humanity, at all times and in all places and societies. The right to work, in the terms in which it is presented in the Universal Declaration and the International Covenant (which correspond closely to the terms in which it is generally thought of in the labour and trade union movement), can only be said to apply to a particular kind of settled and relatively developed economy and society, in which most work consists of employment in exchange for wages. However, vast numbers of people, in vast areas of the globe, live in subsistence conditions (at best) in which 'the right to work' just does not make sense. If anything, what makes more sense, in these circumstances, is a right to freedom from work, to respite from the unremitting toil required to scratch a living from a grudging soil. The right to work may, at a pinch, be said to apply to such people when they move out of their subsistence economy and into the wage economy of the towns and cities. All the same, what is often unthinkingly referred to as a universal human right must be seen as something having a much narrower and more localized application.

There is one sense in which the right to work could be claimed to be universal: that is, when it is said that work (that is, purposive or creative activity) is an essential facet of human nature and human endeavour. This view, which is held, in some form or other, by such diverse theorists as Hegel, Marx, and Pope John Paul II, is not without significance; but in the subsistence economic conditions in which so many millions of people live in the underdeveloped world, it is little more than a pious, perhaps wistful, theoretical observation with no

[11] Brownlie (1971) 201.

practical relevance. I shall return to it in a later section, in the context of the industrialized world.

II

Let me now switch away from the more abstract realm of universal human rights and focus on our own developed, industrialized society. So far, I have couched the discussion in terms of 'human rights', rather than 'legal' or 'civil' rights. Legal or civil rights are rights that are, or ought to be, recognized by law: the most obvious one is probably the right to vote. In a curious way, 'the right to work' *is* recognized as a legal or civil right in the United Kingdom and other states of the European Community, but it is so in a negative sense not much favoured by the labour movement: that is, as the liberty right of an individual not to be prevented from working by some external constraint, for example the restrictive practices of other workers. This issue has made dramatic news in recent years as the right to work without having to belong to a trade union. But this version of the right to work should best be seen as the civil right of a dissenter to *opt out* of an institution that is part of the corporate structure of a given economy or society. As such, it has always been uncontroversially granted by trade unions to conscientious objectors on the grounds of religious conviction.[12] This liberty right to work (a right *not* to have something done to you) would also include the right not to be discriminated against in employment on the grounds, for example, of gender, race, sexual orientation, or religious belief. This is certainly not an irrelevant use of the term 'right to work' (and there is indeed a degree of overlap with the benefit version); but in this paper I am primarily concerned with the positive right to work, a benefit demanded as a protection against the deprivations associated with unemployment.

One of the very few examples, in United Kingdom legislation, of a positive civil right to work is the 1944 Disabled Persons (Employment) Act, which requires every employer of twenty or more persons to give employment to a quota (fixed at three per cent since 1946) of registered

[12] A fuller treatment of this would have to consider the issue of the closed shop and, what is not quite the same thing, the union membership agreement. The most common argument in favour of such agreements is that it is wrong that so-called 'freeloaders' should be permitted to reap the benefits, cost-free, of the collective bargaining conducted by the union. In essence, however, whenever the matter has been legally tested, the right to be exempt from union membership, for reasons of 'deeply held personal conviction' (which does not have to be reasonable), has prevailed over properly validated union membership agreements. For further discussion, see Macfarlane (1981) 49–57, Hyman (1984) 96, and Dunn & Gennard (1984).

disabled persons. However, due to the absence of readily available sanctions, the 1944 act has been an irrelevance for many years and has lain dormant, despite its good intentions. Similar to this legislation (and more directly in line with the traditional trade union conception of the right to work) is the 1967 Dock Workers Employment Scheme. The complex provisions of this scheme sought to protect dockers from the vagaries of the traditional labour market in the industry by creating a permanent registered work-force attached to registered employers, instead of a pool of dock labour employed as and when required, on a casual basis. A registered worker must accept allocation to a specific registered employer and, conversely, a registered employer must use registered workers available for relevant work. Registered workers are paid the agreement rate for the periods during which no work is available to them. In some ways, this provision is analogous to the system of intervention payments under the Common Agricultural Policy of the EEC, whereby payments are made to agricultural producers whether or not there is a market for their produce. It is instructive to note that this scheme was seen by the first Wilson Labour government as one of its great achievements—the kind of scheme that the labour movement would like to have seen and, I suspect, would still like to see implemented throughout industry, as guaranteeing the continuity in employment of dockers, shipyard workers, steel workers, indeed workers in any major industry in which demand for labour is volatile or in structural decline. In this form, the right to work is really the right to be paid for turning up, to be paid for being available to work, whether there is work available or not.[13]

III

It can easily be seen that the right to work as demanded and granted in the Dock Workers Scheme is primarily a defensive demand: the right not to suffer unemployment. And this is the common element in the campaigns of the twenties and thirties, the Upper Clyde in 1971, and the miners' strike of 1984–85. 'The right to work' in all of these campaigns was really a coded demand for the right to be protected from unemployment. But why is unemployment such a major social problem? Why is it almost universally perceived to be such an unattractive

[13] Unions have also negotiated agreements for 'waiting time' payments in many industries in which piece-rate workers are sometimes forced (through no fault of their own) to wait for work from other workers further up the production line. Even in an industry in which compulsory redundancy is illegal, however, the number of registered dockers declined between 1970 and 1987 from 45,542 to 10,123, through retirements and voluntary redundancies.

condition? And why, on the contrary, is work generally deemed to be of value? The evidence suggests there are two main dimensions to these questions and their answers: (1) what I shall call the ethical dimension (with socio-psychological contributory factors); and (2) the financial dimension. I shall consider each one in turn.

(1) At first glance, work is an unlikely cause to be celebrated: it is safe to say that most people get quite enough of it, could do with a lot less of it, are delighted to get away from it at the end of the day or the end of the shift (or even during the tea-break), and look forward with longing to the end of the week or the beginning of the holidays or even to retirement. The old wisecrack that 'if work were all that hot the rich would do a lot more of it' surely has a substantial grain of truth in it. Even the very word we use for working for wages is revealing: when being 'employed', we are, literally, being 'used' by our employer. The language used here expresses what seems to be the correct insight—that work is an unpleasant condition, the circumstances of which are under the control of others and not oneself. It is surprising, therefore, that a highly romanticized and sentimental view of work has tended to predominate in much of the recent discussion about unemployment, among academics, journalists, and politicians: especially with respect to the horny-handed sons of toil who laboured heroically in the traditional heavy industries such as coal and steel, shipbuilding, construction, the railways, and even fishing. What these dewy-eyed commentators seem to forget is that the work that most people actually do day in day out (mostly congregated in unpleasant factories and offices) is deadening (and often deafening), intellectually and spiritually undemanding and unfulfilling, often relentlessly backbreaking, unhealthy and unsafe, and ultimately dehumanizing: most employed people are unhappy in their work (or at the very least, worryingly indifferent to it).[14]

The concept of 'alienated labour' did not, of course, emerge with Thatcherism. Already in 1806, Hegel was describing the process whereby the increasing mechanization of production was making the individual worker more productive, but this increased productivity was

[14] See Studs Terkel's marvellous and disturbing book (1974). This is a kaleidoscope of some one hundred and fifty tape-recorded conversations with Americans about their work, at all levels of the employment hierarchy. While there are glimpses of pride and satisfaction in a job well done, the overwhelming impression is that most people hate their work. The first thing that nearly all pools winners do is give it up! The romantic and heroic vision of a Diego Rivera does not correspond to the harsh, squalid reality of working in a steel mill, in an office or restaurant, or even in a boardroom. For a less racy account of people's experience of work (and non-work), see Littler (1985).

progressively impoverishing the worker's skills and decreasing the value of his or her individual contribution: 'the individual becomes—through the abstractness of labour—more mechanical, duller, spiritless. . . . In the individual's skill is the possibility of sustaining his existence. This is subject to all the tangled and complex contingency in the [social] whole. Thus a vast number of people are condemned to a labour that is totally stupefying, unhealthy and unsafe—in workshops, factories, mines, etc.—shrinking their skills. And entire branches of industry, which supported a large class of people, go dry all at once because of [changes in] fashion or a fall in prices due to inventions in other countries, etc.—and this huge population is thrown into helpless poverty.'[15]

This is not, of course, the end of the story, because the evidence suggests that most people (though not all) currently unable to obtain employment would gladly accept almost any kind of work, if they could find it. And this is so not just for financial reasons. So what is the attraction of work? Many people who say that their work is boring, demeaning, and so on, also point out that being stuck at home is even more boring, demeaning and depressing: in short, when they do not have a job outside the home, they find it impossible to put in the time. Work, and especially work outside the home, seems to satisfy two commonly perceived needs. First, most people are sociable beings, and most unemployed people, paradoxically perhaps (since they have more time on their hands), tend to socialize much less than people in work. Apart from the fact that they simply cannot afford to socialize in the pub or club or any such place that costs money to frequent, this is largely due to the sense of inadequacy and failure commonly associated with being unemployed: one of the words most commonly heard in interviews with the unemployed is 'shame'. Work, on the other hand, is usually a social activity, and it takes people out of the home and out of the narrow confines of the family, into the wider social network. It is impressive that this is claimed to be important even by the people whose work is so noisy or so intensive that communication with their workmates is practically impossible.

Secondly, most people seem to have a need to perform some kind of regular purposive and transformative activity: a need to be creative (in a loose sense of that word). This is the phenomenon already alluded to, whereby the right to work may well be thought of as a human right due to every person, at all times and in all places, insofar as it serves to

[15] See Rauch (1983) 139–40; also Cullen (1979) 66–70. Marx's analysis of alienated labour pervades his whole work, but see especially his (1977) 77–87.

satisfy a widely felt human need.[16] Hegel wrote about this need to work in terms of 'overcoming the resistance of objects'. His whole philosophical system can be thought of as the dialectical confrontation of subjective individuals and the objective world. In his ontology of work, the struggle to overcome the resistance of the external world in work (no matter how unappealing the work and the circumstances may be) is a process of self-development: it is an essential element in the education, growth in self-esteem, and progressive emancipation of the subject, which is denied to individuals who have no employment.[17]

It is interesting to note that a very similar approach to the human being's ontological vocation to work runs through Pope John Paul II's encyclical letter on work, *Laborem Exercens*. Basing his teaching on the biblical injunction to 'subdue the earth' (Gen. 1:28), the Pontiff emphasizes that 'work is a good thing for man—a good thing for his humanity—because through work man *not only transforms nature,* adapting it to his own needs, but he also *achieves fulfilment* as a human being and indeed, in a sense, becomes "more a human being"'.[18] Work certainly gives many people a sense that they are making a useful contribution to the social fabric, even if their work, in itself, is unpleasant. They are participating, in a practical way, in the life of the community. Although people do not like to feel 'used', they do like to

[16] I'm sure Alan Gabbey was correct to challenge me, in discussion, to produce the empirical evidence for my claim that there is such a human need. Like all such claims about general human needs, tendencies, proclivities, etc., this one is based on a wide range of observations I have accumulated fairly haphazardly and reflected on in the course of my lifetime: the sources of these observations include myself (introspection), friends, acquaintances and strangers I have talked to and observed, works of fiction I have read, works of history, sociology, philosophy, and anthropology too. This is my evidence, and it certainly is empirical, although it is difficult to document satisfactorily. It is germane to point out that, in this particular case, it gives special prominence to conversations (written as well as oral) with working people, unemployed people, counsellors of unemployed people, etc. It includes counter-examples; and if a sufficient number of significant counter-examples were to come to my attention, I should certainly abandon my generalization. The sum total of these observations and reflections does not produce an empirical *proof* like a proof in physics or chemistry; but then I'm sure no one would be so foolish as to look for such a proof when inquiring into human behaviour. As Hannah Arendt put it so well: trying to define precisely our own nature would be like jumping over our own shadows.

[17] The *locus classicus* for Hegel's discussion of the ontological significance of work is his *Phenomenology of Spirit,* especially the section on the dialectic of lordship and bondage (see Hegel (1977) 115–19).

[18] Pope John Paul II (1981) 33.

feel 'useful'.[19] The need to work seems to be bound up with the need to be secure in one's standing as a responsible adult member of the community. The unemployed person, by contrast, typically experiences a profound sense of loss of dignity or self-respect.[20] Unemployed people typically see themselves as non-citizens, excluded, cut off from the mainstream. The assertion of the right to work may thus be interpreted as articulating a demand not to be cut off from the economic and social activity of the community.

On the other hand, against the doctrine that work is an essential human activity, and that the human right to work is a reflection of a basic human need to work, it has been argued forcefully that such attitudes merely reflect 'two centuries of propaganda, and an educational system which maintained the idea of work as its main objective, but which singularly failed to teach about leisure and how to use it. . . . The microprocessor allows a far greater degree of economies of scale than any technology hitherto. From this it would follow that the old notions underlying the work ethic are outmoded.'[21] According to the authors, the old enslaving prejudices will take a long time to root out, but the sooner the task is begun, in the schools and in the unions, the better. To the extent that we need to revise radically our ideas of what constitutes a normal working week or a normal working life, and to the extent that we must begin to educate for leisure activities, the argument is persuasive and challenging. To the extent that they seriously contemplate a world devoid of work, the authors grossly (and fancifully) overstate their case.

(2) In the previous section, I have argued that work is generally valued because of its social and creative character—its ethical dimension—and that unemployment exacts terrible costs from its victims in terms of demoralization and loss of dignity and self-esteem. But underlying and exacerbating all the other effects of unemployment is the financial devastation it causes. Furthermore, the common loss of dignity and self-esteem is itself often caused by a man's inability to provide for his wife and his family, to pay his own way; the fact that such feelings are often a reflection of the emotional insecurity of the average

[19] Eric Bogle has written a very poignant song, about the time his father, a railwayman, was made redundant, entitled 'They had no use for him'.

[20] For a brief discussion of the connection between work and self-respect, see Smart (1985) 37–8. The most eloquent account in recent years of the loss of dignity and self-esteem suffered by the unemployed is Seabrook (1982). The testimony of the unemployed themselves, which makes up most of the book, is spellbinding and deeply moving. The author's commentary, however—often sanctimonious and imbued with romantic nostalgia for 'the good old days' of dignified but relentless toil and working-class solidarity—is less satisfactory.

[21] Jenkins & Sherman (1979) 141.

'macho' male does not make them any less real. Peter Townsend's conclusion in 1979 that there is a systematic link between unemployment and poverty has been reinforced in countless studies since then, as unemployment has increased inexorably.[22] These studies indicate that the primary component of the popular demand for the right to work, for most working people, is in fact the right to be protected from poverty. The poverty associated with unemployment is even more important, in the minds of the unemployed themselves, than the sense of uselessness and the loss of self-esteem. This is not hard to understand. We live in a money economy. Employment offers most citizens the best chance of staying clear of poverty, although it provides no guarantee.[23] Perhaps, in these circumstances, 'the right to work' should partly at least be understood as the confused expression of a demand for a basic minimum income for all citizens in the society.

If this conversion were accepted (and the evidence seems quite overwhelming to me), the resulting demand could legitimately be based on a claim to a fair share for each citizen of the wealth produced in a given state (or a group of states, such as the EEC), rather than on what is due to each individual as a human being. Wealth and poverty are preeminently relative concepts, and there are obviously such great discrepancies in standards of living and expectations in different parts of the world that 'the right to a fair share' as applied to someone living in the Sudan is very different from the same right as applied to someone living in Belfast or Dublin or Manchester. Although this raises major moral questions with respect to the international economic order that lie outside the scope of the present paper, the demand makes perfectly good sense when applied to people living in the same political jurisdiction, within which a government has the political and moral authority to legislate, levy taxes, and disburse the resultant revenue so as to ensure the distribution of 'fair shares' of the wealth produced within that politico-economic unit. It should also be clearly understood that, in this context, 'fair share' means a fair-share *minimum* of income, goods and services; it does not necessarily mean that everyone should receive the *same* share.

If we accept the weight of evidence of what the unemployed themselves say, together with workers in vulnerable employment, to the effect that the financial dimension of work and unemployment far outweighs, in practice, what I have called the 'ethical' dimension, it seems reasonable to conclude that the right to work—understood as a

22 Townsend (1979).

23 In 1985, 199,000 families in Great Britain were granted family income supplement, to bring their wages up to the official poverty line (see Becker & MacPherson (1986) 15–18).

benefit right—is really, in the eyes of those who most passionately proclaim it and to whom it is most relevant, a disguised form of claim to social security by right. In other words, the right to work is primarily a right to be protected from the poverty and physical deprivation systematically associated with unemployment. To the extent that many (perhaps most) people prefer not to rely on charity or even public handouts, then the right to a minimum income sufficient to satisfy the basic needs of food, shelter, fuel, clothing, etc., is certainly not unrelated to a 'right to work' for its intrinsic value. In the final section, therefore, I shall consider briefly how the right to work for the sake of its 'ethical' benefits and the right to work for the sake of the financial protection it affords might be given practical effect in tandem; and how their implementation might be managed and financed.

IV

With the exception of the two schemes mentioned in section II, there is no positive legal right to work in the United Kingdom. Although people can, of course, still have rights even though they are disregarded by others, the very contemplation of such a legal provision prompts the question: against whom is one supposed to exercise the right to work, understood as a benefit right? Rights, as we saw above, are moral 'principles' (or demands based upon moral 'principles') that should guide our conduct: for example, 'the right to life' should guide my treatment of others and their treatment of me. If the right to work is to operate in anything like this manner, whose conduct is it supposed to guide? My right, if it is to make any sense at all, must always be correlative with someone else's duty or obligation towards me.[24]

So who has an obligation to *provide* others with the work to which they demand a right? Who has a duty to protect every adult citizen in the relevant jurisdiction from joblessness? It is difficult to envisage how any one of us can reasonably be held to have a moral obligation or a duty to provide work for others (with one possible exception, the voluntary banning of overtime, to which I shall return in a moment). The few among us who happen to own or control means of production, distribution or exchange may have it in their power to 'create jobs' (as the saying goes) on a fairly minor scale, if their business is prospering; or even, if they happen to control a major company, on a relatively major scale. The difficulties of satisfying the demand for work cannot, however, be denied. The privately owned sector of a mixed economy cannot, on its own, provide work for everyone, at least, probably not enough

[24] See Austin (1954) 285n.

worker/hours at a high enough hourly rate to provide each person with an adequate income. The reason for this lies in the very logic of the capitalist economic system, which demands the extraction of surplus value from the productive process at a rate above a certain level; and below this level, for fairly straightforward technical reasons, the enterprise (without public subsidy) would simply go to the wall, thereby ceasing to be in a position to offer *any* employment.

The possibilities of generating employment are, therefore, severely limited within private industry in general, and in the publicly owned industrial sector. It must be emphasized, however, that these strict structural limitations on the creation of employment apply only in a theoretical situation of completely free and unregulated market relations, with no state intervention; and in practice, governments everywhere intervene constantly and substantially in private business transactions, whether through legal regulation of the labour market, the award or refusal of government contracts, or straightforward subsidies to businesses, usually subject to certain conditions (whether explicit or implicit). It is in this area of greatly increased government involvement in the planning decisions of private industrial companies, together with greatly increased government investment in personal and social services, that hope is to be found for the effective elimination of unemployment.

Now we must recall to mind the several interpretations we developed, in earlier sections, of the benefit right to work, which we want to retain. We concluded that the labour movement is committed to asserting the right to work, and unemployment is seen as a major social problem, for two broad reasons. (1) Most people need to perform regular purposive activity of a creative nature so as to assert their personality and take part in the social and economic life of the society as a responsible adult; but most work available hitherto has been tedious and undemanding, or worse, stultifying, unhealthy, dehumanizing. We established that few people are happy in their work, but no one (practically speaking) is happy without any paid work. (2) In our money economy, unemployment means poverty for almost everyone affected. In our society, almost everyone needs employment to generate income: either you work for yourself and sell your goods or services in the market-place; or you must sell your labour-power in exchange for money, to enable you to purchase life's material necessities.

So what is to be done? The slogan 'the right to work', for all its rhetorical power, is seriously inadequate, because it is not differentiated enough. It would be far better if it were abandoned by the labour and trade union movement, and by social reformers in general, and replaced by two related campaigning slogans that are both far-reaching and progressively attainable through political control of the economy: (1) the right to socially worthwhile, healthy and satisfying work for everyone who requires it; and (2) the right to a statutory minimum income.

(1) A certain amount of work is needed for everyone, and the quality of the work done is just as important for people's well-being as the quantity. It must be recognized that the concept of 'full employment' needs to be radically redefined: until quite recently, full employment, for manual workers, meant forty-eight hours per week (plus overtime) for forty-eight weeks in the year for fifty years of a working lifetime. But the days of forty hours a week (plus overtime) as the normal working week for almost everyone in employment are gone for ever, because of increasing automation in production, storage, stock control, and so on. Furthermore, our ideas of what constitutes 'full-time' as distinct from 'part-time' work need to be revised. Regular overtime is still worked by a very high proportion of male manual workers. Although many men probably work regular overtime because they need the extra income, the government must regulate the maximum number of remunerated hours worked per week or per month, so as to maximize genuine job-sharing. The figure could be set immediately (given the present state of automation, low level of aggregate demand, and high rate of unemployment) at thirty-five hours per week; but it could be progressively reduced as automation increased. In ten or fifteen years time, the 'full-time' norm, in conjunction with a statutory minimum wage per hour to take account of the reduced hours worked, could well be twenty-five or twenty hours per week.[25]

Automation should enable us to minimize virtually to the point of elimination the unfulfilling and dehumanizing work that has traditionally been so prominent. Satisfying, socially useful, and healthy work should be maximized, in either production or services.[26] Many

[25] For an illuminating discussion of the likely cost and employment effects of shorter working hours, with lots of interesting figures, see Hill (1987). The author shows that between 1980 and 1985 the proportion of manufacturing employees working overtime in British industry *increased* from 29·5 to 34·5 per cent, with each employee who worked overtime doing so to the extent of nine hours per week on average, while over the same period the size of the employed labour force in manufacturing actually fell by over eighteen per cent; and argues that a reduction of hours worked per person would lead to a compensating rise in productivity per hour. He concludes that worksharing could be used to spread the benefits of greatly increased output per person and per hour amongst a greater number of employed persons. A strong case for the imposition of shorter working time by law, without loss of pay, is presented by Coates & Topham (1986) 245–53; on the need for a statutory minimum wage, see 240–4.

[26] A particularly ambitious example of trade union planning for socially useful employment was the corporate plan developed as an alternative to

services that cannot be afforded on the open market by most people of modest means should be financed by the state; this would provide, for example, work in the health and personal social services, in the educational services, in the provision of facilities and coaching for artistic, sporting and other leisure and recreational activities, or care and companionship for the elderly. These kinds of services are highly labour-intensive, they are socially worthwhile, and even though the work would be sometimes unpleasant (for example, caring for incontinent old people), it would almost always be highly satisfying and fulfilling. Finally, the radical changes in patterns of work outlined in these proposals should provide an opportunity to eliminate the division of labour according to gender, which has been, and still is, so detrimental to the quality of life of so many women.[27]

(2) The provision of a statutory minimum income for every adult citizen, male and female, whether unemployed or employed, full-time (in accordance with the statutory maximum) or part-time, is neither Utopian nor particularly difficult to establish in practice. The actual amount, given the current low level of economic activity in the United Kingdom, could be initially, say, £110 per week, which corresponds roughly to two-thirds of average male manual earnings. A necessary defence against excessive exploitation of the scheme by private employers would be provided by the statutory minimum hourly wage; this would be initially related to the statutory minimum income at, say, £3.25 per hour. Annual increases in both could be linked to either the Retail Price Index or average earnings.

The scheme would require only two basic mechanisms. First, it would involve direct payments from the government to *all* those, including the long-term ill or disabled, not in any kind of remunerative employment: there is nothing new in this mechanism, *except* that now the payment would be non-contributory and thus both more equitable and much easier to administer than the present hopelessly complicated system of benefits. The mass of restrictive legislation that currently prevents certain categories of citizen (such as wives) from receiving state benefits in their own right and makes certain employment rights and related benefits (such as paid maternity leave) conditional on hours worked would have to be repealed. Non-contributory children's allowances could continue to be paid to one parent or the other, usually directly to the mother, as they have been for many years now. The long-

redundancy by the shop stewards of Lucas Aerospace about ten years ago: they developed proposals for some 150 new products, from new kidney machines to the road rail car that has been taken up by British Rail in prototype (see Wainwright & Elliot (1982)). On the general topic, see Coates (1978).

[27] See Knights & Willmott (1986), and Cockburn (1985).

term aim of government policy would be to provide some employment for everyone who requires it; in the meantime, the statutory minimum income would provide for a basic decent standard of living for all, catching all those who currently fall through the net. As an added benefit, since it would be paid to married women in their own right, it would end the traditional 'tyranny of the housekeeping money'.

Secondly, the scheme would involve the mechanism of reverse taxation. A state-contributed supplement to a worker's pay would be included by the employer in the pay-packet instead of going in the other direction in the form of tax, and the effect would be to bring the take-home earnings up to the level of the statutory minimum income. Remember that the state is trying to encourage employees to work less hours, so as to share the work available among a greater number of people. The state-contributed supplement is designed to ensure that those employees who choose to work less than the established norm are not thereby made financially vulnerable; and it also constitutes an indirect subsidy to the employing enterprise for encouraging this degree of working flexibility.

The statutory minimum income (together with the statutory minimum hourly wage) could be introduced tomorrow. I have pitched the level of payments deliberately low because the United Kingdom economy is currently in the early stages of recovery from a severe recession. But as the economy got stronger, with industrial production becoming increasingly automated and increasingly profitable, boosted by the increased demand fed by the statutory minimum income, greatly increased taxation revenue (from employees and successful private employers) would finance the expensive, labour-intensive services and the statutory minimum income. While these measures would certainly not herald the advent of the socialist millennium, they would, all the same, eradicate most of the material deprivation, the misery, and the loss of self-esteem associated with enforced unemployment; and they would provide for every citizen a 'fair share' in the wealth of the community. These would be considerable achievements in themselves. They would also, in the longer term, show people that the material well-being necessary for the development of a fully human life for oneself and one's family can be guaranteed through co-operation and the rational pursuit of a common purpose; and that I consider to be a fundamental lesson in the human possibilities opened up by socialism. With widespread public support and the required political will, there is no reason to believe that a progressive government in a mixed economy could not provide the positive benefit rights to socially worthwhile, healthy and satisfying work, and to a guaranteed minimum income. And that, in my view, is what 'the right to work' is really all about.[28]

[28] I am very grateful to Ann Hope, David Lamb, and Alan Ryan for their comments on earlier versions of the paper.

Surrogacy, Liberal Individualism and the Moral Climate

BOB BRECHER

I attempt in this paper to do two things: to offer some comments about recent discussions of the suggested institutionalization of surrogacy agreements; and in doing so, to draw attention to a range of considerations which liberals tend to omit from their moral assessments. The main link between these concerns is the idea that what people want is a fundamental justification (other things being equal, of course) for their getting it. I believe that this idea is profoundly mistaken; yet it is an inevitable consequence of a liberal notion of the individual and liberals' extremely limited conception of harm. My intention, then, is to illustrate how unease about a concrete problem—whether or not surrogacy agreements should be institutionalized—might interact with dissatisfaction about liberal individualism to make clearer what the unease consists in and to suggest why liberal individualism is inadequate as a basis for moral philosophy.

I

(1) *Harms and Consequences*

The paradigm of the classical liberal notion of harm is the case where one person physically injures another: for physical injury is taken to be recognizable and characterizable regardless of the beliefs, attitudes, and so on, of the people involved. Even if we may allow that such a notion adequately represents one sort of harm, however, it is commonly recognized that there is another sort of harm, well described by Ted Honderich as 'morality-dependent',[1] a sort of harm exemplified by, for example, 'a National Front gathering at a memorial to Jewish war dead',[2] where the fact of harm's being done is in some measure at least dependent on the beliefs of those (allegedly) harmed. Here I shall merely note this, without commenting either on whether or not this sort of harm was properly recognized by J. S. Mill, or on the extent to which it is to be weighed against considerations of liberty where conflict

[1] Honderich (1982).
[2] Honderich (1982) 504.

arises. There is, however, a further sort of harm, which I shall describe as *morality-affecting*. It will be the aim of my argument to clarify the nature of this harm.

Some actions, practices, or events issue not only in direct consequences for specific individuals or groups, but also affect the moral attitudes of people, the moral climate within which direct consequences are characterized and assessed. One example is the Race Relations Act, which has had among its consequences the fact that some people have come to regard racism as a serious moral-political problem who had previously not done so; another is the Wolfenden Report and its attendant legislation, one consequence of which has been a change in public attitudes to homosexuality. The point is, of course, that changes in attitude lead also to changes in some people's activities, as Devlin and others have recognized.[3] Where the impact of an action, practice, or institution on people's moral attitudes, and thus their moral behaviour, is harmful, then I propose that such an action, practice, or institution be described as a morality-affecting harm.

Such a harm may or may not overlap with other sorts of harm; and whether or not something is recognized as such a harm will of course depend on the view of those concerned of the attitude and behaviour engendered, furthered, encouraged, exemplified, or fostered. The notion is clearly not 'neutral' in the way some might regard the sort of harm recognized by classical liberalism, but is, rather, value-laden in the same sort of way as Honderich's morality-dependent harms. What is at issue here can be seen from the following case: if someone walks across a patch of grass with a 'Keep Off' sign, it may not result directly in any damage to the grass, but might encourage, however indirectly, other people to reject injunctions of a similar sort, thereby doing harm. Here, as rule-utilitarians recognize, something which is 'in itself' harmless may nevertheless constitute a morality-affecting harm. Furthermore, a morality-affecting harm may wreak its damage in ways other than straightforwardly causal ones, where by 'causal' is intended a direct relation between one action, event, etc., and another. To anticipate what will be argued later: what three or four consenting adults do in private may neither degrade, nor upset, nor harm the participants in any way whatever; but their playing out, for example, their shared sado-masochistic fantasies may be something which, whatever else it is or results in, encourages other people to do similar (or indeed quite dissimilar) things, the cumulative effect of which might be to help produce a society significantly different from one in which such private activities are illegal. To put it more bluntly, there is no such thing as an activity or practice 'in itself' in any society in which people are able to

[3] Devlin (1959).

communicate, that is, in any society whatever. Whatever we do, whether 'in private' or 'in public', is done in a particular social context, the very distinction which we have come to accept between 'private' and 'public' itself being, of course, part of a particular liberal context. That is why discussions of moral practices, acts, problems, or dilemmas which seek to isolate their subject from the social setting in which it takes place are peculiarly sterile—which is hardly surprising, since our moral relations are after all relations with real people. Furthermore, to take an obvious example, the publication on page three of the *Sun* of photographs of women displayed in certain ways may or may not be part of the causal sequence leading to a particular rape: but even if it is not, it nevertheless exemplifies a set of views, attitudes, and feelings which at the very least help to keep in being a sexist society.[4] Phenomena which reinforce attitudes and their corresponding behaviour are not the same thing as phenomena which cause specific acts (although they may of course coincide): nevertheless, they are not the less important for that.

Attention to morality-affecting harms allows us to take into account the context in which morality-dependent and other harms occur, a context which we might otherwise all too easily overlook. It allows us to recognize as harms phenomena whose effects we otherwise ignore because they 'do not depend for their seriousness on being or resulting directly in acts',[5] having their impact rather in terms of reinforcing, or assisting in the construction of, frameworks within which acts, behaviour, etc., are understood, or fail to be understood, as harms. Perhaps the use of certain forms of language is the clearest example: the use of sexist pronouns, for instance.[6] The notion of morality-affecting harms also affords a mean of avoiding, as well as helping to explain the prevalence of, fruitless arguments about what something is 'essentially' like as opposed to what it is actually like in a specific time and place.[7] Finally, if some harms are morality-affecting harms, it follows that the

[4] Two excellent discussions of this sort of point are Brown (1981) and Mendus (1985a). I return to the idea of exemplification on p. 197 below.

[5] Brown (1981) 13.

[6] For an excellent treatment of the power of naming and related issues, see Spender (1980), esp. Chs 5 and 6; see also Assiter (1983), Shortland and Fauvel (1983), Cameron (1984), and Beezer (1984).

[7] For example, the confusions set off by something like this: 'Prostitution, I suggested, is essentially degrading. It is impossible to imagine a genuine case of prostitution which is not degrading to some extent, even though it may, all things considered, be morally admirable (as with the resistance worker who sets up as a prostitute in order to gain valuable information from soldiers and officials of the occupying power). Surrogacy, I submit, is not essentially degrading' (Lockwood (1985) 182–3). A good corrective is Coward (1982).

consequences of an action need not be limited to its impact on identifiable individuals; so we can see that something might be harmful even though no one can point to a person who has been harmed. This, again, would constitute an advance on the excessive liberal emphasis on artificially isolated individuals, allowing the social contexts in which people act, understand, interpret and respond, to receive their due consideration as parameters of harms suffered by individuals.

(2) *Surrogacy*

> Imagine that the couple who want the child are childless; that by normal standards they are fit people to start a family; that they can produce their own viable gametes; but, for compelling medical reasons, the wife cannot undergo pregnancy; that other possible solutions to their childlessness, such as adoption, are not open to them; and that in any case they are strongly motivated to have a child that is their own genetic offspring. A strong case could be made for saying that if a child from their genetic materials could be brought into existence, they should be helped. So, if another woman who already has children of her own wants to help this couple by gestating their embryo for them, on the strict understanding that the child is theirs and will be handed over to them at birth, should she not be allowed to do so?
>
> I shall call this 'gestatory' surrogacy[8]—so a gestatory surrogate gestates an embryo that is not genetically related to her (E. Page, 'Donation, Surrogacy and Adoption'[9]).

Edgar Page's taxonomy of surrogacy, distinguishing from the 'gestatory' surrogacy outlined above 'genetic' and 'total' surrogacy, and distinguishing each form of surrogacy from the related practice of adoption, I take to be definitive. I agree also with his view[10] that gestatory surrogacy raises fewer and less complex moral difficulties than other forms of surrogacy: and I shall therefore confine my remarks to this, its least controversial form, in order to focus the unease I have about institutionalizing such a practice. While Page offers good reasons why gametes and embryos, unlike children, may be transferred and

[8] Page adds in a footnote: 'Other terms are sometimes used. For example, Peter Singer and Deane Wells (1984) say "full" surrogacy where I say "gestatory" surrogacy and partial surrogacy for what below I shall call "genetic" surrogacy. The terms I propose are clearer and more precise than those proposed by Singer and Wells' (Page (1985) 171, n. 2; see also Page (1986) for a development of his views).

[9] Page (1985) 163, 162.

[10] As stated in conversation.

donated, thereby undermining much of the Warnock Committee's objection to legally enforceable surrogacy agreements,[11] I think there may be other objections to such agreements. These objections are not based on Warnock's failure to distinguish surrogacy from adoption, but they do tell in quite a different way against proposals 'for a coherent system of surrogacy supported by regulative institutions in which surrogacy is seen to facilitate an acceptable form of parenthood'.[12]

Gestatory surrogacy, then, in its reproductively least innovative and morally least controversial form, is this: the female partner of a heterosexual married couple, the male partner of which is fertile, is unable to carry, though able to conceive, whether by artificial insemination or otherwise, a foetus. Another woman is therefore asked to do so on her behalf: the second woman thus agrees to carry to term a foetus brought into being through a union of the egg of the first woman with the sperm of the latter's husband. There are of course many possible variations of this sort of surrogacy: the female and male who wish to co-operate in producing a child might not be married; the male partner might be infertile; and there might be all sorts of other complications. I shall however confine myself to the simplest case. Moreover, I shall assume that the woman who wishes to have a baby is willing, but not able, to undergo a pregnancy—that is, I shall eschew arguments which might be brought to bear, at least in the first instance, against a woman's merely not wishing, for instance, to jeopardize her career as a model by becoming pregnant, and thus having another woman undergo the pregnancy on her behalf. (To the extent that my arguments against the harder case succeed, however, they tell also against such a practice: and even if they do not, they may nevertheless constitute grounds for not permitting surrogacy agreements of convenience, as opposed to necessity.) Rather I shall attempt to argue in relation to cases where the commissioning woman is clearly willing to carrying a foetus; has for

[11] 'Surrogacy tends to be treated as a form of adoption because to achieve its aim, *under existing laws and modes of thought*, the commissioning couple must hope to be able to adopt the child from its legal mother, the surrogate mother, after it is born. The surrogacy agreement, or contract, inevitably appears to be aimed at committing the surrogate mother to giving up her child for adoption at birth or soon after. Clearly the agreement runs contrary to the rules for adoption. However, if we had laws that recognized agreements whereby before conception a woman donates her egg, or embryo, *in utero* the embryo would belong to the commissioning couple from the outset and the resulting child would be theirs. At no point then would there be a question of transferring the child' (Page (1985) 170). For the Warnock view, see Warnock (1985) 6.8, 7.6, 8.18, 8.19; and compare the 'Expression of Dissent A: Surrogacy' (pp. 87–9).

[12] Page (1985) 161.

many years attempted to do so, but without success; has attempted all known alternatives to surrogacy, but again without success; and the couple concerned are genuinely distraught at their inability to have a child in the usual way.

I shall exclude also the case where a friend of the couple concerned undertakes without payment and without any legal agreement to carry the foetus, doing so simply out of friendship and altruism. There are particular difficulties about such a case, especially about the advisability of stretching friendship so far, and the possible emotional impact on a surrogate whose friendship with the commissioning couple extends over the child's life and is not restricted to the time of its birth. Indeed, even if this sort of arrangement on balance benefits from the emotional ties between surrogate and commissioners, it may be that some sort of agreement is indispensable nonetheless. However that may be, my concern here is with suggestions that surrogacy agreements be given an institutional basis and with the sorts of arguments adduced in favour of such a move, rather than with what people might do simply and solely out of love, friendship, or altruism, and without legal safeguards. So if even the people in such cases ought for the sake of all involved to avail themselves of legally enforceable agreements, then, to the extent that objections to such agreements are successful, even these surrogate undertakings are open to objection. Note also that objections to informal arrangements do not of themselves constitute arguments for institutionalizing surrogacy agreements. The fact that such informal arrangements are likely to take place anyway, and that if they remain outside the ambit of the law all sorts of difficulties will arise, not least for the children involved, does not mean that we should accept legal surrogacy agreements as the lesser of two evils without further argument. Doubtless prohibition is always likely to cause problems: but it is not *necessarily* wrong, either morally or pragmatically.

(3) *Surrogacy as an Example*

Having thus indicated my area of concern, namely suggestions that legally enforceable surrogacy agreements should be institutionalized, I should point out that I am not seeking to argue that surrogacy is especially problematic, or even that there are not a large number of practices and institutions which raise similar and related problems even more acutely. Issues such as advertising, pornography, the privatization of health care and of education, the notion of a property-owning democracy and many others may well be far more important. Surrogacy, however, currently seems to provoke standard responses from right and liberal left: in the former case an easily disposed of insistence on keeping women in their place, duly masquerading as objections to 'baby-farming'; and in the latter, too rapid an assent on the basis of letting people have what they want, affording a means of extending the possibility of having children to people outside traditional family structures, and so on. Just because it does so, it is, apart from its own interest and importance, a useful issue on which to focus concerns about what I might describe as the moral philosophy of well-intentioned liberalism. That is to say, I think that some of the ways in which the institutionalization of surrogacy might justifiably be regarded should make us wary about liberal arguments which hang on consequences for identifiable individuals, and especially when those are predicated on people's wants—hence my concentrating on the sorts of justification which might be given for institutionalizing surrogacy, and my analogies with slavery and with prostitution.

II

What I shall discuss, then, is just that sort of surrogacy agreement to which Warnock objects, and which Page advocates. Whether or not financial payment is explicitly envisaged—and I shall return to this, for many insist that consideration of agreements should exclude the question of payment[13]—a surrogacy arrangement which is not simply an understanding between friends must involve some sort of formal agreement; for all concerned have interests at stake. Clearly the commissioning woman or couple (and I leave aside here the question of whether the couple or the female partner alone ought to be party to any such agreement) must insist, minimally, on one condition: that the child gestated be handed over. Against this, Warnock maintains that the surrogate ought to be entitled, because of the obvious emotional problems which might arise, to keep the baby if she wishes to. But this is wrong: for even if the surrogate's emotional state has precedence over the intended recipient's, there would seem to be a *prima facie* case that in the interests of the child it ought to be placed with its parents rather than being forcibly adopted against its parents' wishes and for no good reason to do with its own welfare and safety.[14]

It would appear reasonable also that the recipient should be permitted to stipulate such conditions about the surrogate's activities as she would adopt were she herself pregnant; or, if this is too strong a condition, then at least to seek a surrogate who was willing to accept conditions closest to those which she would wish to have accepted. This

[13] Page insists (in conversation) that the question of money be not brought in until the basic issues have been sorted out, so as to avoid prejudging the issue.

[14] Page's (1986) arguments against Warnock are decisive here.

would of course require making enquiries of potential surrogates and then holding the woman concerned to those conditions. Thus one might not unreasonably envisage surrogacy agreements which, as well as stipulating that the surrogate hand over the recipient's child immediately after its birth, contained clauses about sexual activity; smoking tobacco; mountain climbing; skiing; and taking a range of drugs, including alcohol, both recreationally and medically recommendable. Furthermore the surrogate, however generously motivated, would be well advised to insist on conditions governing Caesarean section; the manner of delivery ('natural', drug-assisted, hospital, home, and so on); and foreseeable circumstances where her own health, or indeed life, might be threatened by the pregnancy. For her agreement to be a surrogate only covers normal medical risk. Further explicit agreement will be needed if the risk exceeds the average; and the same would apply if she were required to conform to traditional Roman Catholic practices concerning the balance of interests between the well-being of the woman and of the foetus. Already, I think, the question alluded to earlier of payment begins to merge with that of proper recompense for inconvenience, expenses incurred, and so on: for the unpaid, highly altruistic surrogate might sensibly be expected to insist on the loosest conditions, so that any commissioner who wanted her to agree to conditions which she, the commissioner, thinks reasonable—and because of the greater than average importance of the foetus in this case, these would be likely to be tighter than average—might well be only too happy to pay rather than to offer due disbursement only. At £20,000 a higher degree of risk-taking is likely to be acceptable than for free. In short, to exclude questions of payment from discussion of surrogacy agreements seems to me entirely unrealistic.

Ought such agreements be entered into? To explore this question, I shall suggest two analogies: one with prostitution, the other with slavery. So as to avoid misunderstanding, however, let me point out at the outset that I am not seeking to suggest that any similarities there might be between acting as a surrogate mother and working as a prostitute or being enslaved are not outweighed by far greater differences. Rather, I wish to draw attention on the one hand to similarities between the sorts of ground adduced in attempted justification of prostitution and those advocated in favour of institutionalizing surrogacy; and on the other, to the implications for our attitude to slavery that certain arguments on behalf of institutionalized surrogacy might properly have. These are not put forward as simple *reductios*; and they are intended to be suggestive, not knock-down. They constitute part of an attempt to outline what might be termed a persuasive description of surrogacy.

(1) *Prostitution*

Consider then how some of my earlier remarks about surrogacy might be transposed to the practice of prostitution. Are there any good reasons why—to take one sort of example—a woman should not sell the use of her body to a man, for the purpose of the latter's sexual pleasure, for a specified period of time, under specified conditions, and for an agreed fee? I shall assume that the woman does so of her own free will; that she feels no personal degradation (whether or not she is as a matter of fact degraded); that the transaction is in fact governed by conditions which she has every good reason to suppose the man will observe (and vice versa); that the fee is exceedingly generous compared with the woman's other available means, if any, of earning a living; and that whatever conditions considered appropriate obtain in respect of privacy and related considerations. Both parties are doing something they want to do; neither is imposing their desires on anyone else; and, for purposes of this discussion, neither party will suffer physical, emotional or any other sort of harm as a result, beyond the explicit expectations, if any, of those concerned. In short, I shall suppose that Mill's conditions for the exercise of the individual's liberty are met:

> The liberty of the individual must be thus far limited; he must not make himself a nuisance to other people,

because

> in each person's own concerns his individual spontaneity is entitled to free exercise.[15]

Is such a transaction objectionable? It will not do merely to insist that prostitution is 'essentially degrading', for one has to give reasons for such a description, rather than merely asserting it.[16] It is hard to imagine, without begging the question at issue, any social practice which is essentially anything out of the context of the society in which it takes place. Specifically religious and related sorts of consideration aside then, the obvious objection is in terms of social impact; the harm done to society by the very existence and instantiation of such a practice constitutes the most serious objection to it. Indeed, it is on such grounds that both Mary Whitehouse and illiberal feminists oppose the practice: the former as well as the latter because their respective visions of a good society do not permit the existence or consequences of prostitution.

What Whitehouse regards as consequences might not be taken to be such by others, and this is a factual matter. Alternatively their relative

[15] Mill (1962) 184, 207.

[16] As is pointed out by Hare (1978/9).

importance or moral-political desirability might be evaluated quite differently; and while such valuation bears some relation to the facts, it is primarily a matter of moral-political conviction. I maintain that such considerations are relevant, that it will not do to shelter behind the closed doors of preference satisfaction, simply because, as a matter of fact, what goes on behind many closed doors may have consequences in the wider world; and no consequentialist can in consistency refuse to countenance the relevance of facts. Arguments in terms of the impact on people's desires and preferences of the mere possibility of their being satisfied, or satisfied in certain ways, cannot be ignored. The legalization of homosexual acts in private between males over the age of twenty-one, for example, has had consequences wider than certain individuals ceasing to be prosecuted who otherwise would have been prosecuted; the advertising of sexual possibilities in contact magazines has made a difference not just to those who actually wished to avail themselves of such a facility before it became available, but also to some who were not even aware of the sexual possibilities in question. As another example, the possibility of transplanting organs from one human being to another has led to, among other things, changes in some people's thinking about what constitutes death, the importance or otherwise of the integrity of the body after death, and so on.

In short, as advertisers and politicians know very well, desires can be created, and with them preferences, satisfactions, and even perhaps forms of happiness. The likely creation of these must therefore be taken into account by the consequentialist in any calculation of consequences. Whether or not the sorts of desires, satisfactions, and so on which prostitution carries with it are morally objectionable, and if so whether or not this outweighs the social importance of individuals' freedoms, is what is at issue. Does the institution of prostitution as a matter of fact have the sorts of consequence, outcome, implication, etc., that either the New Right or illiberal feminists suppose? If so, do these outweigh the arguments on the other side, namely the consequences of individuals being denied the satisfaction of certain wants under certain conditions? This is not the place to argue the substantive case. Instead I shall present a further example where the consequences of the existence of an institution are relevant to its valuation.

(2) *Slavery*

Mill's argument against slavery in *On Liberty* is that 'By selling himself for a slave [a man] abdicates his liberty; he forgoes any future use of it beyond that single act. He therefore defeats, in his own case, the very purpose which is the justification of allowing him to dispose of himself . . .'.[17] It is only on these rather special grounds, that to do so

[17] Mill (1962) 236.

involves some sort of practical self-contradiction, that liberalism can object to a person's voluntarily selling herself into slavery (say for a specified period of time, and to one particular person). But there are at least *prima facie* grounds against permitting a person to sell herself to another even if this argument is unsuccessful, and however much any of those concerned might wish the transaction to go ahead. Regardless of how much she is paid; regardless of how strictly supervised the conditions of the agreement might be; regardless of how short the term of slavery envisaged might be; regardless of the intensity of either her or the potential owner's desires in the matter: it is wrong.

Why? Again (quasi-)religious considerations apart, the sort of society in which such an agreement were permissible, would be the worse for it even if it were initially strictly limited so as to attempt to ensure that a full-blown system of slavery did not develop, that the practice remained at the level of one-off deals; and it would be sufficiently the worse for it to outweigh the limitation imposed on individuals' freedom by not permitting them to exercise it in this way. The mere possibility of one person's owning another would encourage a certain set of power relations to prevail; certain sorts of use to be made by people of each other; certain desires to come into being; and so on. If she allows herself to become a slave, then as a matter of fact, it is thereby more likely that the practice will be accepted and thus, as Mill himself insists in another context, actually acceptable: and from this, all sorts of consequences may reasonably be judged to be likely to follow. Pressures would be put on the poorest people for whom temporary slavery would be a means of pulling themselves out of the poverty they would otherwise remain in; slave owning would become more common, leading to a more rigid division into appropriate classes. Other attitudes to persons would also change; and the community would disintegrate into something resembling a cross between a very enlightened dolphinarium and the Job Training Scheme. One-off deals do not remain one-off deals: individual instances of slavery would lead to a slave society, and a slave society is, in all imaginable instances, wrong.

What is significant about this is that no amount of argument about people's right to spend their money as they wish; do whatsoever they want in private and/or with similarly consenting adults; determine their own lives; make their own choices; or decide their own moral standards, is 'in itself' even relevant to the issue. The only relevant question is the factual one of how the actual consequences of going against these values compare with the actual consequences of prohibiting them from being instantiated in certain forms. Suppose that someone sincerely holds that the likely consequences of people's being permitted to sell themselves into slavery are outweighed—whether in terms of happiness, pleasure, preference satisfaction, needs, natural goods, or whatever else one may posit as among the criteria whereby consequences are to be adjudged harms or otherwise—by the likely consequences of people being denied such a right. She or he then owes us a factual argument for this conclusion, and it is hard to see how one could be supplied.

(3) *Surrogacy Agreements*

If it is not granted that the likely outcome of institutionalizing surrogacy agreements is, for a consequentialist, a relevant factor in the debate, and if it is insisted that only the consequences for the particular people concerned in a particular transaction have any relevance at all in an attempt to form a considered judgment about such agreements, then I have very little to say by way of response—save that such an insistence leaves judgments about slavery, prostitution, pornography, private medicine, private education, mass suicide, genocide, and every form of exploitation whatever simply to those sufficiently powerful to get others to want these things. If, on the other hand, such considerations are admitted as relevant, then it is granted that women's—or men's—desire for such agreements as a means of satisfying the desire to have a child (other than by adoption) but being unable to carry a foetus for whatever reason, does not provide the last word on the morality of the matter. It provides only the first. Consider the suggestion that students who want a degree but cannot, for very good reasons, sit exams, should be provided with surrogate examinees; or the suggestion that people who are not particularly good at tennis because they cannot run fast enough should have surrogates made available for them to compete at Wimbledon. Not all suffering occasioned by not being able to obtain or do what we want is properly eliminable by attempts to give us what we want by circuitous means. One other way of attempting to deal with such problems is to mitigate the desires in question by avoiding, dampening, or substituting them: satisfying desires is not the only choice open. It is of course far easier to say this than for a woman who wants desperately to be a mother but cannot undergo a pregnancy to put it into practice. But it is also the case that this is in part at least a self-generating state of affairs. To the extent that it is not, the benefits wrought by surrogacy need to be measured against the harms generated, for not anything that reduces or counters suffering is simply for that reason a good thing, however tragic the individual circumstances.

First, let me summarize the unease about institutionalizing surrogacy agreements which arise from the consequences that such a practice might reasonably be thought to have. My expectation, as I indicated earlier, is that money would soon come into the picture: a pool of surrogates could well be created on the model of working class prostitution; women would come to be imported from poor countries for the purpose of serving as surrogates on the model of Filipino domestics and Brazilian adoptee producers; and so on. But even if I am mistaken in these expectations, the commoditization of women is not solely a matter of money: making use of women's bodies in certain ways constitutes a sort of commerce in this culture regardless of whether or not money is handed over, and regardless of the voluntariness or otherwise of women's participation. For example, a woman might model for her (male or female) photographer friend without payment, and yet the resulting photographs, despite the intentions of all concerned, nevertheless carry meanings to do with commerce and commodity. Here is a more striking example. The very practice of marriage is beset by meanings of commodity and ownership; so that even an 'enlightened' marriage which was explicitly designed to escape such meanings could not in fact do so. To institutionalize surrogacy would be likely, I think, to lead to an even greater acceptance of people's making use of each other—however voluntarily—either in explicitly commercial terms, or in terms of the power and control exercised by society over women, a phenomenon I would characterize to a large extent in terms of treatment as commodity.

In case this is thought to be an overly commercial view of the matter, ignoring what is really at issue here, namely the regulation in the best interests of all concerned of supererogatory acts of generosity, consider Judith Thompson's example of my perhaps agreeing to remain stuck in bed in order that the famous violinist may remain plugged into my kidneys: although the violinist has no right to this level of care on my part, I might agree to do so in the spirit of the Good Samaritan.[18] Is this not what is being proposed? And surely there can be no suggestion that such admirable self-sacrifice should not be allowed, a self-sacrifice which is far greater than anything contemplated by the surrogate mother? But are there not circumstances in which such apparently laudable behaviour might be wrong? Suppose, what is not after all entirely unimaginable, that such acts of supererogation, if repeated, led to people's having increasing expectations of their friends in the matter of organ function and/or replacement; and this in turn resulted in people's coming increasingly to feel guilty about not wishing to help a friend in this way. If such *were* the consequences of the spread, perhaps enhanced by the practice of instituting agreements to cover them, of such supererogatory acts, would it not be better if people did not undertake them, however admirable, laudable, and altogether good an individual case would doubtless appear to be if considered in isolation from the others? Prohibition, while at first sight quite absurd, might be

[18] Thompson (1971/2). The point was put to me by Edgar Page.

appropriate, just because acts are not thus isolated. Again: compare the different possible circumstances in which one might do something as apparently innocuous as withholding the truth about a person's illness.[19]

My earlier remarks about the commoditizing consequences of institutionalizing surrogacy are linked with a second sort of consequence, which, while even less apparently concrete, seems at least as important: namely that getting what you want would become an even more highly elevated value in our society than it already is. That is to say, attention would be directed even further away from the character of practices and institutions, from what they are like, from their impact on a variety of constituencies—from women and blacks to future generations—and become yet more closely focused on the satisfaction of people's present wants. The questions I am inclined to ask of what is wanted—What is it like? Is it right? How has it come to be wanted? Whose interests are served?—would be pushed yet further into the backwaters of our culture. That is to say, one consequence of progress in the business of getting what we want is that our wants come to assume ever greater importance: and this itself is an important reason for being wary about recommendations based on people's wants.

Whatever benefits it might bring to recipients and/or surrogates, by way of enabling the former to have children and the latter to exercise their altruism or earn some money or both, would be outweighed by the harm done to the general interests of women—and, I would argue, by extension to the general interests of all. The details of this assessment are neither simple nor uncontroversial, and all I have done here is to indicate the sorts of harm I have in mind. In brief, these are: the further commoditization of women; the resulting further commoditization of all of us; the further development of consumerist values, with attendant implications for the idea and practice of community in our society. Here, briefly, is a further consideration. The practice of surrogacy would further entrench the having and raising of children as the central means of women's fulfilment; and this would also push social life in certain directions rather than others. Childlessness, for instance, whether voluntary or otherwise, would become an even greater stigma. Getting what you want affects what others come to want.[20]

[19] I discuss this in Brecher (forthcoming).

[20] Some have suggested that surrogacy be encouraged as a means of widening the range of those who can have children, to include lesbians, single parents, and so on, in order thus to reduce the power of the nuclear family structure as the sole context for children 'ideally' to grow up in. The balance of expectations underlying this difference needs to be explored, and should constitute an important part of the debate.

Finally, as a morality-affecting harm, the institutionalization of surrogacy, because it exemplifies the set of attitudes described above (among others), furthers the attitudes and structures on which such attitudes are built and on the basis of which they gain their power. Just as page three of the *Sun*, in exemplifying a whole range of aspects of women's powerlessness, constitutes a further reminder of that situation and thereby reinforces it, so surrogacy agreements would work in a similar way. They would enhance a climate within which certain sorts of practice, activity, and attitude flourish, a climate which has of course in part given rise to the possibility of surrogacy agreements in the first place. Whatever individuals' intentions, or indeed despite them, activities and practices also exemplify and thus help entrench their meanings and create a climate in which certain things do, and others do not, count as harms. To institutionalize surrogacy would be to help prevent just those harms it would bring about from being recognized as harms.

However, even if I am entirely mistaken in my assessment of the factual likelihoods surrounding surrogacy, and even if I am entirely wrong in the moral judgments I have suggested might well be made about the sort of society which such developments enhance, the central point remains. Any advocacy of or objection to institutionalizing surrogacy agreements must, like discussion of other social practices, address these issues rather than relying on a narrow conception of harm which confines it to identifiable individual acts and persons, and which is based on highly questionable assumptions about the role in moral debate of what people want. It is not what surrogacy is, mythically, like *per se* which is the problem, but the consequences, both direct and indirect, of its being institutionalized: and any discussion of these must take into account the dialectical relationship between 'harms' and the moral climate.[21]

[21] I am particularly grateful to Edgar Page and Roger Crisp for our conversations about surrogacy, and for their comments on earlier drafts; and to David Evans for his helpful editorial advice.

Ethics and Drug Testing in Human Beings

JOSEPH MAHON

In late May 1984, Irish citizens were perturbed to hear that a thirty-one year old man died while participating, as a paid volunteer, in a clinical drug trial at the Institute of Clinical Pharmacology in Dublin. At the inquest, held in September 1984, the State Pathologist, Dr John Harbison, affirmed that the cause of death was the reaction of the trial drug Eproxindine 4/0091 with a major tranquillizer which had been given less than fifteen hours earlier as part of regular treatment for a psychiatric disorder. The mixture of the two drugs, he went on to say, increased their effect by between twenty and thirty times their normal strength, and the volunteer had died of cardiac depression.

This fatal effect was brought about as follows. Eproxindine acts as a suppressant of abnormal rhythms of the heartbeat, while Depixol is a long-lasting neuroleptic agent; in plainer language, the latter is a major tranquillizer, having a duration of action of about four weeks. This major tranquillizer is normally carried in the bloodstream in the human body bound to protein molecules. It is, in the words of a pharmacologist, heavily protein-bound. So, by an unhappy coincidence, is Eproxindine. Thus, as Dr David Nowlan, medical correspondent of the *Irish Times,* explains:

> If these two pharmacologically active substances are present together in the body they will be competing with each other for protein molecules on to which they would bind. Molecules of either drug which were effectively unbound by molecules of the other drug would then be free in the blood serum and maximally active pharmacologically. To have had 'normal' doses of both drugs together could therefore lead to an effective overdose of either or both, by freeing drug molecules from the protein molecules to which they were bound.
>
> One effect of an overdose of Eproxindine, as with other anti-arrhythmic drugs, would be to stop the heart, to throw it into asystole, and render it immune from other drug effects. And one effect of an overdose of a neuroleptic such as Depixol would be to suppress the respiratory centre in the brain and so stop spontaneous breathing.

> Both of these effects—cessation of heart beat and cessation of breathing—were observed in Niall Rush within two minutes of his having received 400 milligrams of Eproxindine within twenty-four hours of his having received forty milligrams of Depixol. Retrospectively, this theory offers a very likely explanation of the cause of death.[1]

I shall discuss the moral status of drug testing in human beings. This is the practice whereby, for a financial or other consideration,[2] new preparations or substances are first tried on a small number of healthy human beings, by clinical researchers, with a view to ascertaining their human pharmokinetics and pharmodynamics. In the broadest terms, pharmokinetics is the study of what the human body does to a drug—how it absorbs it, how it metabolizes it, and how it gets rid of it—while pharmodynamics is the study of how a drug acts on various functions in the human body—how it exerts its therapeutic effect, if any, and how it may cause side-effects.

A shorter, simpler definition of drug testing would be: the practice whereby new drugs are first tried on a small cohort of healthy human beings for the purposes of clinical research, usually with a financial reward for the participants.

The ethically disturbing dimensions of this practice are hinted at by Dr Nowlan in the following passage:

> We feel uneasy when we think about unknown substances being tried out on human beings, doubly uneasy when we hear that the volunteers are being paid (and thus perhaps exploited) and that the institute conducting the trial is making a good profit from its work. Our uneasiness is compounded by ambivalence, because we know that all new drugs must be tested by someone. So we prefer not to consider the issues too carefully, hoping that someone else may make rules and regulations for us.[3]

Other adverse comments at the time were to the effect that most of the volunteers for drug testing come from the lower socio-economic groups, that doubts had to be entertained about the extent of the information given to volunteers prior to testing, and that no one in his right mind would go into a drug testing clinic 'for that sort of money'. The amount in question was IR£20 per diem.

I should now like to look closer at some of these comments, because it isn't always clear what they mean. Then I shall document what are

[1] *Irish Times* 7/9/84.

[2] It could be a remission of sentence, for instance, where the participants were prisoners.

[3] *Irish Times* 7/9/84.

regarded as the beneficial and desirable consequences of the practice of drug testing, as well as the many safeguards which, it is said, are built into it. Finally, I shall give my own opinion on the matter, and in doing so shall discuss a more abstract philosophical issue having to do with the right to privacy, and the extent, if any, to which this right should be recognized when it comes to humans participating in clinical trials.

I

'We feel uneasy when we think about unknown substances being tried out on human beings', says Dr David Nowlan, without further comment or explanation. We are uneasy, I suggest, for the following reasons:

1. Many people have, understandably, some fear of the unknown.
2. Our conception of drug testing in human beings is easily coloured by images of Nazi doctors practising sickening experiments on human beings, by stories of torture meted out to prisoners of fascist and totalitarian regimes, by revelations concerning experimentation with animals, by horror movies, and so on.
3. There is the fear that since the effects of these substances in human beings is literally not (yet) known, those in whom they are infused are being used as guinea-pigs, i.e. are being treated, if necessary, as expendable casualties.

For all, or even any of these reasons, it is no surprise that (as Dr Nowlan says) 'we feel uneasy when we think about unknown substances being tried out on human beings'.

We feel doubly uneasy, he says, when we hear that the volunteers are being paid, 'and thus perhaps exploited'. To be exploited financially is, among other things, to be paid far less than one's efforts are worth, but it isn't the case that payment *per se* involves exploitation. Not everyone who is remunerated is exploited. Another factor, or factors, must be present. So, what exactly engenders the fear about payment for participation in clinical drug trials?

There are, it seems to me, at least four things behind the claim that we feel doubly uneasy when we hear that the volunteers are being paid.

1. The money is seen as an inducement, and this perception gives rise to the thought that if people have to be induced, or tempted (some use the word 'bribed') to participate in drug tests, then the testing must be a really unpleasant business. Alternatively, it gives rise to the thought that in situations where inducements are offered to persons, they have a known propensity to be less cautious in providing themselves with a harm-free human existence.

2. It seems reasonable to suppose that anyone who would submit to hospitalization, blood tests, the administration of unknown drugs orally, by injection or on a drip, for a relatively small amount of money, must be in serious financial difficulties; for, as a rule, human beings do not like to visit discomfort and trauma on themselves unnecessarily. So the impression grows apace that the participants in drug tests are drawn overwhelmingly from the poorest and most abject sections of the population. If that impression is vindicated, then two things follow: (a) one section of the population 'carries the can' for the entire population in this area of medical research; (b) since the cohort in question derives from the lowest income groups, these people who, by definition, are already socially and economically disadvantaged, have *further* unpleasant experiences visited upon them.
3. Where persons need money for the purposes of survival itself, then the record shows that they are very easily exploited, i.e. paid far less than their efforts are worth. In the case of drug testing, the record further shows, it is not simply that participants are open to exploitation: they are, demonstrably, exploited. I shall return to this point later.
4. Where participants are paid relatively little for what involves no small amount of discomfort, loss of freedom, and possible exposure to adverse medical consequences, then a legitimate doubt may be entertained as to whether these same volunteers may properly be called 'volunteers'. A consent given under these circumstances seems something less than the consent which is standardly given in cases involving good and bad consequences for human beings. We standardly consent to suffering bad consequences where we have a reliable guarantee of receiving substantial benefits in return to compensate us for the harm. Where the margin between benefit and suffering gets narrower, so that there is doubt whether one compensates for the other, participation will increasingly appear either stupid, reckless or constrained.

There is, finally, a very different kind of resentment of the financial factor, that which maintains that medical research should be engaged in only for the highest, or purest, of motives. This, by definition, would exclude money which, to this way of thinking, is sordid and base. One doctor interviewed on radio labelled this the 'idealist' approach to drug testing.

Another source of guilt, separate entirely from the uneasiness raised by the financial factor, is that people intuitively realize that drugs must be tested before going into routine medical practice. At the same time very few of us are involved in, or indeed know anything about, the drug testing that takes place. So once again there is the uncomfortable suspicion, amounting in many of us, on reflection, to a real sense of moral guilt, that the majority of us are not pulling our weight in the cause of medical research and human welfare, and that this responsibility is being shouldered by people who have little alternative but to do the unpleasant, and even dangerous, work that the rest of us would rather not even think about.

II

Those who defend the practice of drug testing in human beings do so on the following grounds.

1. Drug testing in human beings is necessary for progress in medicine. Without it there would be no effective medication; by means of it effective medication can be provided, and vital medical discoveries are made. One result of the Niall Rush fatality, for instance, is that the medical world has been alerted to the possibility if not the certainty of death, or at least severe cardiac or respiratory suppression, following the use of neuroleptics and anti-arrhythmics in combination.[4]
2. Those persons on whom the drugs are tested are volunteers. They participate in the trials of their own free will, and they give their consent in writing.
3. The consent given is an informed consent, i.e. it is given in the full, or clear, realization of what the tests involve, including an awareness of the fact that there is always an element of risk attached to what takes place. As Dr Nowlan reports:

   > At the time of admission they are given a four-page document which repeats the description of the study and provides in a dozen or so paragraphs the basis upon which they are being asked to sign their 'informed consent', including the clear statement that there is always an element of risk and no prospect of the health of the volunteer being improved by the trial in which he is to participate.[5]

4. All the drugs tested have been widely and repeatedly metabolized in 'animal body'. In other words, the drug testing in question is not literally first-time testing, only first-time testing in human beings. A great deal is already known about the actual and possible effects

[4] See D. Nowlan in the *Irish Times* 6/9/84.
[5] *Irish Times* 7/9/84.

of these drugs in living creatures. As a result, each drug comes from the manufacturing company with its own protocol attached; this is a list of instructions for trial purposes, setting out maximum and minimum dosages, and so on.

5. The testing is done in phases, i.e. cautiously, with gradual increases made in the doses of the drug being tested. The technique, basically, is to give progressively larger doses, over a protracted period, to healthy male volunteers. In the case of the ICP studies of Eproxindine, for instance, the trial had started in October 1983 and by the time Niall Rush came to receive his dose, Eproxindine had already been administered to seventy-four people, without any evidence of serious side-effects.
6. Drug testing in humans is a carefully graduated affair in the further sense that it is first conducted with healthy humans (these are called Phase One Trials), then on small numbers of patients whose illness the drug is designed to cure or ameliorate (Phase Two Trials). Finally, once the optimal dosage has been established following the Phase Two Trials, they are tried on large numbers of appropriate patients, so that their effectiveness and risk-benefit ratios can be established prior to marketing. The reason why drugs are not first tried on sick people is that they have what is called an 'abnormal physiology'.
7. Fatalities from drug testing are exceedingly rare. Since 1957, for instance, there have been over 10,000 volunteers at the Dublin clinic, and the death of Niall Rush was the clinic's first (and only) fatality. It should also be added that Niall Rush would never have been admitted into the test programme had he revealed to the clinic's medical personnel that he was on treatment for schizophrenia. Volunteers are told, orally and in writing, that they may not take any other medication for two weeks prior to the test. Mr Rush did not communicate the fact that he had been injected with Depixol just prior to entering the test programme and, despite having the most sophisticated laboratory in the country, the clinic would still not have been able, in the usual course of events, to detect its presence in his body, because it is a 'slow release' drug. Asked at the inquest why Mr Rush's family doctor could not have been contacted, seeing that his name had been given on the consent form, the director of the clinic replied that many of the volunteers did not want their doctors contacted. He went on to say, in a submission which I propose to analyse later:

   Yes there is a reason he was not contacted, and that is that in general terms the family doctor is not the custodian of the individual in society. The doctor could only be contacted with the express permission of Mr Rush. Anyway in these circumstances the examination we carried out on Mr Rush is more extensive than any GP might have carried out.[6]

8. There are elaborate procedures laid down by international agencies, such as the Food and Drugs Advisory Board, for the conduct of clinical drug testing in human beings, and clinics scrupulously follow these procedures, whether they are required to by law or not. In Ireland, as it happens, there is no statutory obligation to submit drug protocols or proposals for clinical trials to the National Drugs Advisory Board, though the ICP has always made such submissions in practice. A Bill was recently proposed before the Oireachtas;[7] its purpose was 'to provide for a statutory system of controlling clinical trials which involve the testing on individuals of drugs or other substances to establish whether they may have a medical or harmful effect'. The explanatory memorandum accompanying the legislative proposal makes it clear that the scheme 'would replace the existing voluntary arrangements for the clearance of proposals for such trials through the National Drugs Advisory Board'.[8]
9. Prior to being accepted as a voluntary paid participant in a drug trial, an applicant will do an electrocardiographic examination, and have a blood sample taken for routine testing. The would-be volunteer will return in a day or two when the results of his test will be available to the director or assistant director of the clinic's medical department. Assuming that the preliminary tests are satisfactory, one of these doctors will conduct a full medical examination of the prospective volunteer to ensure that he is, as they say, in the full of his health. Moreover, one of the conditions of participating in ICP trials is a willingness, or preparedness, to submit to random blood or urine tests to screen for the presence of drugs of abuse. In sum, the screening of volunteers is intended to be sufficiently thorough for medical purposes, without at the same time being so invasive as to seriously threaten the privacy or liberty of the individual.

[6] D. Byrne in the *Irish Times* 5/9/84.

[7] Under the Irish parliamentary system, the Oireachtas comprises the Senate and the Dail, the latter of which corresponds to the British House of Commons. The Clinical Trials Bill (first promoted in December 1986) has been given a further reading by the current Fianna Fail government, and is highly likely to become law.

[8] My own views on this legislation (which I welcome in principle) are published in the *Irish Medical Times* 23/5/86.

III

Reviewing the evidence, it seems to me that the defence of drug testing in human beings is a strong one. Without doubt, the practice results in advances in medicine, and the precautions taken are elaborate (which is not the same as saying they are foolproof). It still seems to me, however, that as the practice stands, it exhibits a number of morally objectionable features, and the cumulative effect of these is that it remains a morally objectionable practice.

First, even if we waive any objection to making profit from the labour or discomfort of human beings (as many people are evidently prepared to do), we may still find IR£20–25 unsatisfactory remuneration for the discomfort, loss of freedom due to hospitalization, and the risk to health which drug testing in its very nature brings. Typical side-effects, for instance, are mild, transient facial numbness, nausea, and dryness of the mouth. Looked at in this way, what is involved is not so much a matter of exploitation as one of simple injustice: the participants are not receiving a fair or decent return for what they contribute. To get a better perspective on this, consider the fact that the Institute of Clinical Pharmacology made a pre-tax profit of IR£600,000 in 1983, at which time it had three voting directors, one of whom, Dr Austin Darragh, owned seventy-five per cent of the equity. In 1984, the company made a net profit of just under IR£1·4 million, 'and that was achieved on a total revenue figure of IR£3·8 million which means that net margins are a staggering thirty-seven per cent'.[9] In 1985, the ICP went to the American market and raised 8·9 million dollars with an issue of twenty per cent of its equity. 'So the new American issue clearly puts Dr Darragh into the millionaire status. And he continues to earn a handsome return on his enterprise. The 1984 accounts show that dividends paid out in 1984 were a whopping IR£1 million.'[10]

But there is, at the end of the day, a democratic way of settling this issue. The reader is invited to put himself/herself the following question: 'Would I be prepared to participate in a clinical drug trial for IR£25 a (12 hour) day?' I would not.

If participants were paid a more realistic and equitable sum—say IR£100 a day—then it is a safe bet that the class membership of participants would quickly become more representative, thus removing some of the other objections to this practice.[11] In that event, as well, the screening of applicants could be made even more stringent than it is.

[9] M. Fitzpatrick in the *Sunday Independent* 23/6/85.

[10] M. Fitzpatrick in the *Sunday Independent* 23/6/85.

[11] However, if a much higher remuneration were introduced, the middle classes might become so interested in volunteering for projects that they would begin to displace those who were economically more marginal. In that case a quota system would have to be introduced.

As things stand, a significant proportion of the participants come from the socially and economically less privileged sections of society. Needless to say, clinics are anxious to rid themselves of the reputation of experimenting with down-and-outs, drug addicts, the unemployed, and so forth. So let us see what the evidence has to say. Between February and May 1984, 262 persons took part in drug tests at the ICP. Of these, 239 were involved just once, while twenty-three were involved twice. Of the 262, seventeen were homeless (6·4 per cent) and ninety-two were unemployed (35·11 per cent). The remainder were students, labourers, drivers, loaders, coalmen, porters, clerks and barmen. There was one civil servant, one retired civil servant, one service engineer, one chef, one hotel auditor, and several laboratory technicians.[12] On the Hall-Jones ordinal occupational scale, the bias in the occupations of volunteers clearly points towards social classes 6 and 7. These are the classes designated 'Manual, Semi-skilled', and 'Manual, Routine'.

On the basis of such data, I submit that the burden of responsibility for medical research and human welfare is not being evenly shared among the human population; indeed, a large section of the population (including the entire female segment) does not take *any* responsibility in the area of drug testing. Evidence from practice before and after the Rush case strongly supports the contention that the volunteers are almost exclusively drawn from the ranks of the unemployed. If you think, as I do, that we *all* have some moral obligation in this matter—after all, at some time or other, practically all of us will avail of these drugs—then this is another respect in which the practice of drug testing in human beings is, as it stands, morally objectionable. It might be maintained that volunteering for drug-testing is a supererogatory act, something that it is admirable to do without its being an obligation on everyone. I reply that it is to be viewed as a pan-social obligation, on a par with jury service or voting in general elections and referenda, and as such not to be evaded.

Finally, I wish to draw attention to a feature of drug testing in human beings which raises philosophical as well as clinical issues. It is sometimes said that adult citizens have a right to privacy—understood for the moment as the right to do with their own lives what they please—and that this right should be upheld so long as doing so does not infringe the rights of others. Such a view is implicit in the following extract from the report on the inquest into the Niall Rush fatality:

> Asked why, when Mr Rush's family doctor was named on the consent form, he could not be contacted and Mr Rush's condition

[12] See D. Nowlan, the *Irish Times* 5/9/84.

checked, Dr Darragh said many volunteers did not want their doctors contacted. 'Yes, there is a reason he was not contacted and that is that in general terms the family doctor is not the custodian of the individual in society. The doctor could only be contacted with the express permission of Mr Rush.'

The principle of respect for the privacy, or freedom, of the individual belongs to an intellectual continuity which derives, in the main, from the writings of John Stuart Mill, and, in particular, from Mill's *On Liberty*.[13] In this work Mill argues that subject only to the provision that no one else gets hurt in the process, each individual must be left to do and think as he pleases. The crucial sentences in this celebrated assertion of the right to freedom, or privacy, are the following:

> . . . that the sole end for which mankind are warranted, individually or collectively, in interfering with the liberty of action of any of their number, is self-protection; that the only purpose for which power can be rightfully exercised over any member of a civilized community, against his will, is to prevent harm to others. His own good, either physical or moral, is not a sufficient warrant. He cannot rightfully be compelled to do or forbear because it will be better for him to do so, because it will make him happier, because, in the opinion of others, to do so would be wise or even right. These are good reasons for remonstrating with him, or reasoning with him, or persuading him, or entreating him, but not for compelling him, or visiting him with any evil in case he do otherwise. To justify that, the conduct from which it is desired to deter him must be calculated to produce evil to someone else. The only part of the conduct of anyone, for which he is amenable to society, is that which concerns others. In the part which merely concerns himself his independence is, of right, absolute. Over himself, over his own body and mind, the individual is sovereign.[14]

The striking, and provocative, thing about Mill's principle—what has endeared it to generations of liberals ever since—is that it demands respect for the privacy, or freedom, of the individual *even* when or if respecting such privacy will manifestly not be in the individual's own interest. The individual is to be given his or her freedom in all cases where the exercise of this freedom does not impinge (adversely) on others, *including therefore* those instances where the exercise of such freedom will, in fact or demonstrably, rebound on the agent exercising

[13] I emphasize that my concern here is with the intellectual tradition deriving from Mill, and not with Mill's writings themselves. Obviously I would not wish to ascribe to Mill all the features of late twentieth-century liberalism.

[14] Mill (1962) 135.

that same freedom.[15] This is the full force of the concluding proposition of the quoted passage: 'Over himself, over his own body and mind, the individual is sovereign'.

The standard application of the principle of privacy may be found in the area of pornography and the law. Pornography, it is argued, is not *proven* harmful, and, for that reason, there is no good ground for suppressing it. The willing consumer of pornography must be left to the untrammelled enjoyment of his sexual fantasies. On the other hand, pornography is deeply offensive to many people; there is, as such, good ground for restricting its availability to certain prescribed outlets, which are such that they do not offer gratuitous or avoidable offence to members of the public who do not wish such images thrust upon their psyches. This, in essence, was the argument of the *Williams Report,* a document which is, for the most part, sympathetic to Mill's outlook.[16]

There is at least one other tradition in moral philosophy which sees things differently. Deriving in the end from Plato's *Phaedrus* and *Laws,* it holds that there is no justification for depriving a human being of something which it is vital for any human being to have, when there is nothing equally good, or better, to be received in return.[17] In short, there is no justification for depriving a human being, oneself or anyone else, of a basic human good. On this view, suicide will therefore be immoral, as will any other action in which, or by means of which, the individual does himself a palpable harm, there being no compensating, or insufficient compensating, benefit received in return. The implication of this variant of natural law theory is that the right to freedom, or privacy, cannot have even the limited sovereignty which Mill would demand that it have: the individual is *not* sovereign over his or her body and mind if that is supposed to include the freedom to destroy or injure them. Human welfare is to take precedence over human freedom, even

[15] Mill scholars now tend to hold that while Mill was opposed to strong paternalism, he favoured what Ten calls 'a degree of paternalism' ((1980) 110). Weak paternalism is defined by Ten as 'the doctrine that we are justified in interfering to prevent a person from harming himself only when there is a defect in his decision to engage in the self-harming activity'. Such a defect exists when, for example, the person lacks some relevant knowledge, lacks self-control, or is the victim of undue influence. It is interesting to note that while Mill's favouring weak paternalism is said to be proven by analysis of Mill's arguments and examples, Ten himself does not provide this analysis. Second, if Ten's claim is true, then Mill's principle, in the end, has application only to the perfectly rational, fully informed and psychologically secure individual. But how many human beings fit into this category?

[16] See Williams (1979) 53–8.

[17] I am indebted for this information, and for the insights derived from it, to Levy (1979/80).

if freedom is commonly thought to be intrinsic to the living of a worthwhile human existence.

I do not intend to pursue the purely philosophical discussion any further in this paper. Rather I want to investigate its application to the practice of drug testing in human beings.

A note about the meaning of the word 'privacy' before venturing further. A right to privacy is construed here as a right to personal freedom. It may, *in addition,* be construed as a right to non-surveillance of certain uses one makes of this freedom. Personal freedom itself may be construed (1) as non-interference, and (2) as having plenty of elbow-room. Where drug testing is concerned, the right to privacy has been upheld, and defended, as a matter of principle, in all the various ways depicted by these definitions. The participant or volunteer is not required to contact his family doctor, nor is a family doctor contacted with a view to ascertaining the medical history of the volunteer, except in case of emergency.[18] (I note that the Clinical Trials Bill 1986 does not require the submission of such medical evidence either; in view of what happened in 1984, this omission is, to say the least, alarming.) This, it is said, is out of deference to the individual's right to privacy.[19]

Respect for the principle of privacy is, of course, laudable: a life without freedom would simply not be worth living. Yet clearly there are circumstances where honouring the principle of privacy can have disastrous consequences.

Niall Rush's family doctor was not contacted with a view to establishing his medical history in its entirety. Rush himself chose not to divulge information concerning medication he had received—the slow-release drug Depixol—to the ICP, and it was this drug, in combination with the trial drug, which precipitated his death in such an untimely fashion. In view of this tragic and disastrous occurrence, it is time, I submit, to review the importance we attach to the principle of privacy.

My own view would be that in view of the risks involved, we pay too high a price for this same principle, and that therefore this is one area, or should I say another area, where the privacy of the individual must be invaded. Not to do so in the circumstances under discussion is to leave persons prey to their own ignorance, to their own desperate needs, and to the not negligible hazards of medical experimentation. Anything that can be done to further reduce the risks to the volunteer

[18] But then it would very probably be too late. In Niall Rush's case, as reported at the inquest, the 'emergency' lasted one minute, after which he was dead.

[19] In more recent interviews Dr Darragh has stressed the *confidential* nature of the doctor–patient relationship.

should be done. Lamentably, but unavoidably, this will necessitate depriving certain individuals of a freedom they currently enjoy.

There is a further argument, of a kind which would appeal to Mill, for the same conclusion. Where drug testing respects the privacy of the individual, clinical results could be obtained for a supposedly known cohort of *bona fide* healthy human beings. Yet because the participants were not required to divulge details of their medical histories, and because the clinic did not think it had the right to obtain such information in any event, these same clinical results could, quite conceivably, be misleading and flawed, *if* one or more of the participants decides to conceal clinically significant information, *and* this information is not unearthed throughout the whole of the screening and random testing process. The consequences for later batches of volunteers, and for general medical practice, should this ever occur, might not be very pleasant. The only way to prevent, or at any rate, to further minimize, the risk of this occurring, is to breach the principle of privacy. However, I think I should want to breach it even if this Millian argument could not be invoked.

In conclusion, I disagree with Dr Owen Wade when he says:

> The welfare of the subject must come first, and experiments should not be performed on a man if they are likely to harm him, even if the result might be highly advantageous to science and to the health of others. The difficulty is to decide what constitutes 'harm', and how one assesses whether an experiment is 'likely' to harm. Although the subject needs protection, the community needs knowledge.[20]

Instead I think we should say: the community needs knowledge (in this case, effective medication), while the subject needs protection *and* compensation. If the compensation is sufficiently attractive, then participation rates for the assorted occupational groups will, I strongly suspect, quickly tend to even out. In that event it will be possible to say that society *as a whole,* or at any rate, male society as a whole, is discharging its obligation to human health and human welfare.

[20] See the *Irish Times* 10/9/84.

Genetic Engineering and the Autonomous Individual

SHYLI KARIN-FRANK

The aim of this paper is to expose the unique muddle in which moral philosophy finds itself with regard to genetic engineering. The latter can be essentially defined as the correcting of nature's mistakes at their source, the DNA acid molecule of the gene. I shall discuss the moral nature of genetic engineering with respect to a single issue: the potential harm it may inflict upon the autonomous individual. I shall also consider the distinctions between genetic engineering and other activities affecting human existence, in order to establish that the moral issues presented by genetic engineering are unique to it.

Genetic engineering is often rejected on emotional grounds. I argue that if this emotional rejection of genetic engineering is backed by an intuition, then the latter, when explicated, is false as well as inconsistent with other moral intuitions. It would be possible to reject genetic engineering as an activity that distinctively violates and even destroys a person's autonomy, on the basis of and only on the basis of the genetic definition of individuality: if one's identity is constituted by one's genes,[1] then genetic engineering literally transforms one's individuality and original identity. Thus, it cannot be assumed that genetic engineering is based on the moral good of improving the lot of an afflicted individual, since this objective is not coherent if there is no continuous identity to be improved. Yet, this conclusion will be shown to exact a high price from our fundamental moral convictions; for it would seem to entail the acceptance of other forms of social and political violence, provided they do no harm to the genetic base of the individual.

I

I will first locate the moral issue, concerning the possible harm that may be inflicted upon the individual, in its proper context. Genetic engineering is a subdivision of medical genetics, which until now has

[1] *Gene*: the biological unit of heredity; it is self-reproducing and located in a definite position on a particular chromosome.

been mainly a preventive medicine, involving genetic research, prediction and counselling. In its wider sense genetic engineering includes the application of knowledge and methods employed in microbiology, medicine, biochemistry and genetics, in a way that makes it possible to determine the genotype of a living creature. Genetic engineering also helps to cultivate and improve species in agriculture, as well as playing a central role in the decision to continue a pregnancy when no defects are traced.

In the restricted sense, genetic engineering has been mainly used so far on plants and laboratory animals; as regards humans it is still a matter for the future. It is an intervention directed upon the content or organization of an organism's genetic complement. This would thus include intervention by directed mutation,[2] recombination or molecular construction (presumably to be followed by appropriate selective methods), to isolate organisms with the desired genotype in each case. The medical purpose of the different techniques is to cure inherited disease in animals.

In this paper I do not intend to consider the ethical problems involved in cloning procedures: these are meant to produce a number of genetically identical copies of an organism out of human tissue. Therefore, it cannot be regarded as a case that involves the concept of the autonomous individual (whether pre- or post-natal).[3]

I will refer only to gene therapy, which is the use of biochemical or cell biological methods to add to or replace part of the genetic complement of a plant or a higher animal. Penetration of exogenous DNA into cells and its subsequent expression by transcription and translation have been described most thoroughly in bacteria. There the process is called transformation if the DNA is bacterial, or transfection if viral DNA is involved. A process with the same result can occur in the cells of higher organisms. Here we find some developing methods and techniques which can all be applied to an existing human being (pre- or post-natal) after experiments have been successfully made on laboratory animals.

Transformation and transduction are attempts at inserting genes taken from an external source into the cells of an animal. It is either the insertion of a segment of DNA or the infection with a harmless virus which either has the desired gene or is used as a 'vehicle' for that gene. It can also be the insertion of a whole foreign chromosome into the cell.

[2] *Mutation*: a permanent transmissible change in the genetic make-up of an individual, such that the characteristics of an offspring are different from those of his parents.

[3] I do not wish to imply that clonal processes make no biological sense where humans are concerned. See further Eisenberg (1976).

The 'repair' of cells in a culture involves the possibility of employing techniques of nucleus implanting or transfer and of mending of somatic cells, for the purpose of the repair of hereditary defects. An attempt is made at removing cells from the sick body and transferring them to laboratory culture, where they undergo genetic engineering (transformation, transduction and the insertion of a chromosome), and then are reintroduced into the sick body.

A further technique is the implantation of cells or tissues. If there is a satisfactory solution to the problem of rejection of implanted organs, then it may be possible to cure a person's disease by inserting into his body whole cells with healthy genotype, contributed by another human.

All the above mentioned techniques are meant to be applied to human individuals, whether pre- or post-natal. These techniques are morally problematic not only in themselves but also with respect to general medicine which strives both to remedy different types of cancer or nervous diseases and to replace defective organs.[4]

I will now posit eight limiting suppositions which will define the moral issue now under consideration:

1. Genetic engineering will be considered only as a theoretical possibility. Some have commented that the unrealistic and impractical nature of genetic engineering reduces all the moral issues involved to pseudo-problems. It has been argued, for instance, that we do not have the ability to alleviate inherited disease by introducing the normal form of a particular gene into a person with defects in his copies of that gene (although we can carry out some of the steps involved in such a procedure).[5] Further, it has been argued that only those monogenic defects causing biochemically defined lesions have any real chance of treatment by gene therapy in the foreseeable future. The reason is that the gene therapy will require a large quantity of an isolated gene or chromosomal locus. It is inconceivable that effective gene therapy could result from treatment with unfractionated human DNA, in which the abundance of a typical structural gene is about one in a million DNA segments (depending on the length of the DNA segments). The isolated gene is needed and current schemes for gene isolation require a biochemically defined gene product—an enzymatic activity, an antigenic determinant or, better yet, a messenger RNA. Another argument is that it is difficult to identify a genetic disease, as distinct from other kinds of disease, in the first place; for most diseases have genetic traces.[6] The very act of labelling a disease by its cause

[4] See further Lederberg (1976).
[5] Morrow (1976).
[6] Motulsky (1973).

rather than by its set of pathological symptoms may be considered dangerous; any given set of symptoms constituting a genetic disease inherits not only a genetic make-up but a whole host of other factors. There is no harm in calling the disease after its genetic inheritance if genetic factors are the only significant ones. But this latter point will be extremely difficult to establish.[7]

But even if the label 'genetic disease' is not controversial, it will still be easier to identify such defects than to practise a therapy. Tay–Sachs disease, for example, is caused by the accumulation of fatty matter in the central nervous system, as a result of the lack of enzyme decomposing that matter. We know both the identity of the missing enzyme and the sources of healthy genes (which include information for the creation of the normal enzyme). Suppose we have succeeded in identifying and isolating that gene, and suppose we have found a harmless virus to carry the gene when inserted into the blood of a sick body. The inserted gene should reach the cells of the central nervous system, especially the brain. However, there is a selective block (whose origin is as yet unknown) that does not allow the passage of matter from the blood to the brain. Moreover, even if we could overcome that block, so that the desired enzyme were produced, there remains a problem of guaranteeing the normal operation of the gene by the control system of the cell. The gene could either be paralysed or continue to produce exaggerated quantities of the enzyme and thus cause other damage.

These few examples do something to illustrate how controversial is the scientific value of genetic engineering. Nonetheless, I suggest that for the purpose of our philosophical considerations we regard genetic engineering as a hypothetical enterprise, with certain successful consequences. For argument's sake I will concede that genetic change may possibly cure or alleviate physical or behaviour defects. I do not, therefore, argue for the delegitimization of genetic engineering on the basis of current limits of knowledge.[8] In other words, if we wish to evaluate genetic engineering then we had better construe the latter as a well-established activity, or else we would have to condemn it on the general grounds of sceptical rationality, according to which every action that leads to uncertain consequences ought to be avoided. However, by doing so we would not be able to identify the unique moral issues involved in genetic engineering.

2. I will, for the sake of argument, grant that the intended purpose of genetic engineering is the curing of an abnormality in order to sustain the life of an afflicted individual or to improve the life of such an

[7] Neville (1976).
[8] Ladd (1982); also Callahan (1976).

individual, and that its explicit objective is not eugenic. By that I do not mean to ignore the controversy surrounding the potential causal relationship between the two, or the effect one individual genetic change may have on the human gene pool.[9] However, as our issue is the autonomous individual who undergoes genetic therapy, I will not consider the arguments commonly used against genetic engineering, which are based on the harmful effect of eugenics on the individual and on the values of society.[10]

3. As is implicit in the above, I accept that any potential for moral good that genetic engineering may possess emerges only if its purpose is to remove a defect and thereby enable an afflicted individual to lead a normal human life. The engineering of human genes for the purpose of creating mutants, monsters, paragons or for any similar purpose is, by its very nature, wholly excluded.[11]

4. I assume that genetic engineering is undertaken on behalf of the individual, whose welfare is regarded as an end in itself and not as a mere means. I thereby preclude the manipulation of the individual's genetic base and the control of the human gene pool for social or political reasons; for this is independently considered to be morally wrong, whether the means involved are genetic or of any other kind.[12]

5. I shall consider the moral nature of genetic engineering only from the standpoint of the individual who is its subject. His autonomy may be in danger; so I shall omit the perspective of the rights of the family, society or future generations. Therefore I shall not present the conflict that may arise between the individual and the public interest; this is an important factor in the general moral evaluation of genetic engineering, yet of secondary importance to our particular discussion.[13]

6. I have adopted the postulate that, from the vantage point of full moral rights, both the embryo and the foetus are potentially human. So genetic engineering involves moral issues whether we are concerned with the autonomy of a nascent individual human being or of an adult human being.

[9] Crow (1968).
[10] Murphy (1982).
[11] Hubbard (1982).
[12] *Gene pool*: the gametes of all mating individuals which comprise an assembly from which the genes of the next generation are drawn.
[13] Murphy (1975).

7. The autonomy of the individual person is for me, as for almost all moral theorists, a fundamental premise. The minimal sense of autonomy is free choice based on an intelligent assessment. Thus, another person's autonomy can be violated by simply ignoring his preferences, or by imposing our own preferences against his better judgment and will. On the basis of liberal principles, I also assume that only under special restrictions will it be possible to justify an interference with someone's autonomy (as, for example, in the case of authorized punishment).

8. I choose to consider genetic engineering within a non-religious framework for the following reasons: (a) The basis of the frequent religious rejection of genetic engineering is the idea that one should not interfere with God's creation, rather than the moral idea of protecting a person's autonomy.[14] (b) As such, the religious argument is effective only if it is also fanatic, that is to say, only if it rejects all activities that tend to interfere with God's plans. Hence, genetic engineering is condemned to the same extent as are abortion, contraception and even (in the extreme case) the simple cure of sick people. Once the religious judgment starts to distinguish between what it conceives as legitimate activities like healing or using contraception and non-legitimate activities like abortion and genetic engineering, it should also justify these distinctions. The criteria which will be needed are those which we will be investigating. (c) If the distinction to be made is also to be of a moral nature, then a moral major premise will have to be added to the religious judgments.[15] So the religious point of view is irrelevant to our discussion.

II

The constraints presented above define the moral predicament of genetic engineering on two different levels. On the first level we bypass someone's consent through genetic procedures, simply because it is impossible to obtain it. This happens, for example, in the cases of the embryo or the sick and unconscious adult. Here, on the one hand, the purpose of such procedures is to overcome the subject's disability in order to better his life and, in some cases, even to enable him to take full responsibility for the conduct of personal affairs. This intention is

[14] Ladd (1982).
[15] Anscombe (1970).

morally good and in so far as biogenetic change succeeds in its objective, it has positive moral value. On the other hand, in those cases where it is impossible to obtain the consent of the individual, since his humanness is more of an unexercised moral claim, genetic engineering does not concern itself with the future beliefs and value judgments of the individual. It is at least indifferent to the question of the subject's free choice and it is therefore, at least *prima facie*, morally assailable. Stated simply, the moral status of genetic engineering is essentially controversial, since it aspires towards the benevolent paternalistic objective of enhancing the welfare of another individual, but it does so through the imposition of our own beliefs, standards and preferences. It seems, therefore, that genetic engineering's disregard for any future reservations that the person may have about genetic modification or its consequences, violates the autonomy of the individual.

Now, if the moral problem is presented in this way, it is seen to depend on the factual impossibility of obtaining the embryo's or the adult's consent, as well as on their inability to prevent its implementation. Yet, a different description of genetic engineering may arise if it is compared with birth, for example, a natural process which engenders multiple risks in itself and which paves the way for potential dangers during an entire lifetime. Similarly it could be said that both a pre- and post-natal individual is subject, without recourse, to numerous paternalistic decisions; examples would be the place chosen for the family to reside in, or the life-style selected. Such factors have hereditary and environmental impact on the life of the individual.

It seems now that our former presentation of the problem rests on a fallacy, since it presupposes the existence of alternative circumstances under which the autonomy of the embryo or the unconscious adult is not bypassed. Further, if we now demand respect for the autonomy of the embryo or the unconscious adult under all contingencies, we lose the distinction between genetic engineering and other activities, including harmless ones, which do not conform with that demand; accordingly, the latter would have to be considered morally wrong. If we turn now to examine the second level, we find cases where one's consent or refusal are either being bypassed or even obtained by virtual coercion, even though the individual is in a condition to be fully informed and to make his own decisions. Yet, if we morally condemn genetic engineering simply because it ignores or acts against a person's free choice, that will not be sufficient. The logical terminus of this line of reasoning runs up against a prevalent and basic moral belief: that not all paternalistic actions are of the same kind, given that some are carried out on behalf of the dependent individual while others are actually coercive, violent and thus, *ipso facto*, morally repugnant. In other words, if genetic engineering necessarily involves coercion, then, tautologically it violates the autonomy of the individual. However, this is not a sufficient condition for condemning such an activity. For it could still be judged as one out of many manifestations of social paternalism; and the latter is sometimes judged as justifiable or even as obligatory.

If an essential distinction can be made between genetic engineering and other actions forced on the individual, then certain paternalistic actions could perhaps be justified without prejudicing conclusions concerning the moral defensibility of the former. For it is possible to argue that genetic engineering does more than merely bypass the subject's consent; it constitutes a more drastic external interference, one which is aimed at changing a given natural order, through irresistible force. As the individual subjected to genetic engineering is innocent and harmless, the exercise of power in the therapy cannot be justified by appeal to institutional authority as it is, for example, in the case of punishment. Therefore, the enterprise can be judged to be one of obvious violence and a violation—in a stronger sense—of autonomy. It follows that even if the objective of genetic engineering is good, nevertheless the means by which it is realized are morally inadmissible, as they inflict violence on a defenceless individual while penetrating that person's privacy.

Act-utilitarians provide little help for those who wish to evaluate the principle of genetic engineering. They will raise the question of whether such admittedly violent interference will result in the future happiness of the individual or, at least, minimize the person's suffering so as to compensate for the offence against autonomy. But an empirical approach of this kind presupposes that the desirability of life and of living in the best way possible is as morally important as one's autonomy. A decision not to interfere in order to eliminate or minimize disability, may jeopardize the individual's existence (in the case of life-threatening problems) or result in unavoidable sanctions against the person's liberties (owing to behavioural abnormalities); and this will limit future happiness and autonomous life. So an act-utilitarian appears to require a separate decision regarding every case where genetic engineering is under consideration.

From both rule-utilitarian and deontological perspectives the good or bad consequences of each particular application of genetic engineering are irrelevant to the moral issue; the question is whether or not the activity itself violates a moral rule or principle. Kant's morality, for instance, which has the concept of autonomy at its centre, commits us to treating an individual as an autonomous personality, as an end in and for himself, regardless of other empirical facts, among which the genetic make-up is but one. Two conflicting conclusions seem to follow on this view. Either it is not permissible forcibly to bypass the individual's judgments (whether favourable or unfavourable) about genetic change; or any action or inaction that endangers his existence is disallowed. This conflict makes it inevitable that any decision taken will be immoral, since it will violate the same rule or principle that forbids violence. In this way we get what appears to be a destructive moral dilemma.

Does genetic engineering really constitute a moral dilemma? Kant puts me under obligation to treat the other as if we both belong to the noumenal moral community where neither empirical defects nor empirical advantages are relevant to the concepts of moral obligation and moral intention. Yet one could argue that some behavioural defects may deny the individual the opportunity to exercise his right to belong to a moral community; one may not be able to choose between alternatives and make moral judgments as a result of such disability. Accordingly genetic changes may perhaps serve to free the individual from limitations and allow him to take an active part in human life; and by this means he will be able to exercise his autonomy.

But according to Kant's theory, only one position lends itself to moral judgment and that is the position of the active agent in genetic engineering. It is incumbent on me to treat the afflicted individual as a member of the moral community with full rights—even if he himself cannot understand human existence in moral terms or, for any reason whatsoever, cannot participate in the moral arena.

Thus, we are drawn back to our dilemma, according to which the violation of someone's autonomy is brought about by bypassing his consent in a violent manner. To resolve it I shall compare genetic engineering with education and medical surgery. I have deliberately chosen these analogies not only because we tend to justify such activities—or even make them obligatory—on the basis of our common moral convictions, but also because both have been thoroughly discussed by moral philosophy generally as cases of justifiable intrusion into the domain of the individual. The controversy that surrounds these activities concerns not their basic justifiability but rather the nature of the restrictions we ought to impose on such intrusions.

Can one justify the paternalistic imposition involved in genetic engineering in a way analogous to the justification for education? Even Kant's extreme defence of autonomy permits education for children even though it violates their autonomy. It seems reasonable to argue that education is a moral duty, given that it is the most appropriate means by which to facilitate the child's enfranchisement in the universal moral community and the realization of the child's potential. A proponent of genetic engineering might argue that the status of a defective embryo, for instance, is similar to that of the child who is being educated: both have a right to all possible help in order fully to develop their potential.

This analogy may be challenged. There are differences between education and genetic change despite the paternalistic underpinnings common to both. For example, a distinction between these two sets of activities is that genetic change, unlike education, necessarily utilizes direct force or even violence. Violence in education, one could argue, if present at all, is indirect or sublimated.

But the advocate of genetic engineering can rebut this challenge. If we maintain that the presence of violence is a sufficient or even necessary distinction between the two kinds of paternalistic activity, we assume that violence is an objective fact. But it is far from obvious which acts are genuinely violent and which should be viewed as merely an exercise of power. Moreover there is no way of objectively measuring degrees of violence. So one might judge education to be one of the most violent spheres of human activity, since its oppressive means are so indirect and subtle. The presupposition in this line of argument is that disguised violence is more difficult to identify, and therefore to resist, than are overt forms of violence.

However, simply on the basis of our intuitions, there does not seem to exist a critical point distinguishing genetic engineering from education. Genetic change transforms the individual's characteristics in a way that could not have come about through education or environmental conditions. It replaces—and does not merely modify or condition—the intrinsic potential of the individual. In contrast, education is not a drastic act. It does not change a personality but merely modifies it by eliciting and cultivating what is already immanent in the individual. Even in its most extreme form, where it involves conditioning, education takes into account the individual's faculties and given characteristics and does not create a personality solely on the basis of external feedbacks. No doubt other, less extreme conceptions of education take the genetic complement of the individual to be an inalterable challenge.

Indeed genetic engineering can be seen as the opposite of education, with respect to both the means employed and the underlying presuppositions about human nature. The educational process is premised on the notion that even though environmental conditions are not the sole key to the understanding of human behaviour (for there are also hereditary and other empirical factors), nevertheless they are the means by which it can be made to conform with normative standards. This conception, the basis of many types of socialization, has its root in the belief that evil and suffering are mainly the product of social order, not of the individual (otherwise, there would have been no prospect for educational or political efforts). In opposition to this, genetic engineering implicates the individual as the main source of personal disabilities and poor achievements; society as such is involved to the extent that it is only through personal changes that society may have some hope.[16]

Most liberal theories tend to justify certain restrictions in the modes of education. They embody the belief that paternalism is sometimes necessary and that, ultimately, it does not harm the child's autonomy; for the individual is supposed to remain autonomous both during and after the process of education. Although the proper aims of education can be subverted and abused, education essentially enhances the human faculties of judgment and free choice. Even where education (properly conceived) does not succeed in achieving its goals, it would be wrong to describe it as destroying these faculties. They are assumed as part of the nature of man, so that they made education possible in the first place.[17] Moreover education is a process that occurs gradually and can be changed or stopped at any time.

On the other hand, genetic engineering, whether it be pre- or post-natal, essentially circumvents the individual's discretionary liberty; the influence of its effects will dominate its human subject after birth and throughout his life span. In the relatively brief time that it takes to execute, artificial genetic change is completed with finality. It is not a graduated process, and the modifications it produces in the individual are exceptionally irreversible. On these grounds, while the paternalism intrinsic to education can perhaps be justified, that of genetic engineering should be rejected.

It may be suggested that education can be fruitfully applied only to those who are educable, those who have the capacity to become part of the human community as 'normal adults'. However, as we have already seen, genetic engineering can be justified, if at all, only if it is directed exclusively toward those who are abnormal. For such individuals genetic engineering potentially complements education, from which it must be distinguished. Indeed, it may afford the behaviourally disabled the possibility of becoming candidates for an education that may have not otherwise been possible for them. This argument, though, treads on thin ice when it attempts to distinguish, in a descriptive manner, between defects which will make an individual an outsider to the human community and those which will have almost no effect on his human status. For such a distinction is primarily a normative matter. What is actually involved here is our way of postulating the nature of the moral community as well as the criterion by which someone is included in it.

To conclude, it seems that even if it is true that education is a

[16] I will not consider the controversial issue of the causal connection between an individual genetic change and the gene pool of future generations.

[17] See further Ramsey (1970).

paternalistic process and a violent one (although in an indirect and subtle way), nevertheless in opposition to genetic engineering education is not a drastic act for it does not change one's given characteristics but merely modifies them; and it takes into account, as well as presupposing, the individual's autonomy.

Aside from genetic engineering there are other spheres of activity that seek to remedy human disability. So what distinguishes genetic change from medical surgery, for example? Surgery, like genetic change, is an external, drastic intrusion exercised by force on a person. Unlike education, both processes can be applied to the embryo; and in the case of incapacitated, diseased or injured patients who cannot consent to or refuse treatment, as well as in the case where someone actually refuses treatment, both can be imposed on their subjects. When a person's autonomy is ignored in surgery and genetic engineering, this is presumably done in the person's own interest. Genetic engineering and surgery also share the attribute of irreversibility, at least in the case of some and perhaps most surgical procedures. Open heart surgery, the removal or implantation of organs and even procedures that are cosmetic in purpose, are as radical in their immutability as is artificial genetic change. On the other hand, like education and unlike genetic engineering, a surgical operation cures and shapes the individual without changing his intrinsic make-up. (There exists, however, a whole branch of non-genetic brain surgery which presents similar moral issues with regard to the interference with a subject's given characteristics. I consider this below.)

If, under certain restrictions, both education and the majority of surgical operations are morally justifiable in spite of their paternalistic and violent character, it is mainly because neither destroys the conditions necessary for autonomy. From the moral point of view, human autonomy involves more than simply free choice and intelligence to choose between alternatives. It must also imply the continuous existence of the subject who exercises his autonomy through his actions, for which he is considered to be responsible. We could ask whether genetic engineering inflicts harm on the 'nature' of man—that is, on the conditions by which he is defined as human. If it does, then genetic engineering can be considered as a violation of autonomy—in a stronger sense than merely bypassing consent, even when it is done violently. An examination of traditional definitions of the nature of man reveals that on rationalistic conceptions, for instance, human nature consists of rationality and universality: it is a person's ability to understand as well as to distinguish between right and wrong. Empirical and accidental phenomena have no effect on someone's true nature, since they belong to a totally different category. On this basis there will be no difference between genetic change and an ordinary removal of any organ.

Or consider an existentialist position. If the individual is defined by the plain fact of his existence and his freedom to choose between alternative courses of conduct, then biographical, medical or any other set of factors—like the genetic material of the person—do nothing to eradicate the nature of such an individual.

Or let us take sceptical empiricism as our frame of reference. The empiricist rejects any attempt to attribute an *a priori* nature to man. Then it follows that the genetic code, like any other empirical datum, is no more than an element in the accumulation of experiences through which a person's nature historically grows and develops.

If it is not possible to establish that genetic engineering harms a person's nature, which is a precondition for autonomy, it still does not follow that it inflicts no harm on his identity; by 'identity' I mean a person's unique and distinctive individuality. It is significant that only if we define the individual on the basis of his unique genetic code, will we be able to distinguish between genetic engineering and other paternalistic activities, like education and medical surgery. The latter activities are realized on the basis of the individual's original genetic material; they are limited and dependent on his inherent genes. But genetic engineering only starts from the original genes, which according to the genetic definition of individuality are the core of one's uniqueness. It then goes on to transform them irrevocably; and in doing so it transforms the person's identity as well. The very act of genetic change effectively destroys what its practitioners define as the essence of the individual and converts him to another person. In genetics the existence of the human individual is viewed as starting from a speck of information which is the product of the accidental sexual combination of his parents. Both his pre- and post-natal development are the processes whereby he becomes what he has already been from the moment he was conceived. His unique complement is selected out of a vast number of possibilities. It is certain that no two individuals exist with the same genotype, except for identical twins, and that personal individuality consists of the unrepeatably created complement of the original informational speck.

On these grounds, which are common both to utilitarian and deontological perspectives, we can morally reject genetic engineering, although in a tautological manner only. It is not merely a paternalistic, violent and irreversible intervention into the domain of the individual; more, it inevitably assassinates his identity as well. The tautological judgment is indispensable; for it reveals the contention that morally intended genetic change is directed toward the original individual and undertaken for his benefit, as intrinsically fallacious. Viewed from this perspective, moral intentions in the case of genetic change are, at best, merely a description of the practitioner's state of mind. In reality, the individual is not the subject of the process, since he is essentially eradicated. Enforced genetic alteration does not indicate benevolence towards the defective embryo or concern for his future welfare. So we can now conclude that the lack of consent of the individual is a necessary, as well as a sufficient condition, for rejecting genetic engineering. For even in the case of an adult consenting or requiring to undergo a genetic change, genetic engineering is still to be morally condemned. What is involved here is a case of murder or, at best, assistance in committing suicide. In itself this is morally unjustifiable. Even from a radical liberal position, where there is a moral right to commit suicide without external interference, there is no corresponding duty or right to help another person to achieve this aim. Such allegedly beneficent objectives can only be fulfilled if personal identity and unity are preserved throughout and in the aftermath of such a process.

If human individuality is defined by the genetic code which is unique to and original in each person, we can argue that genetic engineering presents us with distinct moral issues, which are not found in other areas of human endeavour. If we accept the genetic definition of the individual and also try to preserve the autonomy of the individual, then the dilemma mentioned above is resolved and genetic engineering can only be viewed as morally wrong.

III

The advantage of this perspective is that it provides justification for some paternalistic actions, while condemning genetic engineering. But there are problems. (1) The criterion of morality which we have used to comment on the paternalism in genetic engineering is, it now appears, a double-edged sword. For such activities as indoctrination or social and political tyranny, are not rejectable on this basis, since they do not constitute assaults on the genetic base. But our moral intuitions demand the rejection of brainwashing, terrorism and tyranny. (2) The factual existence of identical twins contradicts the genetic definition of individual identity. Identical twins have the same genotype, and they exhibit the only naturally occurring human case that corresponds to the clone of laboratory conditions. Yet each twin is—and knows that he is—a unique and unrepeated human person, something for which the genes drawn from his parents do not account. All the phenotype[18] differences between identical twins necessarily represent environmental influences (except in the case of mutations), so that a human person

[18] *Phenotype*: the outward visible expression of the hereditary constitution of an organism.

becomes himself through an entire lifetime, developing from what he never was at the beginning or by heredity alone. (3) The existence of a genetic code could never suffice to explain the uniqueness of personality. Over an indefinite time all the genetic combinations might be realized, so that we should have two or more genetically identical individuals produced from different genetic sources and existing in different times and places. We could also create separate but identical environments. Still, the individuals in question would each be a unique and distinctive person and could be identified as such.[19] (4) To argue that genetic engineering is the sole activity that results in a change in personality and identity is perhaps false. Brain surgery, or the use of certain drugs, may have the same consequences.[20] Parts of the human brain may be removed by surgery in order to cure disorders where there are clearly identifiable physical causes, such as tumours, blood vessel damage or traumatic head injuries; and psychosurgery is used in other cases where there is virtually no indication of the physical cause of the problem. There are also a number of disorders where there is some experimental or clinical reason to believe that a particular brain structure normally participates in the function that is disturbed, but where there is usually no evidence that the structure is diseased or injured. Nevertheless the symptoms can be alleviated by destroying perfectly healthy brain tissue. Even when behavioural aggression, for instance, is successfully eliminated, the operation is irreversible and may produce intellectual and physiological impairment. None of the stimulation techniques or drugs employed is able to lessen undesirable aggression without also reducing such qualities as sensitivity, ambition and intellectual alertness. The nervous system is not organized in a way that makes it possible to separate functions in terms of their social implications.[21]

Of course, if brain surgery or drug therapy necessarily inflict intellectual injury on the individual subjected to them, their moral justification should be assessed on the same grounds as any other medical therapy; and these would be irrelevant to the point of this paper. But if brain surgery or drug therapy necessarily produce a modification of the personality and if that modification is also defined as a change of identity, then even if it were possible to avoid damage to the subject's faculties, these activities should still be morally condemned for the same reasons as genetic engineering. However, it should be stressed that a moral rejection of brain surgery or drug therapy implies a non-

[19] See further Ramsey (1970).

[20] See Valenstein (1973).

[21] The technique that is intended to avoid damaging consequences, is in fact inadequate; see Valenstein (1973) 238.

genetic definition of individuality—one that is expressed in psychological terms. Such a definition would treat perceptions and emotions as the major components of personal identity, even if these are only necessary, and not sufficient, criteria for identifying a particular person.

By rejecting the genetic definition of individuality we reject a modern version of a traditional definition of the identity of the self. This is the idea of a constant and enduring substance which realizes its potentialities through its own actions and through its interactions with other substances.[22] Yet it would be a mistake to conclude that if the genetic definition of personal identity is in error, then the individual is nothing but the accumulation of perceptions and emotions, and the concept of personal identity is merely a psychological illusion. This conclusion is, moreover, unacceptable from the point of view of genetics. One of the fundamental assumptions of genetics is that with humans, as with most other creatures, individual members of the population can be distinguished.[23] I should point out that my aim in referring to the factual basis of genetics is not to raise questions about the relations between the mental and the bodily. It is simply to cite the genetic base as a necessary, even if not sufficient, condition for personal identity, provided it is taken in conjunction with environmental conditions, psychological characteristics and physical factors. The individual can be regarded as an 'occasion' in which the completed past is grasped and its elements are selected and preserved, so that a new definite fact comes to exist.

A person's distinctive existence can be understood through a grasp of the different elements of which his individuality consists. Genetic inheritance is one element in a whole complex through which the individual, as an occasion, emerges. It follows that whether an animal maintains the same genetic make-up from one day to the next depends on what its occasions inherit each day from both genetic and other environmental influences. When the matter is viewed in this way, genetic continuity is not shown to be more important than other kinds of continuity—for instance, the coherent development of emotional and cognitive life. The price of genetic change together with the discontinuity it brings may be worth paying, if other environmental factors are being successfully balanced. Moreover, a change of genetic base can be viewed as having the same status as the use of new methods in education or the application of new conceptions of psychological therapy. Moral preference for one kind of change over the others will

[22] Neville (1976).

[23] It is also an established fact that the genetic differences between members of the same race are much greater than are those between different races of the same species.

have to be justified in new ways, since it cannot be established on the basis of a definition of autonomous individuality.[24]

In conclusion, we may say that despite the undoubted importance of the concepts of autonomy and individuality for moral judgment, it is not clear whether the enterprise of genetic engineering is discredited by these concepts or, alternatively, provides a novel foundation for them. Central work in moral philosophy remains to be done; but what is certain is that it cannot proceed in ignorance of the issue we have been discussing.

[24] On that issue see Neville (1976).

Brain Death and Brainstem Death: Philosophical and Ethical Considerations

DAVID LAMB

This paper examines the development of the concept of brain death and of the criteria necessary for its recognition. Competing formulations of brain death are assessed and the case for a 'brainstem' concept of death is argued. Attention is finally drawn to some of the ethical issues raised by the use of neurological criteria in the diagnosis of human death.

I. Brain Death: Development of the Concept and Criteria

During the present century until the early 1960s and the advent of techniques for taking over the functions of the lungs and heart, the public had shown almost complete acceptance of medical practice concerning the diagnosis of death. This has not always been the case. Distrust of the profession's competence had been evident in scores of pamphlets and tracts written in the eighteenth and nineteenth centuries.[1] In 1740 it had been suggested by Jean-Jacques Winslow that putrefaction was the only sure sign of death. Such a proposal reflected a total loss of public confidence in their doctors. The prestige of physicians increased however during the mid-nineteenth century as health care became more scientific and professional. The development of certain technological aids, such as the stethoscope, enabled a more accurate detection of heartbeat and respiration, and was an important factor in the growth of public confidence in the ability to diagnose death. In the later twentieth century scepticism has returned in some areas. It will be argued that this scepticism is without foundation, and that refinements in diagnostic criteria have reached the point where public acceptance is justified.

The earliest references in the neurological literature to states resembling brain death go back to 1898, when Sir Dyce Duckworth reported on four cases with structural brain lesions in which 'the function of respiration had earlier ceased for some hours before that of the circula-

[1] Arnold *et al.* (1968).

tion',[2] and in 1902, when Harvey Cushing described a patient whose spontaneous respiration ceased as a result of an intracranial tumour, but whose heart was kept beating for twenty-three hours with artificial respiration.[3] The concept of brain death really emerged in France, in 1959. Early that year a group of French neurosurgeons described a condition which they termed 'death of the central nervous system'.[4] The characteristics of this state were 'persistent apnoeic coma, absent brainstem and tendon reflexes, and an electrically silent brain'. These patients had no detectable electrophysiological activity in either the superficial or deeper parts of their brains.[5] Whilst they looked like cadavers a regular pulse could be discerned as long as ventilation was maintained. Although the authors did not address the issue of whether this state was equivalent to death, they concluded that the persistence of this condition for eighteen to twenty-four hours warranted disconnection from the ventilator. Later that year a more complete account of the condition was published by two Parisian neurologists, Mollaret and Goulon, who called it *coma dépassé* (a state beyond coma).[6] They were not prepared to equate *coma dépassé* with death, and unlike their predecessors, they did not advocate the withdrawal of ventilatory support. The patients had all sustained massive, irreversible, structural brain damage. Patients in a state of *coma dépassé* were in a state of irreversible coma associated with an irreversible loss of the capacity to breathe. They had not only lost all capacity to respond to external stimuli, they could not even cope with their internal milieu: they were poikilothermic, had diabetes insipidus, and could not sustain their own blood pressure. The cardiac prognosis of this condition was at most a few days, but sometimes as little as a few hours.[7]

Outside France the term *coma dépassé* never really caught on. The condition was of course encountered wherever resuscitation was sufficiently well organized, and intensive care units were adequately equipped, to prevent irreversible apnoea immediately resulting in cessation of cardiac action. During this period there was no attempt to relate observations of this condition to any well-founded concept of death. Neither of the two French groups discussed the meaning of death (which is probably why they suggested different courses of action for what was essentially the same condition). By the late 1960s an increasing rate of organ transplantation and greater successes in resuscitation

[2] Duckworth (1898).
[3] Black (1978).
[4] Jouvet (1959); see also Pallis (1984).
[5] Wertheimer *et al.* (1959).
[6] Mollaret and Goulon (1959).
[7] Pallis (1983b).

provided a background to the need for greater philosophical clarity concerning what it meant to be dead. The lack of such clarity was reflected in the ambiguous and often confusing terminology used at that time. The term 'irreversible coma' was sometimes employed to refer to a condition which was equivalent to '*coma dépassé*'. The term 'brain death' referred to the same state. Although terminology was in a state of flux, the construct 'brain death' achieved a degree of precision that allowed it to be used in a popular way.[8]

In 1968 the Ad Hoc Committee of the Harvard Medical School to Examine the Definition of Brain Death published its report, and brain death (which was exactly what the French had described as *coma dépassé*) achieved world-wide recognition.[9] The Harvard criteria for brain death were fourfold: (1) absence of cerebral responsiveness; (2) absence of induced or spontaneous movement; (3) absence of spontaneous respiration; (4) absence of brainstem and deep tendon reflexes. An isoelectric EEG was deemed to be of 'great confirmatory value' but the performance of an EEG was not considered mandatory. The Report specified two conditions which were capable of mimicking the state of brain death and which had to be excluded in each case: hypothermia and drug intoxication. Finally, the Report recommended that tests be repeated over a period of twenty-four hours to document the persistence of the condition. Since then numerous patients throughout the world have been diagnosed as brain dead, maintained on ventilators and observed until their hearts stopped.[10] No patient meeting the Harvard criteria has ever recovered despite the most heroic management. Uninformed reports in the media that physicians do not know the outcome of ventilating the brain dead (see *Guardian,* 6 August 1986) are both false and damaging.

In the years following the publication of the Harvard Report it was gradually realized that the clinically testable component of brain death was death of the brainstem (*brainstem death*). In its upper part the brainstem contains crucial centres responsible for generating the capacity for consciousness. In its lower part it contains the respiratory centre. It is death of the brainstem (which in practice is nearly always the result of a massive increase of intracranial pressure) which produces the crucial signs (apnoeic coma with absent brainstem reflexes) which doctors detect at the bedside, when they diagnose brain death. Since irreversible loss of brainstem function necessarily involves loss of both the capacity for consciousness and of the capacity to breathe a very strong case can be made for linking brainstem death to traditional

[8] Korein (1978).
[9] Harvard Medical School (1968).
[10] Pallis (1984).

philosophical and religious-based definitions of death as the 'departure of the soul from the body' and the 'loss of the breath of life'.[11]

The last twenty years have see the gradual acceptance of the proposition that death of the brain is the necessary and sufficient condition for the death of the individual. The last decade has seen a parallel development; the gradual realization that death of the brainstem is the necessary and sufficient condition for the death of the brain as a whole—and that brainstem death is therefore itself synonymous with the death of the individual. This latter realization first received implicit recognition in statements issued by the Conference of Medical Royal Colleges and Their Faculties in the UK in 1976 and 1979.[12] Proponents of brainstem criteria for death argue that death of the brainstem is itself death (a philosophical position). They also point out that a diagnosis of brainstem death has in every observed case been followed by eventual circulatory arrest (an empirical observation).

The clearly interrelated conditions of whole brain death and brainstem death should not be confused with another clinically, ontologically, and philosophically, very different condition in which massive brain damage is largely confined to the cerebral hemispheres, sparing much of the brainstem and in particular the capacity to breathe spontaneously. This is the *persistent vegetative state.* Such patients have usually been the victims of severe head injury or anoxic insults to the brain (lack of oxygen wrecks the cerebral hemispheres before it destroys the brainstem). Institutions for the chronic sick all over the world are full of such patients. It is important, both scientifically and ethically, to avoid confusing brain death with such non-cognitive states. Patients in persistent vegetative states are said to be 'awake but not aware'.[13] They display no evidence of self-awareness and exhibit no purposeful response to external stimuli. Their eyes may open periodically, and they show sleep–wake sequences. They may exhibit yawning and chewing movements and may swallow spontaneously. A variety of simple or complex reflex responses may be elicited from them. Unlike whole brain death or brainstem death (which signify the 'death of the organism as a whole' and have a cardiac prognosis seldom exceeding a week), the persistent vegetative state has a potential cardiac prognosis of months or even years. The longest recorded survivor in this state was Elaine Eposito. She lapsed into such a condition following surgery on 6 August 1941 and died thirty-seven years later on 25 November 1978.[14] The terms 'cerebral death' and 'irreversible coma'

[11] Pallis (1987).
[12] Medical Royal Colleges (1976) and (1979).
[13] Jennett and Plum (1972).
[14] McWhirter (1981).

have been used in the past to refer *both* to whole brain death *and* to the persistent vegetative state. Such loose usage makes for confusion, and these terms would now be better avoided altogether.

The appropriate formulation of the concept of 'brainstem death' is '*the irreversible loss of function of the organism as a whole*'.[15] This is not the same as 'death of the whole organism', i.e. of every one of its cells. This latter formulation is often implied—although unstated—in arguments which maintain that the concept of death should be left undetermined, or that death is a process with no special point at which a non-arbitrary diagnosis can be factually ascertained.[16, 17] Whereas criteria for '*the irreversible loss of function of the organism as a whole*' (brainstem death) require simple and straightforward tests, criteria for the 'death of the whole organism' could only be met by tests for putrefaction, since cellular life in certain tissues may continue long after the organism as a whole has ceased to function. However, in the contemporary investigation into death putrefaction has not been advanced as a definition of death by either philosophers or physicians.

The argument that death should remain undefined has no place in a world where there is a need for practical decisions. Criteria for '*the irreversible loss of function of the organism as a whole*' can be determined with precision, and appropriate diagnostic tests have been developed.[18] The concept of death so defined presupposes the irreversible loss of the capacity for consciousness and the irreversible loss of the capacity to breathe, and hence to sustain a spontaneous heartbeat. It supersedes (or some would say merely reformulates in secular terms) ethical and religious-based concepts. Its basis is the death of the critical system as measured by tests for the irreversible loss of brainstem function.

II. Higher Brain, Whole Brain and Brainstem Formulations

Although the concept of brain death has been generally accepted by physicians, legislators and the lay public, its precise formulation continues to be a matter of controversy.

Two alternatives to the brainstem concept of death have been argued. Several philosophers have suggested that human death is signified by death of the higher regions of the brain (the cerebrum and cortex) alone.[19] On the other hand the American Bar Association, the

[15] Lamb (1985).
[16] Morison (1971).
[17] Browne (1983).
[18] Pallis (1983a).
[19] Green and Wikler (1981), Puccetti (1976).

American Medical Association, and a report of the President's Commission have endorsed a 'whole brain' formulation of death. This recommends the adoption by Congress (for all areas under Federal jurisdiction) of a statute known as the Uniform Declaration of Death Act. The proposed statute states:

> An individual who has sustained either (1) irreversible cessation of circulatory and respiratory functions, or (2) irreversible cessation of all functions of the entire brain, including the brainstem, is dead. A determination of death must be made in accordance with accepted medical standards.[20]

In the UK the Conference of Medical Royal Colleges has recommended criteria which, like the President's Commission, state that in brain death 'all functions of the brain have permanently and irreversibly ceased'. The recommended tests for loss of brainstem function amount, however, to an implicit acceptance of a brainstem concept of death.

In this section the respective formulations of 'higher brain', 'whole brain' and 'brainstem' death will be examined.

Higher Brain Formulations

In most of the literature on brain death there are references to the higher or lower parts of the brain, which are said to be responsible for cognitive and integrative functions respectively. Terms such as 'higher' and 'lower' do not, however, have very precise physiological meanings. Among neuroscientists there is general agreement 'that such "higher brain" functions as consciousness and cognition may not be mediated strictly by the cerebral cortex; rather, they probably result from complex interrelations between brainstem and cortex'.[21] For convenience and conformity with contemporary usage, the distinction between higher and lower parts of the brain will be maintained in this part of the discussion.

The higher brain, or cerebrum, controls movement and speech. It is concerned with the *content* of consciousness (broadly comprising the sum total of an individual's cognitive and affective endowment). The upper brainstem activates the cerebral hemispheres and is responsible for generating the *capacity* for consciousness. The capacity for consciousness (a brainstem function) is not the same as the *content* of consciousness (a function of the higher brain) but is an essential precondition of the latter. If there is no brainstem function there can be no

[20] President's Commission (1981) 2.
[21] President's Commission (1981) 15.

cognitive and affective life: no thoughts or feelings, and no social interaction. The capacity for spontaneous breathing is also a function of the brainstem. Apnoea is thus a necessary, though not a sufficient, sign of a non-functioning brainstem.

Those who argue that death should be equated with the persistent vegetative state which involves loss of higher brain functions whilst brainstem function persists (ambiguous or misleading synonyms, such as 'cerebral death', 'neocortical death', or the 'apallic syndrome', are sometimes used in this context) base their case on the fact that loss of higher brain functions strips a patient of his or her psychological capacities or attributes. Arguments supporting higher brain formulations of death are therefore concerned with criteria seeking to describe the minimum necessary qualities for personhood, defined in terms of psychological abilities. It is argued that since the loss of higher brain functions entails the loss of continuous mental processes, it must follow that brain-related criteria for death must stress the loss of personal identity.[22] Such a formulation of death does not attribute any significance to the persistence of other functions such as spontaneous respiration and heart beat.

Numerous criticisms can be made (and have been made) of higher brain formulations:

(1) Criteria for personal identity have been extensively discussed by philosophers, theologians, and lay persons, and vary from culture to culture. Arguments in favour of a formulation of death in terms of personal identity often assume an 'essence', the loss of which entails loss of identity. Whether there is such an essence is far from clear and physicians *qua* physicians would be ill advised to seek criteria for detecting its loss.

(2) Higher brain formulations run into difficulties with borderline cases, such an anencephaly or severe dementia. Moreover, there are clinical objections to a diagnosis of death when there is persisting function in the brainstem. What is the ontological status of patients with damage to neocortical or subcortical areas but who nevertheless retain spontaneous breathing and circulation? The case of Karen Quinlan is significant here. For several years Ms Quinlan retained brainstem function and an ability to breathe spontaneously. According to arguments based on higher brain formulations she would have been fit for burial, from the very onset.

(3) It is still uncertain whether fragments of consciousness or awareness may be mediated by subcortical structures. It is particularly difficult to prove that there is total absence of sentience when the brainstem is still functioning. Moreover, what is meant by the expres-

[22] Green and Wikler (1981).

sion 'loss of cognitive faculties'? Does it exclude any type of perception that may, in part, be mediated by the lower part of the brain? If patients in persistent vegetative states are to be considered dead then how much neocortical damage would be necessary for a patient to be labelled vegetative? Although such patients do not satisfy tests for whole brain death (and *a fortiori* for brainstem death), their loss of cognitive faculties is usually irreversible. Usually, but not invariably. This potential variation in clinical outcome probably reflects the lack of clinical homogeneity in vegetative patients. This further reflects a lack of firm criteria for defining the vegetative state. No physician should diagnose death in such cases.[23]

(4) While death of the brainstem is relatively easy to diagnose, the same cannot be said for death conceived of in terms of the loss of higher functions. 'It is easier to test pupils than to be certain about sentience'.[24] Diagnosis of the persistent vegetative state may be difficult.[25] What constitutes a permanent loss of the content of consciousness requires careful definition. And even if a suitable definition could be found, a determination of the precise time of 'death' in such cases (if one ever accepted that such patients were dead) would be even more difficult. Veatch has stressed what appear to be insoluble problems in the determination of non-cognitive states. He concludes:

> We must come to grips with the possibility, indeed the probability, that we shall never be able to make precise physiologic measures of the irreversible loss of mental processes. In this case we shall have to follow safer-course policies of using measures to declare death only in cases in which we are convinced that some necessary physical basis for life is missing, even if that means that some dead patients will be treated as alive.[26]

(5) There are many ethical objections to higher brain formulations. The notion of a still-breathing corpse *is* morally repugnant. How, for example, does one bury such a patient? Should burial or cremation take place whilst respiration continues? Or should someone take responsibility for suffocating the 'corpse' first? And what would happen if a distraught family member suffocated a relative who had been vegetative for months? Would it be murder? Or would it be unacceptable treatment of a corpse? As Lynn[27] points out in a criticism of higher brain formulations, society cannot afford the kind of ambiguity

[23] Pallis (1983a).
[24] Pallis (1983b).
[25] Beresford (1978).
[26] Veatch (1978).
[27] Lynn (1983).

inherent in them. At best higher brain formulations require the advocacy of benign neglect. At worst they imply the advocacy of active euthanasia. Between the two is a slippery slope strewn with conceptual and moral uncertainty. The cognitive and affective components of consciousness may be essential for a meaningful and pleasant life, but they are not necessary and sufficient conditions for the functioning of the organism as a whole.

(6) Many physicians have advanced 'slippery slope' objections to higher brain formulations of death. The relevance of such objections is obvious once we realize that a definition of death based on the loss of higher brain functions can be extended to include a wide range of disorders that should not be considered as death—or even remotely close to death. As Pallis says:

> I am opposed to 'higher brain' formulations of death because they are the first step along a slippery slope. If one starts equating the loss of higher functions with death, then, which higher functions? Damage to one hemisphere or to both? If to one hemisphere, to the verbalizing dominant one, or to the 'attentive' non-dominant one? One soon starts arguing frontal versus parietal lobes.[28]

It might be objected that arguments of this kind involve a mode of fallacious reasoning which illicitly conjoins today's proposed uses with tomorrow's possible abuses. But this objection applies only to the empirical predictions of the slippery slope argument. These may either be sustained or rebutted by further empirical evidence. The ultimate force of the slippery slope argument (which is too often ignored) lies in its exposure of inherent conceptual and clinical uncertainty and ambiguity.[29] It is the inherent indeterminacy of higher brain formulations of death which limits our ability to derive from them adequate clinical criteria or tests.

The Whole Brain Formulation

Despite the popularity with philosophers of higher brain formulations of death very few if any physicians are willing to accept them. The Report of the President's Commission[30] stressed the 'irreversible cessation of all functions of the entire brain, including the brainstem' and opposed criteria for death that only covered the loss of the higher brain functions:

> Extending the 'definition' of death beyond those lacking *all* brain functions to include, for example, persons who have lost only cogni-

[28] Pallis (1983a) 2.
[29] Lamb (1987).
[30] President's Commission (1981) 2.

tive functions but are still able to breathe spontaneously would radically change the meaning of death.[31]

Such a change, it was argued, would run counter to existing religious beliefs.

The commission saw an affinity between traditional religious concepts of death and criteria for whole brain formulations. For example, although Jewish writings do not deal directly with brain death, some passages were deemed to support whole brain formulations. They identified the decapitated state with death, whatever might be happening to the body below the severed head. Both Catholic and Protestant theological doctrines maintain that the human essence or soul departs at the moment of death. This is not incompatible with diagnosing death on neurological grounds. Although no early religious source mentions loss of heartbeat or pulse (let alone an isoelectric EEG, or an absence of cerebral blood-flow), both the Old Testament and Muslim sources explicitly refer to the association between breath and life. Contemporary religious sources are not opposed to neurological criteria for the determination of death. A Papal address states that '(It) remains for the doctor to give a clear and precise definition of "death" and the "moment of death" of a patient who passes away in a state of unconsciousness'.[32]

There have nevertheless been several criticisms of the whole brain formulation.

(1) Exponents of higher brain formulations have accused exponents of the whole brain concept of inconsistency and irrationality in relation to the persistence of respiratory function after irreversible damage to 'higher' structures. In a criticism of the Report of the President's Commission, Youngner and Bartlett[33] say that its rejection of higher brain formulations (and endorsement of the whole brain concept) is based on emotional grounds; namely on a reluctance to treat those with spontaneous heartbeat and respiration as corpses. The Commission is accused of equating 'an emotional reaction to the treatment of a breathing body with the rational determination of whether the patient is dead'.[34] 'Emotional forces', Youngner and Bartlett argue, 'are also influential partly because they are not rational.'[35]

This account of an 'emotional reaction' cannot go unchallenged. An emotional response, like any other response, takes place in a context where it has to justify itself. One can then decide whether the reasons offered provide the appropriate justification. In the case at issue there

[31] President's Commission (1981) 7.
[32] Pope Pius XII (1957).
[33] Youngner and Bartlett (1983).
[34] Youngner and Bartlett (1983) 254.
[35] Youngner and Bartlett (1983) 254.

are very good reasons for an emotional objection to preparing a still-breathing patient for burial or organ removal. The canons of contemporary practice are unambiguous and uncontested. Such a course is universally recognized as homicidal and an emotional objection to homicide is perfectly rational. The reasons which justify the Commission's 'emotional reaction' are that according to both the traditional cardio-respiratory concept of death and the whole brain formulations, patients with spontaneous respiration and heartbeat are still alive.

(2) Youngner and Bartlett also see inconsistency in the way the Commission does not attribute significance to chest movements, arterial pulsations and bodily warmth of patients meeting whole brain criteria of death, but then goes on to cite the very persistence of these functions as an objection to higher brain formulations.[36] This inconsistency is, however, more apparent than real. Having met criteria for whole brain death, the ex-patient has no capacity for spontaneous respiration, heartbeat or temperature control. In so far as these functions persist they are performed by the technical apparatus, not by the patient. Once it has been shown that the loss of these functions is irreversible, there should be no problem in recognizing death. This is markedly different from the state of affairs in patients whose brainstem function persists and where spontaneous respiration, heartbeat, and the control of body temperature may continue for years provided really good nursing attention is available.

The preference for whole brain over higher brain formulations is not simply based on emotional grounds, conservatism or appeals to tradition. Its strength lies in the contrast between whole brain formulations (which lead to diagnostically clear-cut tests) and higher brain formulations (where diagnostic uncertainty prevails and where dubious criteria for 'personhood' are rampant). As Lynn points out:

> At most, with no blood flow studies and with barbiturates present, confirming death of the entire brain may take a week; however, confirming irreversible absence of consciousness and cognition may take years even if one can develop an adequate definition of what consciousness and cognition are.[37]

The 'whole brain formulations' have recently been challenged, at the conceptual level, by the 'brainstem formulation' implicit in the UK guidelines. The next section will argue that this concept differs in substance from 'higher brain formulations', while more accurately and honestly reflecting what is really known than do the 'whole brain formulations'.

[36] Youngner and Bartlett (1983) 254.
[37] Lynn (1983) 266.

The Brainstem Formulation

Whilst extensive damage to the cortex, from trauma or anoxia, may not cause permanent unconsciousness, there is one functional unit without whose activity consciousness cannot exist. This is the ascending reticular activating system, or ARAS, which is situated in the upper part of the brainstem. Acute, strategically situated, bilateral lesions in the paramedian tegmental area of the rostral brainstem entail loss of the capacity for consciousness, whilst lesions of critical areas in the lower part of the brainstem are associated with the permanent cessation of the ability to breathe which in turn deprives the heart and cerebral hemispheres of oxygen, causing them to cease functioning. Whole brain formulations of death recognize that survival of the brainstem is incompatible with a diagnosis of the death of the person as a whole.

Survival of the brainstem is needed to generate a capacity for consciousness and a capacity to breathe. This role of the brainstem is often overlooked by exponents of higher brain formulations—particularly by those who have not done their physiological homework. In this respect, support for higher brain formulations in some philosophical circles seems to be a case of philosophers rushing in where neurologists fear to tread.

Any valid concept of death must necessarily be linked to an irreversible change in the state of the organism as a whole. Life depends on the integration of physiological functions, such as ingestion, digestion, absorption, respiration, distribution (circulation), metabolism, excretion, and egestion or elimination. The concept of the irreversible loss of function of the organism as a whole implies the irreversible loss of integrated functioning. In these purely biological aspects the death of a human is no different to the death of a dog, for what is lost is the ability to organize and integrate component systems. Essential to any definition of death in terms of the loss of integrated functioning is the role of the critical system which organizes and integrates other systems and which cannot be replaced by an artefact.[38] This critical system is the brain, whose integrating function depends on an intact brainstem. The brainstem can be thought of as the critical system of the critical system, without whose function the organism as a whole could not survive as an independent biological entity. Pallis has described brainstem death as the 'physiological kernel' of brain death.[39] Since destruction of the brainstem precludes integrated functioning of the brain as a whole, a diagnosis of irreversible loss of brainstem function is the quintessence of whole brain death. In the overwhelming majority of cases brainstem death is not a primary event. It is the ultimate pathological repercussion

[38] See Lamb (1985) esp. 33–40.

[39] Pallis (1983a).

of processes above the tentorium[40] which cause massive increases in intracranial pressure. A concept of brainstem death yields unambiguous clinical criteria which can be objectively tested. It is both clinically and conceptually superior to traditional heart-related concepts. It is also superior to dualistic formulations which, by offering a choice between brain or heart-related concepts, cannot be said to be derived from any well-founded concept of death.

The explicit brainstem formulation of death, which I am arguing for here, has not yet been fully understood or addressed. For instance, the Report of the President's Commission states that: 'The prevailing British viewpoint on the neurological diagnosis of death is closer to a *prognostic* approach (that a point of no return has been reached in the process of dying)'.[41] It presents the American approach as being 'more *diagnostic* in seeking to determine that all functions of the brain have irreversibly ceased at the time of death'.[42] Neurologists and neurophysiologists in the United Kingdom would reply that brainstem criteria are prognostic in relation to the heart, not in relation to the patient, who is deemed already dead when brainstem function has irreversibly ceased. They have, moreover, drawn attention to the impossibility of demonstrating 'cessation of all functions of the entire brain' which the Uniform Declaration of Death Act (supported by the President's Commission) requires.[43] The UK Code[44] only requires that loss of certain specified *critical* functions be documented (namely those of the brainstem) which, as a matter of fact, are the only ones that can be tested in the usual clinical context.

The differences between the recommendations of the President's Commission and the UK Code amount to a distinction between 'death of the whole brain' and 'death of the brain as a whole'. In so far as the brain as a whole cannot function without a functioning brainstem it follows that once reliable criteria for loss of brainstem function have been met, the patient can be diagnosed as dead. Signs of residual electrical activity in isolated neuronal aggregates in the higher regions of the brain do not indicate persistent functioning of the organism as a whole, or even of the brain as a whole. The Commission's commitment to the whole brain formulation conveys every indication of an abundance of caution. But in this very caution it is seeking to achieve what cannot be achieved. There is strictly no way, in the clinical context of

[40] The tentorium is a fibrous ring which separates the cerebral hemispheres (above) from the cerebellum and brainstem (below).

[41] President's Commission (1981) 28.

[42] President's Commission (1981) 28.

[43] Pallis and Prior (1983).

[44] Medical Royal Colleges (1976) and (1979).

suspected brain death, that loss of cerebellar or thalamic function could be directly demonstrated, for instance. The caution itself may be an important defence against proposals in favour of higher brain formulations. But it has no relevance as a counter to the brainstem formulation.

The Commission recognized that with an intact brainstem life may persist (even in the absence of higher brain functions). But with the irreversible cessation of brainstem function the continuance of consciousness or of integrated life is impossible. The Commission recognized the centrality of brainstem function. But the apparent clumsiness of its whole brain formulation (which refers to the whole while needlessly specifying one of its parts) is an indication of theoretical uncertainty. No argument so far produced has shown that the intentions behind the Commission's proposed Uniform Declaration of Death Act would be thwarted if adequate criteria were met for the irreversible loss of brainstem function.

Conclusion

We have considered three formulations of brain death and have established (1) that higher brain formulations are inadequate since they do not require the irreversible cessation of brainstem function; (2) that whole brain formulations meet this requirement, but in doing so do not provide anything that is not covered by brainstem formulations. Insofar as the only acceptable formulation of death is one which requires a permanently non-functioning brainstem, the distinction between whole brain and brainstem formulations has less significance than that between higher brain and brainstem formulations.

III. Ethical Aspects of Brain Death

The concept of brain death is a by-product of medical science which has generated serious ethical questions regarding the physician's duties and the patient's rights. Notoriously the following four questions have been confused in recent medical literature:

1. Is the patient dead?
2. Should the patient be allowed to die?
3. When should resuscitation cease?
4. When, and under what circumstances, should decisions be taken to allow the removal of organs?

It is important to recognize that these questions are fundamentally different in kind.

1. Is the Patient Dead?

Once the concept and criteria for human death have been clearly established this question becomes one of medical diagnosis. According to the concept of death defined as '*the irreversible loss of function of the organism as a whole*' the patient is dead when tests have demonstrated that the brainstem has irreversibly ceased to function. Anything short of brainstem death (for example, destruction confined to the hemispheric regions of the brain) is unacceptable. Damage restricted to these regions does not satisfy the necessary and sufficient conditions for the death of a human being. Those who advocate the identification of the vegetative state with death, whether they know it or not, are asking for a change in the current homicide laws and the acceptance of euthanasia.

2. Should the Patient be Allowed to Die?

This question is bound up with the problem of prognosis and the planning it implies. It calls for a comparison of alternatives. Whereas the scope of the first question is limited to eliciting and ascertaining objective clinical evidence, the second question involves ethical, religious and economic considerations. Answers reflect different moral attitudes towards the quality of residual life. Questions concerning whether a patient is alive or dead, like queries concerning pregnancy or meningitis, demand a yes-or-no response. But answers to the question 'Should a patient be allowed to die?' do not. They entail a consideration of a wide spectrum of alternatives, ranging from the continuance of intensive life-support to the withdrawal of some, but not all, forms of treatment. In deciding whether the patient is dead, deference to the expertise of the physician is needed. When deciding whether the patient should be allowed to die one will need as accurate a prognosis as possible from the physician. But one may then have to consider legal, ethical, economic, and political matters. One must take into consideration the known wishes of the patient, the relatives, and others. When the first question (is the patient dead?) has been answered affirmatively, the second is obviously meaningless.

Distinctions between the two questions have not always been maintained. The Harvard Report of 1968 implicitly confused ventilation after brain death with the prolongation of life. The Report invoked the statement of Pope Pius XII to the effect that there was no obligation on the part of the physician to employ extraordinary measures to prolong life. But as the Task Force on Death and Dying of the Institute of Society, Ethics and the Life Sciences[45] pointed out, this confused the factual question of the determination of death with the ethical question of when, if ever, a patient should be allowed to die.

The possibility of prolonged attempts at resuscitation raises the question of death with dignity. Must the patient be subjected to a

[45] In Weir (1977) 90–102.

hopeless and futile regime of intravenous alimentation, dialysis, drug-dependent maintenance of the blood pressure, 'prophylactic' antibiotics, and control of the heartbeat by electrical means, in order to survive for another day or week? Are a few statutory hours on the ventilator to become the last rite of modern medicine?

Giving up when the prognosis is hopeless cannot be interpreted as a form of passive euthanasia. One is not 'allowed to die', if all treatment is 'hopeless'. The physician in such circumstances is not in a position to 'allow' anything. All he or she can do is to cease to apply a useless treatment. In such cases the choice facing the doctor is not whether to allow the patient to die, but to choose *how* the patient shall die: either after a prolonged period in institutional isolation wired up to a mass of electrical gadgetry, or in relative dignity, possibly within a few hours or a day or two. To discontinue treatment in hopeless cases is not 'letting die', but allowing to die in a more acceptable manner. The statement 'I let him die' only has meaning if it was ever possible to specify an alternative.

3. When Should Resuscitation Cease?

Criteria for brain death are ethically necessary because it is now possible to maintain organs alive in a cadaver after integrated life has ceased. Thus the moment when the brain has been determined as dead is the moment beyond which further attempts at resuscitation are pointless. Korein describes the maintenance of certain functions in the brain-dead patient (merely because the technical means exist to do so) as a 'moral and economic atrocity that has evolved through a perversion of modern science'.[46] He was among the first in favour of discontinuing ventilation or cardiovascular support after brain death.

How one treats a corpse after death is a problem which affects relatives and social agencies as well as the physician. The physician has a primary duty to maintain life. Once he is satisfied that the patient is dead he has no moral duty to ventilate a cadaver. If he is responsible for the ventilator his duty is to disconnect and either save electricity or use the machine for another patient. To do so in this context is neither active nor passive euthanasia. 'Disconnecting the respirator should seem no more significant than drawing the sheet over the body once all the conditions for declaring brainstem death have been met.'[47] At this point the physician has a duty to inform the relatives that death has occurred and that there is no individual life for further ventilation to prolong. Current reports in the media of relatives instructing physi-

[46] Korein (1978) 33.
[47] Pallis (1980).

cians to 'give up' or 'let the patient go' after a diagnosis of brain death only exacerbate confusion and uncertainty regarding the finality of brainstem death.

Could problems arise if relatives or responsible social agencies wished to provide alternative means of ventilation, despite an assurance that the patient was dead? Should they be free to do so? This is not the kind of 'service' that should be provided in a hospital, at the taxpayer's expense. Those with responsibility for hospital patients have an ethical duty to ensure that facilities are kept available for the living and that wards are not treated as mortuaries. Under these circumstances a decision by the relatives to continue ventilation would be a personal decision (with all the implications that entails) akin to a decision as to where to bury the deceased. A ventilated cadaver would not be alive but 'treated as alive'. This might suggest immaturity or bad taste, but probably no more than embalming, mummification, the preservation of Jeremy Bentham in University College, London or the public display of Lenin's remains in Moscow. It would however be considerably more expensive. And it is doubtful whether relatives could persuade physicians to undertake such a grisly task for long. When ventilation after brainstem death is carried out, as it is in some cases, it is simply as a gesture to the relatives. Needless to say no such ex-patient has ever recovered.

4. *When and Under What Circumstances Should Decisions be Taken to Allow the Removal of Organs?*

The fourth and final issue concerns separating questions related to the need to obtain organs for transplantation from questions related to the conceptual and factual aspects of defining death. Tremendous pressure exists for more donors, and this pressure will certainly grow. Physicians can be subjected to conflicting moral obligations when the organs of one patient can be used to save the life of another. To avoid potential conflicts between the attending physician and the requirements of the transplant team, practices have evolved which ensure that the donor's physician should have no role in the transplantation procedure itself. For the same kind of reason the Judicial Council of the American Medical Association requires that the donor's death be determined by someone other than the recipient's physician. Similarly the Committee on Morals and Ethics of the Transplantation Society of the USA says that 'acceptance of death should be made and declared by at least two physicians whose primary responsibility is care of the potential donor and is independent of the transplant team'. The same situation obtains in the UK.

The motive behind these requirements was to ensure that the need for organs never interfered with the objective judgment that a patient was dead. A clearly defined concept of death (and appropriate criteria for diagnosing death) would help procure cadaver organs in optimal condition for transplantation. But it is important that statutes or guidelines on brain death should avoid the serious risk of running together criteria for diagnosing brain death with legislation and/or guidelines for the removal of organs. In 1976 the European Committee on Legal Co-operation fell into precisely this trap. It underwrote the following positions:

(1) It should be possible for the removal of cadaver organs to be effected from the moment when it was established that the donor had irreversibly lost all his cerebral functions even though the function of other organs might have been preserved.
(2) Legislation should move towards the adoption of presumed consent for the removal of cadaver organs if circumstances give reason to believe that the family or the donor do not or would not have objected.[48]

These two statements illicitly conjoin proposals for brain-related criteria of death and legislation permitting the removal of cadaveric organs. The proposals are then linked with a particularly dangerous attempt to shift the burden for permission to remove cadaveric organs.

Confusion of this sort stems from earlier attempts to come to terms with the phenomenon of brain death. The need to define brain death was presented in terms of factors extraneous to the patient's welfare. The Harvard Report (1968) itself, for example, gave two practical reasons for a definition of death.

(1) Relief of the patient, kin, and medical resources from the burden of indefinitely prolonged coma.
(2) Removal of controversy with regard to the obtaining of organs for transplantation.

There is nothing objectionable in these proposals insofar as the primary rationale behind the redefinition of death was to enable a physician to terminate treatment when it was no longer in the patient's interests. There is, clearly, an ethical imperative to reduce the period of anxiety for relatives. There have been cases of relatives paying over $2000 a day to keep a corpse ventilated.[49] But objections to the second reason adduced in the Harvard Report were raised by Hans Jonas,[50] who argued that freedom for organ use is not covered by the primary rationale, that is the interest of the patient. Jonas stressed that the

[48] Cited in Walton (1980) 13.
[49] President's Commission (1981) 24.
[50] Jonas (1974) 133.

theoretical requirement to define death is one thing (and an essential thing if the patient's interests are uppermost) but that the requirement for organ transplants (even to save lives) is the intrusion into the situation of another interest. Commenting on the Harvard Report, Jonas said:

> I contend that pure as this interest (viz. to save lives) is in itself, its intrusion into the *theoretical* attempt to define death makes the attempt impure; the Harvard Committee should never have allowed itself to adulterate the purity of its scientific case by baiting it with the prospect of this *extraneous* though extremely appealing gain.

Jonas's concern was not with theoretical purity for its own sake. He was rightly worried about the policy consequences of this impurity, once a need for the harvesting of organs is built into the definition of death. Stories about 'human vegetables' lingering on for months (while their organs could be used to save other lives) must never be allowed to influence criteria for determining death. Wherever such arguments are raised they must be seen as advocacy for euthanasia or dissection of the living, and their pros and cons evaluated in this light. The fact that other humans might benefit from organs obtained from patients in vegetative states is no reason for the assimilation of these states to death. Discussions regarding the *worth* of a life should never replace discussions about the *existence* of a life. The term 'vegetative state' refers to the clinical condition of a living being; there is no way in which it can be seen as anything other than an instance of life.

It is clearly important to define death with some precision in order to know when to stop expensive forms of treatment, in order to keep intensive care facilities available for living patients and in order to seek authorization to harvest cadaver organs. In this paper such a definition (the brainstem concept of death) has been articulated and defended. But this defence does not require the consideration of cost-benefit factors or of the need for cadaver organs. Such considerations should not be allowed to interfere with judgments concerning the nature or the moment of death.

Bibliographical Index

Anscombe (1970): Anscombe, G. E. M., 'Modern Moral Philosophy', in G. Wallace and A. D. M. Walker (eds), *The Definition of Morality* (London: Methuen, 1970), *211–34*. 218.

Aquinas (1966): Aquinas, *Summa Theologiae*, T. Gilby (ed.) (London: Blackfriars, 1966), Vol. 18. 135–40, 144, 146–7.

Aristotle (1915): Aristotle, *Nicomachean Ethics*, trans. W. D. Ross (Oxford: Clarendon Press, 1915). 35–6, 41, 55, 107–12, 115–16, 133, 135, 148, 151, 157–64.

Aristotle (1921): Aristotle, *Politics*, trans. B. Jowett (Oxford: Clarendon Press, 1921). 20–2, 157.

Arnold *et al.* (1968): Arnold, J. D., Zimmerman, T. F. and Martin, D. C., 'Public Attitudes and the Diagnosis of Death', *Journal of the American Medical Association* **206** (1968), *1949–54*. 231.

Assiter (1983): Assiter A., 'Did Man Make Language?', *Radical Philosophy* **34** (1983), *25–9*. 185.

Attfield (1984): Attfield, R., 'Work and the Human Essence', *Journal of Applied Philosophy* **1** (1984), *141–50*. 166.

Austin (1954): Austin, J., *The Province of Jurisprudence Determined*, H. L. A. Hart (ed.) (London: Weidenfeld & Nicolson, 1954). 177.

Baier (1985a): Baier, A., 'Doing Without Moral Theory?', in *Postures of the Mind* (London: Methuen, 1985), *228–45*. 88–9.

Baier (1985b): Baier, A., 'Theory and Reflective Practices' in *Postures of the Mind* (London: Methuen, 1985), *207–27*. 55, 58, 91.

Becker and MacPherson (1986): Becker, S. and MacPherson, S., 'Staying Poor', *Labour Research* (July 1986). 176.

Beezer (1984): Beezer, A., 'More on Man-Made Language', *Radical Philosophy* **36** (1984), *16–19*. 185.

Benn (1975/6): Benn, S. I., 'Freedom, Autonomy and the Concept of a Person', *Proceedings of the Aristotelian Society* **76** (1975/6), *109–30*. 167.

Beresford (1978): Beresford, H. R., 'Cognitive Death: Differential Problems and Legal Overtones', *Annals of the New York Academy of Sciences* **315** (1978), *339–48*. 238.

Berkeley (1948–57): Berkeley, G., *Collected Works*, T. E. Jessop and A. Luce (eds) (Edinburgh: Thomas Nelson, 1948–57). 37, 40, 48, 50–3.

Black (1978): Black, P. M., 'Brain Death', *New England Journal of Medicine* **299** (1978), *338–44*, and *393–401*. 232.

Blake (1966): Blake, W., *Complete Writings*, G. Keynes (ed.) (London: Oxford University Press, 1966). 53.

Blum (1980): Blum, L. A., *Friendship, Altruism and Morality* (London: Routledge, 1980). 55.

Bibliographical Index

Bradley (1962): Bradley, F. H., *Ethical Studies* (Oxford: Clarendon Press, 1962). 9, 75.

Brecher (forthcoming): Brecher, B., 'On Not Caring About the Individual', in G. and S. Fairbairn (eds), *Ethical Issues in Caring* (Aldershot: Gower, forthcoming). 196.

Brenkert, G. G., 'Marx's Critique of Utilitarianism', in K. Nielsen and S. C. Patten (eds), *Marx and Morality: Canadian Journal of Philosophy* Supplementary Volume 7 (1981), *193–220*. 30.

Brown (1981): Brown, B., 'A Feminist Interest in Pornography', *m/f* **5/6** (1981), *5–18*. 185.

Browne (1983): Browne, A., 'Whole-brain Death Reconsidered', *Journal of Medical Ethics* **9** (1983), *28–31*. 235.

Brownlie (1971): Brownlie, I. (ed.), *Basic Documents on Human Rights* (Oxford: Clarendon Press, 1971). 167–9.

Buchan (1972): Buchan, A., *The Right to Work: The Story of the Upper Clyde Confrontation* (London: Calder & Boyars, 1972). 165–6.

Buchanan (1982): Buchanan, A. E., *Marx and Justice* (London: Methuen, 1982). 10–11, 16, 134.

Callahan (1976): Callahan, D., 'Ethical Responsibility in Science in the Face of Uncertain Consequences', in *Annals of the New York Academy of Sciences*, M. Lappé and R. S. Morison (eds), **265** (1976), *1–12*. 216.

Cameron (1984): Cameron, D., 'Sexism and Semantics', *Radical Philosophy* **36** (1984), *14–16*. 185.

Campbell (1983): Campbell, T. D., *The Left and Rights: a Conceptual Analysis of the Idea of Socialist Rights* (London: Routledge & Kegan Paul, 1983). 166.

Campbell (1985): Campbell, T. D., 'The Rights Approach to Mental Illness', in A. Phillips Griffiths (ed.), *Philosophy and Practice* (Cambridge University Press, 1985), *221–53*. 167.

Caplan (1982/3): Caplan, A., 'Can Applied Ethics Be Effective in Health Care and Should it Strive to Be?', *Ethics* **93** (1982/3), *311–19*. 82, 84–5.

Clark (1983): Clark, S. R. L. 'Morals, Moore and MacIntyre', *Inquiry* **26** (1983), *425–45*. 49.

Clark (1985): Clark, S. R. L. 'God-appointed Berkeley and the General Good', in J. Foster and H. Robinson (eds), *Essays on Berkeley* (Oxford: Clarendon Press, 1985), *233–53*. 40.

Clark (1986): Clark, S. R. L., 'Icons, Sacred Relics, Obsolescent Plant', *Journal of Applied Philosophy* **3** (1986), *201–10*. 49.

Clark (1987a): Clark, S. R. L., 'Animals, Ecosystems and the Liberal Ethic', *Monist* **70** (1987), *114–33*. 49.

Clark (1987b): Clark, S. R. L., 'The Land We Live By', *Ecos* **8** (1987), *7–12*. 44.

Coates (1978): Coates, K (ed.), *The Right to Useful Work* (Nottingham: Spokesman, 1978). 179–80.

Coates and Topham (1986): Coates, K. and Topham, A. J., *Trade Unions and Politics* (Oxford: Blackwell, 1986). 179.

Cockburn (1985): Cockburn, C., *Women and Technology* (London: Workers' Educational Association, 1985). 180.

Cohen (1967): Cohen, B., 'An Ethical Paradox', *Mind* **76** (1967), *250–9*. 137.

Cohen (1971/2): Cohen, G. A., 'Karl Marx and the Withering Away of Social Science', *Philosophy and Public Affairs* **1** (1971/2), *182–203*. 121.

Cohen (1973/4): Cohen, G. A., 'Marx's Dialectic of Labour', *Philosophy and Public Affairs* **3** (1973/4), *235–61*. 26–7, 29.

Cohen (1978): Cohen, G. A., *Karl Marx's Theory of History: a Defence* (Oxford: Clarendon Press, 1978). 29, 119, 127.

Cohen (1978/9): Cohen, G. A., 'The Labor Theory of Value and the Concept of Exploitation', *Philosophy and Public Affairs* **8** (1978/9), *338–60*. 128.

Cohen (1983): Cohen, G. A., review of A. Wood, *Marx*, in *Mind* **92** (1983), *440–5*. 118.

Cohen and O'Hear (1984): Cohen, B. and O'Hear, A., 'Editorial: A Note on Policy', *Journal of Applied Philosophy* **1** (1984), *3–4*. 72.

Coward (1982): Coward, R., 'Sexual Violence and Sexuality', *Feminist Review* **11** (1982), *9–22*. 186.

Crow (1968): Crow, J. F., 'Rates of Genetic Change under Selection', *Proceedings of the National Academy of Sciences* **59** (1968), *655–61*. 217.

Cullen (1979): Cullen, B. A., *Hegel's Social and Political Thought* (Dublin: Gill & Macmillan, 1979). 173.

D'Arcy (1961): D'Arcy, E., *Conscience and its Right to Freedom* (London: Sheed & Ward, 1961). 136.

Devlin (1959): Devlin, P. A., *The Enforcement of Morals* (London: Oxford University Press, 1959). 184.

Duckworth (1898): Duckworth, Sir Dyce, 'Some Cases of Cerebral Disease in which the Function of Respiration Entirely Ceases for Some Hours Before That of the Circulation', *Edinburgh Medical Journal* **3** (1898), *145–52*. 231–2.

Dunn and Gennard (1984): Dunn, S. and Gennard, J., *The Closed Shop in British Industry* (London: Macmillan, 1984). 170.

Eisenberg (1976): Eisenberg, L., 'The Psychopathology of Clonal Man', in A. Milunsky and G. J. Annas (eds), *Genetics and the Law* (New York: Plenum Press, 1976), *387–95*. 214.

Elster (1985): Elster, J., *Making Sense of Marx* (Cambridge University Press, 1985). 10–12, 19–20, 22–5, 27, 29, 33, 121, 125, 130, 134.

Elster (1985/6): Elster, J., 'Self-realization in Work and Politics: the Marxist Conception of the Good Life', *Social Philosophy and Policy* **3** (1985/6), *97–126*. 31–3.

Elster (1986): Elster, J., *An Introduction to Karl Marx* (Cambridge University Press, 1986). 19.

Evans (1977): Evans, J. D. G., *Aristotle's Concept of Dialectic* (Cambridge University Press, 1977). 135.

Feyerabend (1968): Feyerabend, P. K., 'How to Be a Good Empiricist—a Plea for Tolerance in Matters Epistemological', in P. H. Nidditch (ed.), *The Philosophy of Science* (Oxford University Press, 1968), *12–39*. 90.

Bibliographical Index

Finnis (1980): Finnis, J., *Natural Law and Natural Rights* (Oxford: Clarendon Press, 1980). 136, 138, 147.

Geach (1969): Geach, P. T., *God and the Soul* (London: Routledge, 1969). 36.

Geras (1985): Geras, N., 'The Controversy about Marx and Justice', *New Left Review* **150** (1985), *47–85*. 121.

Gewirth (1983): Gewirth, A., *Human Rights: Essays on Justification and Applications* (University of Chicago Press, 1983). 57.

Giddens (1976): Giddens, A., *New Rules of Sociological Method* (London: Hutchinson, 1976). 127.

Graham (1986a): Graham, K., *The Battle of Democracy* (Sussex: Wheatsheaf Books, 1986). 7–8, 17.

Graham (1986b): Graham, K., 'Morality and Abstract Individualism', *Proceedings of the Aristotelian Society* **87** (1986/7), *21–33*. 3, 8.

Gray (1967): Gray, J. Glenn, *The Warriors: Reflections on Men in Battle* (New York: Harper & Row, 1967). 50.

Gray (1982): Gray, C. S., *Strategic Studies: a Critical Assessment* (London: Aldwych Press, 1982). 106–7.

Green (1966): Green, P., *Deadly Logic: the Theory of Nuclear Deterrence* (Columbus: Ohio State University Press, 1966). 106.

Green and Wikler (1981): Green, M. B. and Wikler, D., 'Brain Death and Personal Identity', in M. Cohen, T. Nagel and T. Scanlon (eds), *Medicine and Moral Philosophy* (Princeton University Press, 1981), *49–77*. 235, 237.

Hare (1978/9): Hare, R. M., 'What is Wrong with Slavery?', *Philosophy and Public Affairs* **8** (1978/9), *103–21*. 191.

Hart (1955): Hart, H. L. A., 'Are There any Natural Rights?', *Philosophical Review* **64** (1955), *175–91*. 167.

Harvard Medical School (1968): Harvard Medical School: Ad Hoc Committee, 'A Definition of Irreversible Coma', *Journal of the American Medical Association* **205** (1968), *337–40*. 233, 245, 248.

Hegel (1952): Hegel, G. W. F., *Philosophy of Right,* trans. T. M. Knox (Oxford: Clarendon Press, 1952). 119–20, 123, 130–2.

Hegel (1977): Hegel, G. W. F., *Phenomenology of Spirit*, trans. A. V. Miller (Oxford: Clarendon Press, 1977). 169, 172–4.

Hill (1987): Hill, S., 'Working Time Changes and Employment Growth', *Lloyds Bank Review* **163** (January 1987), *31–46*. 179.

Hobbes (1962): Hobbes, T., *Leviathan*, J. Plamenatz (ed.) (London: Fontana, 1962). 72–3, 111.

Hollis (1977): Hollis, M., *Models of Man* (Cambridge University Press, 1977). 2.

Honderich (1982): Honderich, T., '"On Liberty" and Morality-dependent Harms', *Political Studies* **30** (1982), *504–14*. 183.

Hubbard (1982): Hubbard, R., 'Some Practical and Ethical Constraints on Genetic Decisions About Childbearing', in D. Teichler-Zallen and D. C. Clements (eds), *Science and Morality* (Lexington: Lexington Books, 1982), *37–47*. 217.

Hume (1888): Hume, D., *A Treatise of Human Nature*, L. A. Selby-Bigge (ed.) (Oxford: Clarendon Press, 1888). 4–5, 43, 74–5.

Hyman (1984): Hyman, R., 'Wooing the Working Class', in J. Curran (ed.), *The Future of the Left* (Cambridge: Polity Press, 1984), *90–9*. 170.

Jenkins and Sherman (1979): Jenkins, C. and Sherman, B., *The Collapse of Work* (London: Methuen, 1979). 175.

Jennett and Plum (1972): Jennett, B. and Plum, F., 'Persistent Vegetative State After Brain Damage: a Syndrome in Search of a Name', *Lancet* **i** (1972), *734–7*. 234.

Jonas (1974): Jonas, H., 'Against the Stream: Comments on the Definition and Redefinition of Death', in *Philosophical Essays: From Ancient Creed to Technological Man* (Englewood Cliffs, New Jersey: Prentice Hall, 1974), *132–40*. 248–9.

Jones (1977): Jones, G. (ed.), *The Oxford Book of Welsh Verse in English* (Oxford: Clarendon Press, 1977). 44.

Jouvet (1959): Jouvet, M., 'Diagnostic electro-souscortico graphique de la mort du système nerveux-centrale aux cours de certains comas', *Electroencephalography and Clinical Neurophysiology* **11** (1959), *805–8*. 232.

Kant (1929): Kant, I., *Critique of Pure Reason*, trans. N. Kemp Smith (London: Macmillan, 1929). 58.

Kant (1948): Kant, I., *The Moral Law*, trans. H. J. Paton (London: Hutchinson, 1948). 42, 55, 57, 60–2, 68, 75, 90, 120, 133, 145, 220–1.

Kant (1970): Kant, I., 'What is Enlightenment?', in H. Reiss (ed.), trans. H. B. Nisbet, *Kant's Political Writings* (Cambridge University Press, 1970), *54–60*. 60.

Kant (1978): Kant, I., *Critique of Judgement*, trans. J. C. Meredith (Oxford University Press, 1978). 69.

Keat (1981): Keat, R., 'Individualism and Community in Socialist Thought', in J. Mepham and D.-H. Ruben (eds), *Issues in Marxist Philosophy* Vol. 4 (Sussex: Harvester Press, 1981), *127–52*. 27.

Knights and Willmott (1986): Knights, D. and Willmott, H. (eds), *Gender and the Labour Process* (Aldershot: Gower, 1986). 180.

Korein (1978): Korein, J., 'The Problem of Brain Death', *Annals of the New York Academy of Sciences* **315** (1978), *19–38*. 233, 246.

Ladd (1982): Ladd, J., 'Aspects of Genetical Ethics', in D. Teichler-Zallen and D. C. Clements (eds), *Science and Morality* (Lexington: Lexington Books, 1982), *129–38*. 216, 218.

Lamb (1985): Lamb, D., *Death, Brain Death and Ethics* (London: Croom Helm, 1985). 235.

Lamb (1987): Lamb, D., *Down the Slippery Slope: Arguing in Applied Ethics* (London: Croom Helm, 1987). 239.

Leary (1977): Leary, D. E., 'Berkeley's Social Theory: Content and Development', *Journal of the History of Ideas* **38** (1977), *635–49*. 52.

Lederberg (1976): Lederberg, S., 'Law and Cloning: The State as Regulator of Gene Function', in A. Milunsky and G. J. Annas (eds), *Genetics and the Law* (New York: Plenum Press, 1976), *377–86*. 215.

Levy (1979/80): Levy, D., 'Perversion and the Unnatural as Moral Categories', *Ethics* **90** (1979/80), *191–202*. 209.

Lewis (1952): Lewis, C. S., *Out of the Silent Planet* (London: Pan, 1952). 51–2.

Littler (1985): Littler, C. R. (ed.), *The Experience of Work* (Aldershot: Gower, 1985), 172.

Locke (1959): Locke, J., *An Essay Concerning Human Understanding,* Vol. 1, A. C. Fraser (ed.), (New York: Dover, 1959). 36.

Locke (1985): Locke, D., 'The Right to Strike', in A. Phillips Griffiths (ed.), *Philosophy and Practice* (Cambridge University Press, 1985), *173–202*. 166.

Lockwood (1985): Lockwood, M., 'The Warnock Report: a Philosophical Appraisal', in M. Lockwood (ed.), *Moral Dilemmas in Modern Medicine* (Oxford University Press, 1985), *155–86*. 185.

Lukes (1985): Lukes, S., *Marxism and Morality* (Oxford: Clarendon Press, 1985). 3, 14, 19, 117, 121, 134.

Lynn (1983): Lynn, J., 'The Determination of Death', *Annals of Internal Medicine* **99** (1983), *264–6*. 238–9, 241.

Macfarlane (1981): Macfarlane, L. J., *The Right to Strike* (Harmondsworth: Penguin, 1981). 170.

MacIntyre (1981): MacIntyre, A., *After Virtue* (London: Duckworth, 1981). 25, 43–4, 46, 48–9, 55, 69, 108–12, 115.

MacIntyre (1984): MacIntyre, A., 'Does Applied Ethics Rest on a Mistake?', *Monist* **67** (1984), *498–513*. 82.

Mackie (1977): Mackie, J. L., *Ethics: Inventing Right and Wrong* (Harmondsworth: Penguin, 1977). 3.

Maritain (1943): Maritain, J., *The Rights of Man and Natural Law,* trans. D. C. Anson (New York: Scribner's, 1943). 167.

Martin (1975): Martin, G. D., *Language, Truth and Poetry* (Edinburgh University Press, 1975). 38.

Martin (1981): Martin, G. D., *The Architecture of Experience* (Edinburgh University Press, 1981). 38, 46, 51–2.

Marx (1967): Marx, K., *Writings of the Young Marx on Philosophy and Society,* L. D. Easton and K. H. Guddat (eds) (New York: Anchor Books, 1967). 31, 33.

Marx (1973): Marx, K., *Grundrisse: Foundations of the Critique of Political Economy (Rough Draft)* (Harmondsworth: Penguin, 1973). 26–9.

Marx (1975): Marx, K., *Early Writings* (Harmondsworth: Penguin, 1975). 119, 132.

Marx (1976): Marx, K., *Capital* Vol. 1 (Harmondsworth: Penguin, 1976). 14–18, 30, 117–18, 119, 124–8.

Marx (1977): *Karl Marx: Selected Writings,* D. McLellan (ed.), (Oxford University Press, 1977). 166, 169, 173.

Marx and Engels (1962a): Marx, K. and Engels, F., *Selected Correspondence* (Moscow: Foreign Languages Publishing House, 1962). 118.

Marx and Engels (1962b): Marx, K. and Engels, F., *Selected Works,* Vols 1–2 (Moscow: Foreign Languages Publishing House, 1962). 118, 123, 127–30.

Marx and Engels (1965): Marx, K. and Engels, F., *The German Ideology* (London: Lawrence & Wishart, 1965). 28–9, 133.

Marx and Engels (1967): Marx, K. and Engels, F., *The Communist Manifesto* (Harmondsworth: Penguin, 1967). 15, 27–8.

Marx and Engels (1975): Marx, K and Engels, F., *The Holy Family* in *The Collected Works of Marx and Engels,* Vol. 4 (London: Lawrence & Wishart, 1975). 120.

Maxwell (1980): Maxwell, N., 'Science, Reason, Knowledge and Wisdom: a Critique of Specialism', *Inquiry* **23** (1980), *19–81*. 85.

Maxwell (1984): Maxwell, N., *From Knowledge to Wisdom* (Oxford: Blackwell, 1984). 93.

McDowell (1986): McDowell, J., discussion of B. A. O. Williams, *Ethics and the Limits of Philosophy, Mind* **95** (1986), *377–86*. 75.

McLellan (1973): McLellan, D., *Karl Marx: His Life and Thought* (London: Macmillan, 1973). 134.

McWhirter (1981): McWhirter, N. (ed.), *The Guinness Book of Records* (New York: Bantam, 1981). 234.

Medical Royal Colleges (1976): Medical Royal Colleges and their Faculties, Conference of, 'Diagnosis of Brain Death', *British Medical Journal* Part 2 (1976), *1187–8*. 234, 236, 243.

Medical Royal Colleges (1979): Medical Royal Colleges and their Faculties, Conference of, 'Diagnosis of Death', *British Medical Journal* Part 1 (1979), *332*. 234, 236, 243.

Mendus (1985a): Mendus, S., 'Harm, Offence and Censorship', in J. Horton and S. Mendus (eds), *Aspects of Toleration* (London: Methuen, 1985), *99–112*. 185.

Mendus (1985b): Mendus, S., 'The Practical and the Pathological', *Journal of Value Inquiry* **19** (1985), *235–43*. 63.

Mill (1962): Mill, J. S., *Utilitarianism, On Liberty, Essay on Bentham,* M. Warnock (ed.) (London: Collins, 1962). 57, 62, 183, 191–3, 208–11.

Miller (1984): Miller, R. W., *Analyzing Marx: Morality, Power and History* (Princeton University Press, 1984). 14, 17.

Mollaret and Goulon (1959): Mollaret, P. and Goulon, M., 'Le coma dépassé, *Revue Neurologique* **101** (1959), *3–15*. 232.

Mooney (1985): Mooney, M., *Vico in the Tradition of Rhetoric* (Princeton University Press, 1985). 37, 41.

Morgenthau (1972): Morgenthau, H. J., *Politics Among Nations* (New York: Knopf, 1972). 109, 111.

Morison (1971): Morison, R. S., 'Death: Process or Event?', *Science* **173** (1971), *694–8*. 235.

Morrow (1976): Morrow, J. F., 'The Prospects of Gene Therapy in Humans', *Annals of the New York Academy of Sciences,* M. Lappé and R. S. Morison (eds) **265** (1976), *13–21*. 215.

Motulsky (1973): Motulsky, A., 'The Significance of Genetic Disease', in Hilton, B., Callahan, D., Harris, M., Candliff, P. and Berkley, B. (eds), *Human Genetics: Genetic Counselling and the Use of Genetic Knowledge* (New York: Plenum Press, 1973), *59–65*. 215.

Mulgan (1977): Mulgan, R. G., *Aristotle's Political Theory* (Oxford: Clarendon Press, 1977). 22.

Murphy (1975): Murphy, E. A., 'The Normal, Eugenics and Racial Survival', *Johns Hopkins Medical Journal* **136** (1975), *98–106*. 217.

Murphy (1982): Murphy, E. A., 'Genetic Engineering: Eugenic Consequences', in D. Teichler-Zallen and D. C. Clements (eds), *Science and Morality* (Lexington: Lexington Books, 1982), *49–60*. 217.

Nacht (1985): Nacht, M., *The Age of Vulnerability: Threats to the Nuclear Stalemate* (Washington: Brookings Institution, 1985). 107.

Nagel (1970): Nagel, T., *The Possibility of Altruism* (Oxford: Clarendon Press, 1970). 6.

Nagel (1986): Nagel, T., *The View from Nowhere* (Oxford University Press, 1986). 6–7.

Neville (1976): Neville, R., 'Gene Therapy and the Ethics of Genetic Therapeutics', *Annals of the New York Academy of Sciences,* M. Lappé and R. S. Morison (eds) **265** (1976), *153–61*. 216, 228–9.

Newman (1979): Newman, J. H., *An Essay in Aid of a Grammar of Assent* (Notre Dame, Indiana: University of Notre Dame Press, 1979). 39, 49.

Newman (1887): Newman, W. L., *The Politics of Aristotle,* Vol. 1 (Oxford: Clarendon Press, 1887). 22.

Nielsen (1973): Nielsen, K., 'Alienation and Self-Realization', *Philosophy* **48** (1973), *21–33*. 20.

Nozick (1974): Nozick, R., *Anarchy, State and Utopia* (New York: Basic Books, 1974). 7, 78.

Olson (1965): Olson, M., *The Logic of Collective Action* (Cambridge, Mass.: Harvard University Press, 1965). 10.

O'Neill (1984): O'Neill, O., 'How Can We Individuate Moral Problems?', in Attig. T., Callen, D. and Frey, R. G. (eds), *Social Policy and Conflict Resolution* (Bowling Green: Bowling Green State University, 1984), *104–19*. 83.

O'Neill (1986): O'Neill, O., 'The Power of Example', *Philosophy* **61** (1986), *5–29*. 65, 84.

Page (1985): Page, E., 'Donation, Surrogacy and Adoption', *Journal of Applied Philosophy* **2** (1985), *161–72*. 186–7.

Page (1986): Page, E., 'Warnock and Surrogacy', *Journal of Medical Ethics* **12** (1986), *45–7*. 186, 189.

Paine (1969): Paine, T., *Rights of Man,*, H. Collins (ed.) (Harmondsworth: Penguin, 1969). 165.

Pallis (1980): Pallis, C., in 'News and Notes', *British Medical Journal* **281** (1980), *1220*. 246.

Pallis (1983a): Pallis, C., *ABC of Brainstem Death* (London: British Medical Journal, 1983). 235, 238–9, 242.

Pallis (1983b): Pallis, C., 'Whole-brain Death Reconsidered—Physiological Facts and Philosophy', *Journal of Medical Ethics* **9** (1983), *32–7*. 232, 238.

Pallis (1984): Pallis, C., 'Brainstem Death: the Evolution of a Concept', in P. J. Morris (ed.), *Kidney Transplantation* (London: Grune & Stratton, 1984), *101–27*. 232–3.

Pallis (1987): Pallis, C., 'Death', *Encyclopaedia Britannica* (Chicago, 1987), *1030–42*. 233–4.

Pallis and Prior (1983): Pallis, C. and Prior, P. F., 'Guidelines for the Determination of Death', *Neurology* **33** (1983), *251*. 243.

Parfit (1984): Parfit, D., *Reasons and Persons* (Oxford: Clarendon Press, 1984). 2, 4, 6.

Paskins and Dockrill (1979): Paskins, B. and Dockrill, M., *The Ethics of War* (London: Duckworth, 1979). 111.

Péguy (1961): Péguy, C., *Victor Marie, Comte Hugo,* in *Oeuvres en Prose, 1909–14* (Paris: Gallimard, 1961), *659–840*. 57.

Peirce (1931–5): Peirce, C. S., *Collected Papers,* C. Hartshorne and P. Weiss (eds) (Cambridge, Mass.: Harvard University Press, 1931–5). 42.

Pennock and Chapman (1981): Pennock, J. R. and Chapman, J. W. (eds.), *Human Rights: Nomos XXIII* (New York University Press, 1981). 166.

Plamenatz (1975): Plamenatz, J. P., *Karl Marx's Philosophy of Man* (Oxford: Clarendon Press, 1975). 20.

Plato (1952): Plato, *Phaedrus*, trans. R. Hackforth (Cambridge University Press, 1952). 209–10.

Plato (1956): Plato, *Republic,* trans. H. D. P. Lee (Harmondsworth: Penguin, 1956). 36, 99–101.

Pope John Paul II (1981): Pope John Paul II, *Laborem Exercens: On Human Work* (London: Catholic Truth Society, 1981). 169, 174.

Pope Pius XII (1957): Pope Pius XII, 'The Prolongation of Life', in *The Pope Speaks* (London: Catholic Truth Society, 1957 Summer). 240.

Popper (1945): Popper, K. R., *The Open Society and Its Enemies* (London: Routledge & Kegan Paul, 1945). 100.

President's Commission (1981): President's Commission for the Study of Ethical Problems in Medicine and Biomedical and Behavioural Research (Morris B. Abram, Chairman), *Defining Death* (Washington: US Govt Printing Office, 1981). 236, 239–41, 243–4, 248.

Prichard (1966): Prichard, H. A., 'Duty and Ignorance of Fact', in J. N. Findlay (ed.), *Studies in Philosophy: British Academy Lectures* (London: Oxford University Press, 1966), *41–64*. 139–42, 147.

Puccetti (1976): Puccetti, R., 'The Conquest of Death', *Monist* **59** (1976), *249–63*. 235.

Quine (1961): Quine, W. V., 'Two Dogmas of Empiricism', in *From a Logical Point of View* (New York: Harper & Row, 1961), *20–46*. 75–8.

Ramsey (1970): Ramsey, P., *Fabricated Man* (New Haven: Yale University Press, 1970). 223, 227.

Rauch (1983): Rauch, L., *Hegel and the Human Spirit* (Detroit: Wayne State University Press, 1983). 173.
Rawls (1972): Rawls, J., *A Theory of Justice* (Oxford: Clarendon Press, 1972). 25, 78, 90, 130.
Roemer (1982): Roemer, J., *A General Theory of Exploitation and Class* (Cambridge: Mass.: Harvard University Press, 1982). 130, 134.
Roemer (1986): Roemer, J. (ed.), *Analytical Marxism* (Cambridge University Press, 1986). 130, 134.
Rorty (1980): Rorty, R., *Philosophy and the Mirror of Nature* (Princeton University Press, 1980). 96.
Rorty (1982): Rorty, R., *Consequences of Pragmatism* (Sussex: Harvester Press, 1982). 95, 97–8, 100–1, 104–5.
Ruddick (1980): Ruddick, W., 'Philosophy and Public Affairs', *Social Research* **47** (1980), *734–48*. 65.
Russell (1983): Russell, D. A., *Greek Declamation* (Cambridge University Press, 1983). 39.

Sandel (1982): Sandel, M. J., *Liberalism and the Limits of Justice* (Cambridge University Press, 1982). 56.
Sartre (1948): Sartre, J.-P., *Existentialism and Humanism,* trans. P. Mairet (London: Methuen, 1948). 55, 59–60.
Seabrook (1982): Seabrook, J., *Unemployment* (London: Quartet Books, 1982). 175.
Seidler (1986): Seidler, V., *Kant, Respect and Injustice* (London: Routledge, 1986). 55–6.
Shortland and Fauvel (1983): Shortland, M. and Fauvel, J., 'Sexist Language: Fatherfuck or Genderspeak', *Radical Philosophy* **34** (1983), *29–32*. 185.
Shue (1980): Shue, H., *Basic Rights: Subsistence, Affluence and U.S. Foreign Policy* (Princeton University Press, 1980). 57.
Singer and Wells (1984): Singer, P. and Wells, D., *The Reproduction Revolution* (Oxford University Press, 1984). 186.
Skinner (1978): Skinner, Q. R. D., *The Foundations of Modern Political Thought* (Cambridge University Press, 1978). 108–9, 111.
Smart (1985): Smart, B., 'The Right to Strike and the Right to Work', *Journal of Applied Philosophy* **2** (1985), *31–40*. 166, 175.
Spender (1980): Spender, D., *Man-Made Language* (London: Routledge & Kegan Paul, 1980). 185.

Ten (1980): Ten, C. L., *Mill on Liberty* (Oxford: Clarendon Press, 1980). 209.
Terkel (1974): Terkel, S., *Working: People talk about what they do all day and how they feel about what they do* (New York: Pantheon Books, 1974). 172.
Thompson (1971/2): Thompson, J. J., 'In Defence of Abortion', *Philosophy and Public Affairs* **1** (1971/2), *47–66*. 195.
Thompson *et al.* (1983): Thompson, I. E., Melia, K. M. and Boyd, K. M., *Nursing Ethics* (Edinburgh: Churchill Livingstone, 1983). 86.

Townsend (1979): Townsend, P. B., *Poverty in the United Kingdom* (London: Allen Lane, 1979). 175–6.

Valenstein (1973): Valenstein, E. S., *Brain Control* (New York; Wiley, 1973). 227.

Veatch (1978): Veatch, R. M., 'The Definition of Death: Ethical, Philosophical and Policy Confusion', *Annals of the New York Academy of Sciences* **315** (1978), *307–21*. 238.

Vico (1982): Vico, G., *Vico: Selected Writings,* L. Pompa (ed.) (Cambridge University Press, 1982). 37, 40–1.

Wainwright and Elliot (1982): Wainwright, H. and Elliot, D., *The Lucas Plan* (London: Allison & Busby, 1982). 179–80.

Walton (1980): Walton, D. N., *Brain Death* (Purdue, Indiana: Purdue University Press, 1980). 248.

Walzer (1983): Walzer, M., *Spheres of Justice* (Oxford: Martin Robertson, 1983). 55.

Warnock (1971): Warnock, G. J., *The Object of Morality* (London: Methuen, 1971). 3, 134.

Warnock (1985): Warnock, M., *A Question of Life* (Oxford: Blackwell, 1985). 186–9.

Weinsheimer (1984): Weinsheimer, J., *Imitation* (London: Routledge & Kegan Paul, 1984). 36, 42, 45.

Weir (1977): Weir, R. F. (ed.), *Ethical Issues in Death and Dying* (New York: Columbia University Press, 1977). 245.

Wertheimer *et al.* (1959): Wertheimer, P., Jouvet, M. and Descotes, J., 'A propos du diagnostic de la mort du système nerveux', *Presse Medicale* **67** (1959), *87–8*. 232.

Whateley (1832): Whateley, R., *Elements of Rhetoric* (Oxford: Parker, 1832). 38.

White (1981): White, M. G., *What Is and What Ought to be Done* (Oxford University Press, 1981). 77–8.

Wilkes (1980): Wilkes, K. V., 'The Good Man and the Good for Man in Aristotle's Ethics', in A. O. Rorty (ed.), *Essays on Aristotle's Ethics* (Berkeley: University of California Press, 1980), *341–57*. 157.

Williams (1973): Williams, B. A. O., 'Ethical Consistency', in *Problems of the Self* (Cambridge University Press, 1973) *166–86*. 137, 148.

Williams (1979): Williams, B. A. O. (Chmn), *Report of the Committee on Obscenity and Film Censorship* (London: HM Stationery Office, 1979). 209.

Williams (1981a): Williams, B. A. O., 'Internal and External Reasons', in *Moral Luck* (Cambridge University Press, 1981), *101–13*. 4–5, 7, 120.

Williams (1981b): Williams, B. A. O., 'Moral Luck', in *Moral Luck* (Cambridge University Press, 1981), *20–39*. 148.

Williams (1984): Williams, B. A. O., 'Morality, Scepticism and the Nuclear Arms Race', in N. Blake and K. Pole (eds), *Objections to Nuclear Defence: Philosophers on Deterrence* (London: Routledge & Kegan Paul, 1984), *99–114*. 107.

Williams (1985): Williams, B. A. O., *Ethics and the Limits of Philosophy* (London: Fontana, 1985). 55, 75, 90, 120, 133–4.

Winch (1972): Winch, P. G., 'Moral Integrity', in *Ethics and Action* (London: Routledge & Kegan Paul, 1972), *171–92*. 63.

Wittgenstein (1958): Wittgenstein, L., *Philosophical Investigations,* trans. G. E. M. Anscombe (Oxford: Blackwell, 1958). 55, 65–6, 101–2, 104.

Wood (1981): Wood, A., *Karl Marx* (London: Routledge & Kegan Paul, 1981). 134.

Yeats (1955): Yeats, W. B., *Autobiographies* (London: Macmillan, 1955). 40.

Youngner and Bartlett (1983): Youngner, S. J. and Bartlett, E. T., 'Human Death and High Technology: the Failure of Whole-brain Formulations', *Annals of Internal Medicine* **99** (1983), *252–8*. 240–1.

Notes on Contributors

David Archard is Senior Lecturer in Philosophy at the University of Ulster at Jordanstown. He is the author of *Marxism and Existentialism* and *Consciousness and the Unconscious.* His current research is on the moral philosophy of socialism.

Bob Brecher is Senior Lecturer in the Humanities Department at Brighton Polytechnic, where he teaches applied philosophy. He is the author of *Anselms's Argument* and of articles on ethics and social philosophy which have been published in the *Journal of Medical Ethics.*

James Brown is Senior Lecturer in Philosophy at the University of Ulster at Coleraine. He has contributed articles on themes in ethics to *Philosophy, Mind* and the *Proceedings of the Aristotelian Society.* He has taught ethics in degree courses in nursing for a number of years, and is currently writing a book on ethics for nurses.

Stephen Clark is Professor of Philosophy at Liverpool University. His most recent book is *The Mysteries of Religion.* He is currently giving the Stanton Lectures at Cambridge and will publish the first series under the title *Limits and Renewals.*

Desmond Clarke is Associate Professor of Philosophy at University College, Cork. He has published *Church and State: Essays in Political Philosophy,* and has edited *Morality and the Law.* His current research is on freedom of thought as a fundamental human right.

Bernard Cullen is Lecturer in Scholastic Philosophy at Queen's University, Belfast. He is the author of *Hegel's Social and Political Thought* and editor of *Hegel Today.* He is founding Editor of the *Irish Philosophical Journal,* the first four volumes of which have now been published.

David Evans is Professor of Logic and Metaphysics at Queen's University, Belfast. He is the author of *Aristotle's Concept of Dialectic* and of *Aristotle,* which contain discussions of Aristotle's moral theory. He is a Member of the Royal Irish Academy.

Jonathan Gorman is Senior Lecturer in Philosophy at Queen's University, Belfast. He is a member of the executive committee of the Society for Applied Philosophy. He has written extensively on social philosophy and has published *The Expression of Historical Knowledge.* He is currently writing a book on the philosophy of economics.

Keith Graham is Lecturer in Philosophy at Bristol University. His most recent book, *The Battle of Democracy,* is an attempt to bring together conceptual, empirical and normative thinking. He is currently working on a book about the philosophical foundations of Marx's theories.

Notes on Contributors

Shyli Karin-Frank is Lecturer in Philosophy at Tel-Aviv University. She is the author of *Utopia Reconsidered* and (with L. Barash) *Uri Givon's Discovery,* a philosophy book for children.

David Lamb is Senior Lecturer in Philosophy at Manchester University. He is General Editor of the Avebury Series in the History and Philosophy of Science. He has written and edited a number of books on Hegel and on medical ethics, most recently *Down the Slippery Slope: Arguing in Applied Ethics.*

Joseph Mahon is Lecturer in Philosophy at University College, Galway. He is the author of *An Introduction to Practical Ethics* and is a regular contributor to the *Irish Medical Times* and *In Dublin* on topics in medical ethics and on issues in legislative policy.

Onora O'Neill is Senior Lecturer in the Philosophy Department at Essex University. Her books include *Having Children* and *Faces of Hunger;* and she is currently working on Kantian topics and problems in international justice. She is President of the Aristotelian Society for 1988–9.

Barrie Paskins is Lecturer in the Ethical Aspects of War at the Department of War Studies, King's College, London. He is the co-author of *The Ethics of War* and of *The Church and the Bomb;* and he has published articles in the *Proceedings of the Aristotelian Society* and the *British Journal of International Studies.*

Alan Ryan, who is a Fellow of the British Academy, has recently moved from New College, Oxford, to Princeton University. He has written extensively on the philosophy of the social sciences, J. S. Mill, and theories of property. His most recent book is *Property.*

Elizabeth Telfer is Senior Lecturer in Philosophy at Glasgow University. She is author and co-author of a number of books on moral philosophy and medical ethics, the most recent being *Happiness* and *Caring and Curing.*